**W9-CDC-541**

# LATIN AMERICA IN THE WORLD ECONOMY: NEW PERSPECTIVES

# LATIN AMERICA IN THE WORLD ECONOMY: NEW PERSPECTIVES

Edited by
Diana Tussie

Contributors:
Carlos F. Diaz Alejandro,
Peter B. Evans,
Aldo Ferrer,
E. V. K. Fitzgerald,
Carlos Fortin,
Stephany Griffith-Jones,
and
G. Philip

**St. Martin's Press    New York**

Library of Congress Cataloging in Publication Data

Main entry under title:

Latin America in the world economy.

    Bibliography: p.
    1. Latin America — Economic policy — Addresses,
    essays, lectures. 2. Latin America — Foreign economic
    relations — Addresses, essays, lectures. 3. Economic
    policy — Addresses, essays, letctures.
    I. Tussie, Diana
    HC125.L345   1982b   338.98     82–47501
                           AACR2

ISBN 0 312 47333 8

*8221198*

# Contents

# Tables

# Figures

# Acknowledgements

Most of the chapters contained in this volume were presented at a conference held under the auspices of *Millennium, Journal of International Studies* at the London School of Economics at the end of April 1981. Early versions were extensively revised in the light of the discussion which also provided the inspiration for additional contributions.

I would like to thank Professor Ralf Dahrendorf, Director of the School and Professors Susan Strange and Fred Northedge, Convenors of the Department of International Relations, for the support which they gave to the project and for their help in steering the way over the numerous obstacles.

Funds for the conference were provided by the Centro de Estudios Economicos y Sociales del Tercer Mundo, the Third World Foundation, the British Council and the US Embassy in London. I am grateful to Oswaldo Rivero of the Peruvian Embassy in London for his assistance in this initial phase.

My deepest thanks are due to the Editorial Board of *Millenium* without whose continued support the project would never have seen the light. Mark Hoffman was the ideal colleague to lean on, always forthcoming with enthusiasm and sound advice at all stages. I also owe a special debt to Wolfgang Deckers, Steve Singer and particularly Carla Garapedian for her organisational skill in running the conference and for her aid in preparing the index. Hilary Parker and Gill Portwine provided patient and diligent secretarial assistance throughout the project.

Lastly I wish to thank all the contributors to this volume for liberally giving their time to illuminate my muddled ignorance, for their friendly acceptance of ill-informed suggestions and for their tolerance towards my nagging about deadlines.

Diana Tussie

# 1 Introduction*

DIANA TUSSIE

The process of transnationalisation of capital since the war has shown two central tendencies: the growing integration of central economies alongside discontinuities between these and the periphery of the world economy – the dependent or underdeveloped countries, exporters of cheap primary commodities. The seventies seemed, however, to show possible points of fracture in centre-periphery relations. First, there was the emergence of the oil-rich countries wielding the 'oil weapon' which seemed not only to enhance their bargaining power but also to trigger a redistribution of income in international terms. Second, there was the rise of a group of semi-industrialised countries showing impressive dynamism and high rates of industrial growth on the basis of foreign investment and the export-orientation of their economies. The advancement of industrialisation in the periphery was hailed by many as the new success story – the emergence of new Japans that were also posing a challenge to the post-war economic order. For others the important question to be addressed was whether these trends denoted a real abridgement of the gap between centre and periphery and a mitigation of underdevelopment, or merely another form of dependence on international business and finance within a new international division of labour.

Alongside these changes in the periphery, the international financial system also underwent significant restructuring. In addition to the

* I wish to thank A.G. Frank, Faruk Yalvac and the contributors to this volume for suggestions on an earlier draft.

1

devaluation of the dollar in 1971 and the abandonment of fixed exchange rates, there was the notable expansion of transnational banking which jointly entailed an erosion of the hitherto IMF-dominated financial system. An increasing volume of liquidity was manipulated by agents with a high degree of autonomy — banks only loosely subject to the direct control of national monetary authorities — and credits became progressively available for the less developed countries to cover their balance of payments deficits. Only when the smooth service of their loans seemed endangered by mid-1982 did these private banks call back a revitalised IMF to save them and oversee debt-rescheduling.

The essays in this volume are an attempt to make a critical review of such changes and from that point to draw a more accurate picture of the interplay between internal and external factors in Latin American development. Part II also analyses aspects of state behaviour in the context of this changing external environment.

## Monistic analyses of centre-periphery relations

Analyses of dependency in vogue in the Anglo-Saxon world mostly have their roots in A.G. Frank's work, who in his insightful *Capitalism and Underdevelopment in Latin America*, described endless chains of metropolises and satellites extending

> the capitalist link between the capitalist world and national metropolises to the regional centers (part of whose surplus they appropriate), and from these to local centers, and so on to large landowners or merchants who expropriate surplus from small peasants or tenants, and sometimes even from these latter to landless laborers exploited by them in turn (1967, p.7).

Dependency implies participation in the chain as a satellite and the draining of surplus from satellite to metropolis. This exploitative chain has existed since the sixteenth century. Changes since then in the form of surplus expropriation are not changes of substance because the basic causal mechanisms of dependency have been kept intact but rather changes of appearance which highlight the 'principle of continuity in change'.

The studies emanating from this starting point were valuable firstly, in underlining the external factors that contributed to underdevelopment and secondly, in demonstrating the relevance of history for the comprehension of both development and underdevelopment. This marked an important point of departure from traditional analysis of social change which relied on linear explanations and on the assumption that all countries followed a similar path of development, albeit at different paces. Scholars of development and social change had for long felt frustration with this concensual perception of 'modernising societies' proceeding autonomously through the universal 'stages of economic growth', with the advanced nations extending a benevolent hand in the form of aid, trade, finance, technology or investment so as to reduce the time span required to reach the last stage of modernisation.

This dependency approach provided a pivotal point from which to shift the emphasis from single modernising societies as the principal units of analysis to relations between societies. With the publication in the United States of Immanuel Wallerstein's *The Modern World System* in 1974 a further change in the academic trend began. Wallerstein started from the point correctly analysed by dependency studies that countries are not isolated enclosures, and from there asserted that the world system constituted the only valid unit of analysis, thus rendering distinctions between exogenous and endogenous forces meaningless. The focus of Wallerstein's work is in effect an expansion

3

of A.G. Frank's model, moving the focus from country to country relations to the complex of relational webs themselves. He has attempted to trace 'structured constellations of relational networks' (Wallerstein and Hopkins, 1981, p.237) at a global scale, and he argues that these relations constitute a system with patterns of regularity. Systemic change is furthermore time-specified; periodicity and duration are determined by the Kondratieff cycles of expansion and contraction.[1] Changes in a particular area of the system do not merely imply the economic growth or development of that area. They signal

> a complex structural transformation of the system as a whole, of which the changes in question are but one part and the area in question but one locus (Wallerstein and Hopkins, 1981, p.242).

Like Frank, Wallerstein claims that since the sixteenth century the market has united the different parts of the world in a system of exchange relations. Wallerstein incorporates, however, a new dimension; the extension of the world market has entailed the expansion of its network of governance and rule, the interstate system. These market relations have led to the division of the world into three tiers of states: the core; the periphery; and the semi-periphery. The core is characterised by strong states, and relatively limited supplies of high-skilled labour; the periphery by weak states, and relatively unlimited supplies of unskilled labour. The semi-periphery is a transitory stage between the core and periphery and combines features of both. State formation is the result of the process of expansion of the world market, and its logic is dictated by the world division of labour. The state in the periphery must be strong enough in relation to its internal forces to assure the constant outflow of economic surplus from across its boundaries to core states, but in relation to the core it must be weak enough to be incapable of blocking such flows. Conversely, the core states must be strong to extract the surplus from the periphery.

The system of exploitative relations between core and periphery is sustained by the power of the core states to manipulate market exchanges in order to maintain their supremacy. They preclude the periphery from pursuing autonomous paths; they protect their own markets but force free trade on the periphery; and they aim to perpetuate weak states on the periphery so that these countries keep their place within the system and the system is thereby continually reproduced.

As a result of the emphasis in carving out the relational context between the core and the periphery, the world system approach has lost sight of the internal structures that lend dynamism to the process of state formation. Indeed, for Wallerstein the peripheral state is reduced to an epiphenomenon of a global economic base, a sort of conveyor belt between the international and the domestic market. There may be variations in the form of surplus extraction and internal restructuring in the periphery, but the substance of the system as a whole is kept intact.

Despite the multitude of studies influenced by this perspective the greatest pitfall is that broad brush strokes depict long-term trends at a macro level and all concrete situations are deprived of their particularities. It has been rightly pointed out that one-sided reliance on this line of thought tends to produce a circular argument:

> dependent countries are those which lack capacity for autonomous growth and they lack this because their structures are dependent ones (P. O'Brien, 1975, p.24).

Dependency is reduced to an unrelenting condition in which differences of degree do not modify the underlying essence. The overconcern with the reproduction of the system has led to neglect the limits to its functioning. Furthermore, the cyclical explanation of change (both past and future) entails the double danger of smothering national particularities by over-homogenisation as well as relegating political conflict to an automatic outcome of the rhythms of the world economy.

## The centre-periphery relationship

The essays in Part I are an attempt to review aspects of the centre-periphery relationship that may appear obscured by monistic interpretations of Latin American integration into the world economy. The external dependence or vulnerability of the third world is a matter of degree since all countries are dependent upon one another and all economies are conditioned by the world economy. The attempt to draw a precise boundary between a dependent and an interdependent relationship is surely an idle academic exercise and is bound to be excessively value-laden. Yet it is clear that not all countries in the periphery can be lumped together in the same dependent compartment, nor is any one country in the same situation for ever. Changes in the world economy as well as domestic transformations may open the possibility of enhanced capacity for independent action. The central concern, however, is not empirical measurement of degrees of dependence for a behaviourist analysis of governmental decision making. In addition to dwelling on external constraints, the enquiry must proceed to identify structural linkages – linkages which impose limits but do not determine outcomes.

Chapter 2 by Carlos F. Díaz Alejandro examines the hypothesis that insertion into the international division of labour necessarily requires an authoritarian political regime to maintain a cheap labour force under control.[2]

Díaz Alejandro extracts evidence from an overview of openings and closings in Latin American economic history to argue that protectionism, just as open economies, can operate in either a progressive or regressive direction. In other words, degrees of openness to the world market do not have unequivocal political correspondences. He points out that since the mid-1960s governments moving in the direction of promoting exports have included both the Frei and the Pinochet administrations in Chile, the second Belaúnde government in Peru and Castroist Cuba, as well as Peronist and post-Peronist Argentina. Díaz Alejandro concludes that few generalisations may be drawn from the historical review. But the historical review shows that both paces and policy instruments have varied and it is perhaps these factors that may hold a stronger clue to the link between economics and politics than just the foreign sector on its own. If high rates of capital formation are desired (be it in an open or closed economy) consumption and real wages will need to be limited. If hyper-inflation and unsustainable balance of payments disequilibria must be checked a natural alliance may be forged by 'those used to discipline, command and punishment with those emphasising order and soundness in budgetary and monetary policies' (p.1). Orthodox, anti-inflationary prescriptions do require a stable social order and a measure of control over social forces by which some policy-makers and entrepreneurs may feel attracted to an authoritarian expedient.

Díaz Alejandro's attack on a form of economic reductionism to explain the link between openness and the spread of authoritarianism unfolds the matter into several layers. First, there is the level of economic thought in which associations between the left and protectionism on one hand and the right and free trade on the other, are a simplification of the issue. Arguments for free trade can be founded on Ricardian comparative advantages and on Marx's position that free trade was progressive in so far as it was the 'natural, normal atmosphere' for the historical evolution of capitalism (Marx and Engels, 1976, p.269). Second, politics whether authoritarian or democratic do not unequivocally mirror a particular economic strategy. There have been democracies with both high and low degrees of openness to the world market and the same holds for authoritarian rule. Third, there is the concrete situation in which a policy is adopted to move away from an orthodox import-substitution model with a bias against exports to one which attempts to restore a balance between protectionism and export incentives. Such 'Japanese approach' to dynamic export growth need not entail the elimination of all protection and has been followed by Brazil, Mexico and Colombia with the state actively and extensively involved in the export drive. Such an approach results in a gradual shift that does not necessarily bring about social upheaval. Factors other than freer trade will be needed to explain authoritarianism should it emerge in such conditions. Fourth, there is another type of concrete situation, that in which a drastic transformation of the economy is undertaken with a radical liberalisation of imports in a short time span. In this context

> there *is* a serious gap in the array of analytical tools provided by mainstream trade theorists, who typically rely on the methodology of comparative statics. The path between two equilibrium situations is seldom discussed because standard models are not suitable for those explorations (p.26).

The political implications of this type of transition become more complex when the trade opening is an instrument of an anti-inflationary package, as could be said to have been the case in the Southern Cone. Nevertheless, there is no prima facie reason to assume that closer integration of less developed countries into the world economy will be necessarily and directly correlated with the emergence of authoritarianism. Authoritarianism does require economic and political analysis, but it is a multi-faceted phenomenon that merits more complex explanations than just its correlation with degree of openness to the international market.[3]

From the discussion of the implications of export-led growth, we now turn to the chapter by S. Griffith-Jones which tackles the financial dimension of Latin American incorporation into the world economy – a hitherto neglected area. In attempting to break down the concept of financial dependence, she first traces the evolution of international capital flows to Latin America since the Bretton Woods system was instated and then examines how different countries in the periphery are subject to varying degrees of financial dependence. She outlines three phases that roughly correspond with the three post-war decades. In the fifties, foreign direct investment by trans-national corporations provided the main source of external finance, in the sixties flows were mostly in the form of aid channelled through the Alliance for Progress, and more recently, in the seventies, in the form of private bank loans. In each phase US based institutions or enterprises took the lead in initiating the flows, and only at a later stage did the process become truly 'multinationalised' as other countries joined in. The changes in US initiatives were motivated by its foreign policy interests and the evolution of its balance of payments.

Latin American capacity to import remained on a precarious footing until a less rigid situation evolved as a result of the emergence and expansion of the Eurocurrency markets and transnational private finance. Though the recycling of petro-dollars only accelerated a process that was already in motion, the rapid jump in the price of oil in 1973 marked an important landmark in international financial relations. On one hand, the oil-exporting countries acquired unprecedented and vast financial surpluses practically overnight. Given the relatively low absorptive capacity of several of these economies, most notably the Middle Eastern ones, these surpluses were deposited with the private banks in the Eurocurrency market. On the other hand, the need of the oil-importing less developed countries to obtain finance to cover balance of payments deficits increased sharply. The banks faced with vast OPEC deposits and dwindling demand from the recession-ridden industrialised countries became keener to provide finance to third world borrowers in conditions so lax as to appear invisible. As a result of 'financial permissiveness' Argentina, Brazil and Mexico jointly owed the international financial system around 200 billion dollars by the end of 1982 and held a significant bargaining chip. The stability of the international financial system depended more than marginally on the willingness and capacity of these countries to continue servicing their debt. As *The Economist* anxiously reflected, they could wield "debtor power".

During the seventies the access to substantial volumes of funds with no apparent conditionality increased the short-term flexibility of deficit countries in dealing with their external accounts. From this point Griffith-Jones contends that financial dependency remains a valid concept only for those countries whose access to international liquidity remained restricted throughout the seventies. The larger semi-industrialised countries of Latin America that had an active role in international capital markets gained a greater margin of short-term external manoeuvre and were able significantly to delink their growth from the fluctuations of the metropolitan cycle. Some governments found in the banks' preferences for financial equilibrium a natural source of legitimisation for their own policy objectives. Yet over-emphasis on financial equilibria to the detriment of all other economic objectives (as in the case of the Southern Cone countries' disregard for the disequilibria in the real economy that may ensue) was a function of domestic political dynamics rather than a direct imposition of the international financial sector. Mexico and Brazil provide ready examples of governments that borrowed actively abroad to finance industrial development and to sustain high rates of exports and growth through the world recession. Argentina and Chile followed the opposite course and, in search of 'efficiency', drastically opened their economy to external competition which, coupled with the swift appreciation of their exchange rates, gave way to an extreme bias in favour of imports and de-industrialisation. Obviously for all borrowing countries the increase in debt service has entailed a new set of structural constraints, an area in which further research is urgent. Yet the assessment of the long term implications of indebtedness in each country will be related to the ultimate purpose of the debt and not merely with the absolute volume reached. In this sense, the determinants of national development strategies cannot be explained solely as the unfolding of global order being forced on the periphery.

The chapter by Aldo Ferrer argues that the ties of dependency are being lessened as a consequence of world economic restructuring. He pins his argument on several related trends. Since the immediate post-war period the accelerated expansion of Japan and Western Europe has eroded the hegemony of the United States. This has led to a tilting of the balance among industrialised countries, and a world order under-pinned by American hegemony has evolved to one based on economic interdependence. For Latin America this entails the multiplication of sources of supply of capital goods, technology and finance. Moreover, the developed countries are confronted with mounting internal tensions that erode the foundations on which their collective supremacy rested. In addition, the level of development achieved by some Latin American countries no longer allows the simplistic view that their economies are totally structured for the benefit of metropolitan powers. The semi-industrialised countries of the continent have been successful in expanding their industrial output, in diversifying their trade structure and their export markets — factors which have enhanced their external flexibility. Latin America has become more closely integrated into the world economy as a whole and developed closer links with the developed countries in particular. Though he does not specify this caveat, Ferrer is particularly referring to Mexico and the semi-industrialised countries of South America.

The argument that crisis and recession within the developed centres lessens their capacity for involvement in the periphery may at first glance bear points of resemblance with A.G. Frank's interpretation of the respite provided for Latin American development during the Great Depression and the two World Wars (Frank, 1967, p.297). But Ferrer does not support his case by only pointing to the greater breathing space provided by the crisis-ridden metropolises; he also looks at the other side of the coin, the strengthened economies and states of the larger Latin American countries which gives them greater leverage in negotiating both with foreign capital and with other states. To the extent that the Latin American economies are more closely incorporated into the world economy, reciprocal influences are possible.

An important point which these chapters bring out is that closer integration has opened new options and increased the external scope of action of the state. A corollary to this argument may well be that backwardness was not a result of integration of the periphery into the world market but of its incomplete integration (Kay, 1975, p.x). Most writing on dependency has tended to assume the desirability of economic autarky. Dudley Seers, for example, in an attempt to identify sources of dependency, pointed to reliance on oil, cereals and technology as important yardsticks. From this premise the conclusion was drawn that the countries best able to withstand the breakdown of their trade were the least dependent:

> The emphasis suggested by this approach would be to aim at greater national self-sufficiency, by policies aimed at consumption as well as production (Seers, 1979, p.109).

The pitfall of this line of thought (which stems from the over-concentration on international trade relations in the line of Frank, Emmanuel and Amin) is that countries as disparate in the world economic and political order as West Germany (dependent on oil and cereals) and Thailand (dependent on oil and technology) may be lumped together in the same category of semi-dependent countries. Moreover, an acceptable degree of self-sufficiency can only be attained by a few resource-rich countries.

Ferrer, like Seers, points in the direction of domestic reform rather than international reform to overcome backwardness and poverty, though not in the direction of autarky. Here a semantic clarification is pertinent: autarky refers to the ability to be self-sufficient, whereas autonomy is the capacity to be self-centred. There is no necessary correlation between the two, even though one may ease the other. Drawing on the experience of the advanced industrialised economies, Ferrer highlights that their autonomy was related to their mutual interdependence, the intimate interconnections of their economies. Post-war economic expansion was not only based on the domestic market but also on a high level of international transactions, on intra-industrial specialisation within the centre or 'the trilateral system' made up of Western Europe, North America and Japan.

## The state and the domestic structure

The first three chapters of Part II review aspects of national development in Latin America. They highlight the complex interaction between the domestic setting and the international context and provide the analytical tools to correct certain misconceptions about the role of the state.

Few analysts would dispute the crucial role played by the state in the process of economic development, yet there is little agreement on what that role is. Some approach the subject making a clearcut distinction between state and civil society; implicitly or explicitly the state is viewed as an autonomous agent acting upon society which, except in cases of corruption or inefficiency, is able to carry out the interests of the community as a whole. Others, influenced in various degrees and by different strands of Marxian thought, have tended to be more wary about taking for granted the neutrality of state intervention.

The world-system perspective takes the view that the peripheral state is a direct instrument of international capital, passively adjusting to the unfolding of the international division of labour. Moreover

> the duality of state and economy (market) reflects a nineteenth-century historical interlude, a brief contradiction in a small part of the world which was generalised into a principal ground of liberal social thought. It has no place as a basic theoretical duality in political economy (Wallerstein and Hopkins, 1981, p.246).

Chapter 5 by E.V.K. FitzGerald disputes the interpretation of the peripheral state as a neocolonial instrument − an interpretation which by identifying economic and political spheres, reduces politics to the manifestation of market relations. The thrust of the essay is aimed in two directions. Since both the conflict between core and periphery and the conflict between classes collide in the peripheral state, the essay examines the relative autonomy of the state vis-à-vis internal forces and vis-à-vis international forces.

FitzGerald contends that although the state acts to preserve the interest of capital it is not and cannot be subject to its direct control. He grounds his argument on the characterisation of semi-industrialised economies developed by Oscar Braun (Braun, 1973) as an extension of the trade theory formulated by the Economic Commission for Latin America (ECLA). In semi-industrialised economies the expanded reproduction, and even the simple reproduction of capital is obstructed because a significant part of the machines and inputs required for production are controlled by other countries. Since the process of capital accumulation is neither self-regulatory nor self-sufficient the state is called upon to play a crucial role. Derived from the incomplete nature of these economies, state intervention has particular features; it must intervene not only in production but in circulation as well. Thus it has two sets of tasks to fulfill: the better known and more 'instrumentalist' ones related to the regulation of the labour supply and investment in infrastructure and production of essential inputs; and the hitherto less examined but probably more crucial tasks of 'macroeconomic management' at the level of circulation. The incompleteness of these semi-industrialised economies entails, in effect, the subordination of production to circulation — a reversal of the logical relation which occurs at the global level. In the periphery this reversal is reflected in recurrent foreign exchange shortages, fiscal crises[4] and inflation. Management of these falls within the role of the state and state autonomy is required to deal with them so that accumulation is not obstructed. As foreign trade conditions deteriorate the state has increasing saliency in the management of exports (both primary goods and manufactures) and imports (particularly fuel, food and capital goods). In the financial sphere the scope for intervention and relative autonomy is particularly evident. To solve the fiscal crisis and counter the foreign trade bottlenecks the state increases external borrowing and 'becomes a financial intermediary in its own right, locked into the international system but at the same time gaining freedom to manoeuvre domestically and in the case of larger borrowers, even internationally' (p.111). Internally this special role of the state is enhanced by the virtual absence of domestic capital markets, and externally by the need for domestic borrowers to obtain government underwriting for foreign loans.

The last part of the chapter moves away from the logic of capital to a complementary route to the concept of state autonomy: the discretionary intervention of managers of the state apparatus. Given the part played by the state in macroeconomic management this is not only a theoretical possibility but also a necessity in order to sustain accumulation. Yet the intimate connection between the state and economic development implies that the conflict between the different fractions of capital is reflected in the conflict between what may be called the 'financial fraction' of state managers versus the 'production and trade fraction'.

Obviously there are limits to the functioning of relative autonomy. Under the growing influence of domestic finance capital and its intimate connections with the international financial system, the financial fraction of state managers has acquired greater leverage in the formulation of economic policy making. In practice the process may well be mutually supportive and implies that the state itself is a terrain for struggle. This conclusion suggests, therefore, that the room for bureaucratic politics and the impact of these on policy making are probably more significant than commonly assumed. For example, Cardoso views his construct of 'bureaucratic rings' (Cardoso, 1978, p.18) as applicable only to particular periods of political life when the relation between civil society and the state seems to dispense with the mediation of parties. From a different perspective and attempting to establish a comparison with the political system of the United States, J.S. Migdal suggested that the state in less developed countries does not 'have enough stability of structure or form' to guarantee a fruitful analysis of bureaucratic interests (J.S. Migdal, 1974, p.514).

A different perspective on the role of the state is offered in the chapter by Peter B. Evans. From the economic analysis of the logic of capital at a relatively high level of abstraction, we shift to sociological analysis applied to a particular country – Brazil. From the concern with the regulation of foreign trade and finance we now move to the role of the state at the level of production. In a conscious effort to unite the macro/micro dialectic the chapter highlights the inherent contradictions of a development model which relied simultaneously on the transnational corporations and the expansion of the state sector. The pact of domination that emerged and profited from the impressive growth records of the Brazilian 'economic miracle' holds together a particular balance of interests. It is a threefold pact composed of foreign, local and state enterprises, the 'triple alliance' in Evans's more graphic terminology. This pact functioned to promote rapid capital accumulation with the exclusion of popular forces from significant benefits.

The chapter brings to the fore the qualitative change in the relationship between the state and society as a result of the evolution of state capitalism and the central role that the state has acquired in production. This entrepreneurial role is not restricted to a mere gap-bridging exercise which covers low profit areas. It has also expanded into highly profitable sectors where the state has become an economic agent – an individual profit-seeking capitalist – in its own right. A result of this expansion is that one of the fractions that constitute the pact of domination, the 'state bourgeoisie' (the social sector engaged in accumulation in public enterprises), has in effect been created by the state itself.[5] The state has formed a class fraction of its own and *mutatis mutandis* it has gained a greater degree of freedom from the two other components of the alliance.

The process has complex implications. On the one hand, far from being a direct instrument of private capital, the state has entered into competition with it albeit not at a level of an all-out antagonistic conflict. Rather the competition takes place within certain implicit parameters that do not undermine the interests of capital. On the other hand, there can be said to be a partition of the state, as an institution, into two segments each with relative autonomy from the other: the central bureaucratic machine and the entrepreneurial segment. The overall state institution has acquired what could be described as a split personality. The two other partners of the alliance, multinational and local capital, can feed upon and fuel this potential division leading to the possibility that one part of the state may turn against the other.

Yet, much as it may be deceptive to analyse the state as a unified whole, the two parts of the state are not absolutely divorced from each other. By virtue of the same process whereby it has become an entrepreneur, induced the emergence of the state bourgeoisie and increased its command over economic resources, the state has augmented its degree of freedom from the direct control of private capital. This holds true in spite of the nature of state capitalism in Brazil, which far from operating as a spearhead for a social revolution with a redistributive programme, has been intimately associated with the private sector.[6]

Finally, in so far as the state in its entrepreneurial guise is actually a member of the triple alliance it is neither a neutral third force nor an umpire. The sociological insight into the complex interweaving of interests within the alliance puts into question the notion of the state as a passive entity with, to borrow from Raymond Vernon, 'sovereignty at bay' as well as that of a state that has fused into a single mechanism with transnational corporations as a consequence of dependent development.

Chapter 7 by G. Philip analyses the possibilities opened to Mexico and Venezuela by their vast oil revenues. Mexico and Venezuela are two other cases where the model of the 'triple alliance' could be fruitfully applied. Whereas in Brazil certain external and internal dimensions of autonomy were enhanced with the profitable expansion of the public sector, in Mexico and Venezuela oil revenues have made that process all the more viable. Philip starts by providing a critical review of the weaknesses of economies heavily reliant on the revenues generated by the exports of primary products, and then points in the direction of three variables that may play a central role in averting a similar outcome for the apparently more fortunate oil exporters: the steady expansion of export revenues, the achievement of effective import substitution and efficient state expenditure. The external variable, the successful long-term expansion of their export revenues appears dubious. Oil exports have enjoyed a monopoly price; but as a consequence of recession, conservation and diversification output will need to be restricted in order to sustain price levels, in which case Mexico and Venezuela will be unable significantly to expand their export volumes in the next decade. If an agreement on export volumes is not attained, export revenues will tend to fall. In either case there is a foreseeable ceiling to growth based on the steady expansion of oil revenues.

The two domestic variables may however offset the damage done by the fall of export revenues. Oil may generate national income on a large scale, and thereby facilitate an accelerated expansion of the domestic market providing a ready stimulus for local industrialisation. In this respect Mexico and Venezuela are better placed compared to other oil-exporting countries as they already possess a relatively sophisticated industrial base. In addition, a crucial role can be played by state expenditure. It can follow two alternative courses which are obviously not mutually exclusive, direct capital investment or redistribution of national income. Oil revenues have tended to make both alternatives comparatively easier. The state has gained access to a greater proportion of the economic surplus by-passing the political difficulties of carrying out a fiscal reform. Consequently, room to manoeuvre domestically has also increased. Yet this may be short-lived and the fiscal gap reopened due to the probable halt to a steady expansion of oil revenues. Thus, the state will be confronted in the not too distant future with the typical bottlenecks of semi-industrialised economies outlined by FitzGerald, only at a higher level of economic activity and with higher popular expectations than before.

The closing chapter by Carlos Fortin examines the extent to which the Marxist concept of relative state autonomy can illuminate the analysis of Latin American development. He points out that as a first step a distinction must be drawn between two aspects of the state. At a high level of abstraction, it is an implicit *pact* among the dominant classes to affirm their power on the rest of civil society. At a more concrete level, the state is also the *set of institutions* which expresses and guarantees that pact. From the viewpoint of this distinction the relative autonomy of the state may be defined as the degree of independence of the institutional apparatuses and their personnel from the pact or social base on which they lie, in other words, the extent to which the state is legitimately a creator of its own socio-economic environment.

Fortín also points out that another route to define and circumscribe relative autonomy refers to the logic underlying the emergence of the state and its role. As such this closing chapter serves as a guide to some of the theoretical issues raised by the preceding chapters and illuminates areas for further research.

The authors in this volume have begun with different questions and ideological persuasions. They have pursued different approaches, at times contrasting, at others complementary. The purpose of this exercise was not to draw a conclusive synthesis, nor can it be claimed that this has occurred. Perhaps the value of this exchange lies in inject-ing caution into two sorts of views: first, the one that blames every-thing that is wrong on external constraints; and second, the one hoping that from increased bargaining power autonomous development, justice and welfare will spring. As Díaz Alejandro would put it, 'it all depends (to the dismay of the lazy, the impatient or the seeker of mass mobilising slogans) on the circumstances' — circumstances that can be shaped by correctly and creatively analysing a specific reality in such a way as to transform it.

# Notes

1   For a review of the theoretical implications of economic cycles see *Review*, Vol.II, No.4, Spring 1979.

2   See, for example, F. Block's argument that 'an open economy is in the net interests of the capitalist class' (Block, 1977, p.1). See also Appendix.

3   See D. Collier (1979) for further questioning of the relationship between authoritarianism and economic development.

4   Fiscal crisis, following J. O'Connor (1973), is the persistent tendency for government expenditure to grow against a constrained tax base.

5   The concept of state bourgeoisie as a distinct feature of state capitalism must be distinguished from the concept of state managers used by FitzGerald. Stage managers refers to the personnel in charge of managing the administrative and organisational functions of the state. As such they do not have a direct relation with capital, by definition they are relatively autonomous. State bourgeoisie refers to the social sector directly engaged in generating surplus in public enterprises. They do not express the general interests of capital as do stage managers, but only the individual interests of their enterprises (see Chapter 8).

6   In contradistinction to the governments of Allende in Chile, Velasco Alvarado in Peru and Peronist Argentina where state capitalism operated as a spearhead for income redistribution and social transformations. Ironically, since then, those now dreaming with the 'withering away of the state' in these countries are right wingers rather than left wingers.

# Part I


# The Centre-Periphery Relationship

Perhaps because of this limited aim, it is not easy to find clear statements of revisionist hypotheses and arguments linking open economies with authoritarian regimes. One line of reasoning argues that to compete in international markets and to attract investments the domestic labour force must be kept cheap and docile. Investments with long gestation periods are also said to require more predictable political environments; openness may be accompanied by more of those investments, calling forth authoritarian leaders eager to supply stability and order. Another line of reasoning emphasises not the steady-state political requirements of openness, but the political preconditions for a *transition* from a closed to a more open economy. Such a change, the argument goes, will inevitably hurt vested interests which can only be disciplined by an authoritarian regime. Once the transition is accomplished, the need for authoritarianism would presumably disappear. While the first line of reasoning is usually found in the neo-Marxist literature, the latter is often suggested in the capitalism-now-freedom-later literature.

Both approaches frequently make reference to what contemporary mainstream academic economics says and does not say regarding openness and several economic variables which may influence a country's political regime. The next section of this chapter will sketch my (perhaps idiosyncratic) understanding of that matter. It should be useful in such an exercise to differentiate between what may be termed the academic and practical orthodoxies of mainstream economics (Bacha and Díaz Alejandro, 1981). The former is the product of leading academic centres, is careful in stating its assumptions and conclusions, and tends towards flexibility and agnosticism. Its leading thinkers often are its own major critics, frequently curious about heterodox notions. For the topic at hand, glittering examples include James Meade, Bertil Ohlin and Paul Samuelson. Practical orthodoxy is more assertive: it is found in editorials of the business press, among those who seek only 'bottom-line' knowledge or just a smattering of paradigmatic 'common sense' from their Master or even PhD degrees, and among some of the more politically or financially ambitious, or simply lazy, academics away from the rigour of their chairs. The main focus of the next section will be on academic orthodoxy; practical orthodoxy will not receive much attention, although its importance in the political world and in confusing the topic at hand is not denied.

The third section of the chapter will be a rather quick overview of key events in Latin American economic history to the mid-1960s which have helped to mould perceptions about openness. Since the discovery of the continent, Latin America has undergone a number of economic openings and closings, each leaving behind crucial memories which naturally influence one's gut reaction in discussing the topic of openness (say 'sugar' to Cubans and many will reply 'slavery').

The economic history of various Latin American countries should also provide, if not rigorous tests, at least some notion of the robustness of generalisations about links among openness, domestic economic variables and authoritarianism.

The fourth section will extend the historical narrative to the rest of the 1960s and to the 1970s, a period singularly traumatic for the region, when discussions about openness and authoritarianism became particularly urgent. A final section will present what may be regarded as the few valid generalisations arising from the rest of the chapter and the many questions left open.

## From the mainstream: sturdy propositions or chimerical fantasies?

Openness may refer to international trade in goods and services, or to international flows of capital and labour. Modern academic orthodoxy, contrary to popular impressions, has had surprisingly little to say about the welfare consequences of international factor flows. Until fairly recently, the bulk of serious research on international economics referred to commodity trade: the profession analysed nations exchanging wine for cloth, apples for blankets.

For many years I have been puzzled by the animosity shown by some heterodox economists toward the Heckscher-Ohlin-Samuelson models of international trade developed since the Second World War. Compared with earlier mainstream views of international trade, the modern formulations are much more modest about what can be claimed in favour of free trade and contain results which earlier orthodox economists regard as troublesome. For example, the Stolper-Samuelson theorem rigorously showed that freer trade policies could make some members of a nation *absolutely* worse off; in other words, not only were the gains from trade unequally distributed within a country, but for some groups there could also be losses under laissez-faire Post-war welfare economics also emphasised that unless those benefiting from a certain policy actually compensated those made worse off by it, one could not say that the policy was desirable.

A recent interchange between Ronald Findlay and Gottfried Haberler illustrates this contrast between the new and the old. Haberler first stated that income distribution within the less developed countries had nothing to do with the international economic order. Findlay invoked the Stolper-Samuelson theorem. Haberler replied:

> As far as the Stolper-Samuelson theorem is concerned, I would say that it is ingenious from the purely theoretical standpoint but is of no help in the present context, because it is based on a two-factor model and breaks down, as Stolper and Samuelson recognize, when we introduce, as we surely must, more than two factors and two types of income, different types of labour, salaries, profits, interests and so on. I therefore conclude that my statement that inequality of income has very little to do with the international order has emerged pretty much unscathed from the discussion. And the little systematic influence trade may have on income distribution may ... go in either direction ... (1979, p.87).

Whether an assumption is judged to be a brilliant simplification or an unexcusable distortion of reality very much depends on whether one likes the conclusions drawn from it. The Findlay approach is an example of modern academic orthodoxy at its best; using its analytical tools it opens the way to systematic exploration of links between trade and income distribution, replacing the somewhat obscurantist older view, so timid in granting the possibility that anybody may be hurt by openings. The Findlay approach will not reach simple conclusions such as 'trade benefits everybody' or 'trade hurts everybody'. It all depends (to the dismay of the lazy, the impatient or the seeker of mass-mobilising slogans) on the circumstances in which the trade takes place. But modern academic orthodoxy goes beyond boorish sceptical ignorance.

Take a country whose most abundant factor of production is land; a trade opening should witness land-intensive exports and benefits to landowners. This could improve income distribution if land is scattered evenly among sturdy Jeffersonian families and if the other major factor of production is a bundle of urban capital and labour, made up of a minority of families who had benefited from trade prohibitions. Under these circumstances, a plausible conjecture is that freer trade will also strengthen democratic forces and contribute to a freer flow of ideas. Latin American history does not provide many examples of this possibility, although Costa Rica and some Colombian coffee-growing areas approach it. But the point here is that one cannot say much about the link between trade and income distribution without knowing something about the distribution of land. To put it bluntly, if only one family owns the land, it seems foolish to blame free trade for a bad income distribution. Decreasing trade without touching land tenure will be an expensive and probably short-lived way to improve income distribution.

The Heckscher-Ohlin-Samuelson positive theory of the structure of international trade assumes that a given production function for each industry is known to all economic agents all over the world. The model can accommodate differences and changes in technology, but not gracefully. Continuous innovations, both in production processes and in products, and their international diffusion seem best handled in other models, which may include economies of scale and product differentiation. Technological change not instantly diffused will naturally generate quasi-rents to those originating it; leaders may have to innovate continually not just to grow but even to maintain their real income in the presence of technological borrowing by follower countries. The market for technology will show obvious differences from markets for cloth and wine; it is not clear that free trade in technology will benefit both sides, and leaders will be tempted to restrict their sales. As noted by Paul R. Krugman:

> Success by less developed countries in accelerating their adoption of new techniques can leave workers in developed countries

worse off; and it is easy to imagine that by encouraging protectionism such success could be self-defeating (1979, pp.253–266).

It is interesting that these words appeared not in the *Journal of Radical Political Economics*, but in a publication not famous for its heterodoxy.[3]

Other post-war theoretical developments have added to the need for care in making the case for openness. Second-best theorising opened a Pandora's box of models that, by noting that some markets were either missing or incomplete, by assuming this market imperfection or that instrument limitation, could lead to a disconcerting variety of results regarding the effects of freer trade on welfare and desirable policies. Under certain assumptions, without the need to abandon modern orthodox methodology, it can be shown that free trade would lead to a worsening of a country's welfare; autarky would be preferable to free trade. Even technological change and growth can be shown to be immiserising for a country under some circumstances. True, the major message of these models is that while government actions are required to correct distortions, and thus laissez-faire is out, it is unlikely that first-best policies would involve trade restrictions, so free or freer trade was still desirable. But if first-best policies are not feasible, a great deal can be justified depending on one's judgement on particular constraints and willingness to accept non-economic considerations (Díaz Alejandro, 1978; Díaz Alejandro, 1975a). Judgements will differ on whether one can expect the required finesse from public officials in charge of these matters, but mainstream academic economics does provide the analytical tools to establish non-dogmatically a hierarchy of policies, ranging from first to nth-best.

There *is* a serious gap in the array of analytical tools provided by mainstream trade theorists, who typically rely on the methodology of comparative statics. The path between two equilibrium situations is seldom discussed because standard models are not suitable for those explorations. The policy maker who wonders what will happen on the way to freer trade may get some sensible advice but few firm predictions from the scrupulous trade theorist. Practical-orthodox quacks have often rushed in to fill this gap in academic analysis.

Just as the period 1914–1950 bred pessimism regarding the net benefits of international trade, so the period 1950–1973 was conducive to optimism. The sturdy academic proposition that some trade can potentially make everyone better off, as compared with no trade, was increasingly turned by some practical orthodoxy into the conviction that more trade at all times, places and conditions will not only improve efficiency and accelerate growth, but also increase employment, improve income distribution and reduce governmental corruption. The question that naturally followed was: If all of these good things, why not political democracy also?

It was perhaps the exaggerated claims made for the benefits of freer trade that led some observers to wonder how such a marvellous economic engine could often be associated with monstrous political machines. It was only a small further step in the dialectical crescendo to argue that authoritarian politics was a necessary condition, and to some perhaps not too high a price to pay, to obtain such wondrous economic results for at least part of the population.

The 1950–1973 period also witnessed the blooming of transnational enterprises (TNEs). 'Apple Inc.' and 'Cloth Inc.' spanned the world and every year came out with a 'new apple' and a 'new cloth'. The question that must be asked is whether this is irrelevant institutional detail or something likely to modify even sturdy mainstream propositions. Does it matter for economics or politics whether exporters are Jeffersonian family farmers or Differentiated Apples Inc., an integrated agrobusiness which handles apples from seed to mouth and hires the Mid-Ocean Auctioneer as PR man? This is a tougher challenge to mainstream orthodoxy than complicated neo-Ricardian models of steady-state growth and heterogeneous capital goods, which can generate ahistorical chimerical fantasies of their own (Dixit, 1981).[1] Indeed, several kinds of traditional economic theories, from neoclassical to Marxist, are uneasy in the presence of imperfect competition and its modern corporation; and standard democratic theory has little room for 'corporate citizens'.

That so much of technical change is generated or diffused by oligopolies further complicates the analysis. Given the diversity of special assets and of the stimuli triggering foreign investment, one may doubt a priori claims regarding unambiguous welfare implications of TNE activities (Díaz Alejandro, 1981a; Lindblom, 1977). This is reinforced by noting the heterogeneity of the less developed countries, not just in domestic market size and natural resource endowment, but also in the responsiveness of their government officials to different domestic social groups and in the bargaining ability of those officials. Such an agnostic approach is in the spirit of that line of economic thought which teaches that private profit-seeking behaviour may lead to socially desirable results, but only if certain conditions are met, conditions which involve both economic and political variables, and whose presence in less developed countries can neither be taken for granted nor regarded as impossible.

The analysis of trade and investment in the context of specific historical circumstances should clear up at least some of the uncomfortable mists of agnosticism left by the 'it all depends' of theorists. We have not discussed mainstream theoretical analysis of international flows of labour, a topic that only recently is being rediscovered in major academic centres. Many have noted the contrasting reactions to a freer flow of capital versus a freer flow of labour among observers, including academic ones, in the industrialised world. Market imperfections, non-economic reasons, or just 'common sense' are more readily found to justify limiting the flow of the latter (Díaz Alejandro, 1975b). This is how Gottfried Haberler reacted to Ronald Findlay's observation that a truly liberal international order should provide free movement not only of goods and capital but also of people:

> I, for one, simply took it for granted that there is no free migration from the LDCs [less developed countries] to the DCs [developed countries], and only in a few rare cases between the DCs, nor is there free migration between the LDCs for that matter. One may deplore this, but it would be unrealistic to expect a change. It is even doubtful whether a greater international mobility of labor can be regarded as desirable from the standpoint of international peace and harmony, despite the economic benefits for all participants that may be expected (Haberler, 1979, p.82).[2]

## Some openings and closings in Latin American history

Writers on the political economy of Latin America seem almost obsessed with the external sector as the source of all that is good or bad in the region.[3] This is not surprising given the history of Latin America. The conquest of the continent was a *sui generis* forced opening of native economies making most local residents terribly worse off. (So far no bright cliometrician has challenged this conventional wisdom; Iberian *conquistadores* are perhaps less charismatic than the slave-owners of the US South.) No fancy algebra nor definitional exercises are needed to call the system that emerged one of exploitation or unequal exchange. *Encomiendas*, slavery and debt-peonage characterised 'the labour market'; royal favours, legal trickery and the force of arms cleared 'the land market'. Trade was limited as to countries, commodities and even harbours. Future generations were to remember not only the trauma of forced opening but also the peculiar prosperity it yielded the conquering nations. Thoughtful Mexicans and Venezuelans, contemplating their present oil riches, wisely recall the melancholy rise and fall of Spain during the sixteenth and seventeenth centuries.[4] An opening based on exhaustible natural resources, whether silver or oil, may make you very well off today but may induce habits and economic and social structures that, when the silver and oil run out, will make you sink back to a poverty perhaps worse than that of pre-bonanza days. Judicious intertemporal trade among generations of the same society, i.e. maintaining a prudent balance between consumption today and tomorrow, must accompany international trade based on exhaustible natural resources, otherwise openings may not lead to permanent gains. Even in the case of trade based on non-exhaustible natural resources yielding easy rents there are obvious dangers that a society may fail to expand into other sources of profitable trade.

The Bourbon liberalisation of decrepit Iberian mercantilism during the second half of the eighteenth century led to export-led booms in many parts of Latin America. As the appetite grew with the eating, local elites became increasingly restless and resentful of the still extensive trade restrictions. Most of the leaders of the Latin American independence movements blamed Iberian crowns for artificially delinking the region from promising external markets. An 1800 tour of the 'de-linker' Samir Amin[5] through the flourishing 'Economic Societies of Friends of the Country' might have required an escort of loyalist troops (or of poor but royalist *pardos*). To the patriotic intellectuals it was clear at that point that the less enlightened a despot and the greater the degree of political tyranny, the more trade restrictions one would find. Arrogant and often ignorant Iberian bureaucrats had more to do with the popularity of such an idea than the writings of the peripheral Scot.

The excessive hopes of the liberal patriots were dashed during the chaotic 1820s. The destruction and disorganisation caused by the wars of independence, veritable civil wars and unfavourable international market conditions combined to make post-liberation openings weak or ambiguous in their impact on growth. Even if the supply was willing, the demand was weak: as noted by Arthur Lewis, before the second half of the nineteenth century the British and European industrial revolutions needed few inputs from today's third world (Lewis, 1978, pp.5–6). The south of the United States dominated the cotton trade, and only a few luxury products, such as sugar, could overcome high transport costs, thanks largely to slavery and the 'mining' of new soils. The post-independence decades are one of the most obscure periods in Latin American economic history, but one may conjecture that in most of the region per capita incomes in 1850 were below those of 1800. After a burst of libertarian measures, immediately following independence, a conservative and traditionalist reaction spread throughout most of the new nations, generating titanic despots, who to this day exert enormous fascination.

Indeed, in the feverish intellectual climate of the 1960s, those great tyrants, who had allied themselves with a very pre-Maryknoll Church and had opposed public education, were rediscovered and glorified by some segments of the left. The obscurity of the period encouraged their being perceived as great industrialisers and opponents of 'the imperialism of free trade'. The liberals were cast as the destroyers of local crafts and manufactures, in an unholy alliance with British imperialism. By some of these revisionist accounts, a good share of the time of British leadership during the first half of the nineteenth century was devoted to snuffing out Paraguayan industrialisation. This type of revisionism has not spread to Mexico, whose nineteenth-century conservatives ended not with the courageous stand of a Lopez but behind the weak shield of a Maximilian.

By the last third of the nineteenth century growing demand in Europe and North America for primary products and a drastic lowering of ocean freight costs presented tempting trade options to most Latin American countries. Local resource endowments and probably domestic politics influenced the rapidity and degree of the openings that took place and which continued at least until the First World War. Thus, the Argentine and Uruguayan openings came earlier and went further than that of Colombia, whose civil wars continued until the beginning of this century.

By the late 1920s Latin America actively participated in international trade, was an important recipient of international capital flows, and some countries had witnessed large inflows of labour. Monetary arrangements by the late 1920s tended to conform with the restored international gold standard. Relative to its past and future history, the region probably reached its maximum degree of opening toward trade, capital and labour during the 1920s. The crude indicators of opening and development shown in Table 2.1 emphasise the heterogeneity found in the region regarding both opening and development; compare the figures for Argentina, Chile, Cuba and Uruguay, at one extreme, with those for most of the Caribbean and Central America, Bolivia and Ecuador at the other.

We do not have indices of political democracy for those years; nor do we have estimates of per capita income for more than a handful of countries. The per capita imports shown in the table are likely to be highly correlated with two variables: positively with per capita income and negatively with size of country, measured by population. Bearing these two offsetting influences in mind and leaving aside colonial or quasi-colonial territories, the table suggests that the degree of political democracy in Latin America in the 1920s was correlated with per capita income. But the correlation is unlikely to be very high, and as later years were to show, far from robust. Table 2.1 offers the stronger hint that in the 1920s relatively high per capita incomes went together with a high degree of opening to both trade and investment, even if openings were to be measured not as per capita trade and investment but as trade as a share of gross national product, and as foreign investment as a percentage of all capital. Again, however, such gross correlations are unlikely to take us very far, at least using ranges observed in Latin America. Specific features of national histories, are likely to dominate the explanatory power of macroeconomic variables.

Take, for example, the cases of Chile, Cuba and Uruguay as they stood in the late 1920s. Their per capita incomes were probably roughly similar, as were their populations and opening to trade. Yet both the extravagant Cuban opening to foreign capital and its miserable politics must be explained by its quasi-colonial status and by geography. Domestic income distribution and politics in these three countries also had something to do with the characteristics of major export products: mineral, tropical and temperate staples surely had different Hirschmanesque linkages. Post 1929 history for these three countries also shows the bewildering variety of political paths which may be taken even by economies similar in per capita income and their degree of opening to trade. But a detailed comparison of these three fascinating economies and polities cannot be undertaken here.

There are additional measures of openings besides the ones suggested in earlier paragraphs. An important one would be a country's *policies* towards trade and international flows of capital and labour. One could, for example, compare levels and structures of tariffs and subsidies on traded goods and quantitative restrictions on investment and migration.

Domestic policies, factor endowments and other domestic variables interacting with external conditions will in fact yield such observed measures of opening as imports as a percentage of gross product. Regarding tariffs, the then predominant instrument to restrict trade, it would be difficult to argue that in the 1920s protectionism was a general banner of progressive political movements in Latin America. The Argentine Socialist Party was firmly for free trade in goods (and for the gold standard as well). One of the most interesting protectionist experiments during that decade in Latin America occurred, of all places, in Cuba, and was sponsored by General Gerardo Machado, known otherwise as 'the Butcher'. The Leguia dictatorship in Peru was frankly protectionist, at least since 1922. Contrary to widespread misconceptions, Latin American countries did not embrace free trade absolutely even during export booms. In most countries tariffs were fairly high both for revenue and for mildly protectionist purposes. A modest but significant import-substituting industrialisation process had started in many countries before 1929. Argentina and Brazil witnessed in the 1920s tariff-jumping direct foreign investment in manufacturing. In many countries there were severe criticisms of monoculture and the concentration of exports on a few markets. But these legitimate preoccupations typically led to prescriptions for diversifying export products and markets rather than delinking from the international economy.

A clearer picture existed regarding foreign capital, where the need to bargain and regulate more effectively was felt from the Rio Grande to Patagonia. Modern mainstream theorists, aware of the oligopolistic nature of many industries in which foreign capital is concentrated, and of the Ricardian and Hotelling rents yielded by natural resources being exploited by foreign enterprise, may find little to quarrel about with the modest Latin American aspirations of those years. Some types of international labour flows were also viewed with disfavour among progressives and others; most democratic Cuban opinion disliked the inflows of labour from elsewhere in the Caribbean during the sugar harvest. Such species of labour protectionism was not without racist overtones, like that practised in Australia for many years, and that which marked the end of laissez-passer in the United States during the 1920s.

In spite of the obvious flaws in Latin American societies — skewed incomes and wealth distribution, vulnerability to shocks from the world economy, an irritating reliance on foreign capital and limited political participation by broad segments of the population — a comparison between Latin America and Africa or Asia circa 1928 would suggest net positive dividends for Latin America in terms of economic and political welfare due to sovereignty and a sustained non-preferential opening to global international trade. A comparison between the

Latin America of 1928 with that of 1878 would have yielded a similar feeling of relative satisfaction, in contrast with an 1828–78 comparison and, alas, also in contrast with a 1928–78 Southern Cone comparison.

Depression and war generated external demand and supply shocks to Latin American economies during the 1930s and 1940s. Trade declined absolutely and relative to gross national product; capital flows practically disappeared as early as 1929; and domestic rural-urban migrations dwarfed any international ones. The relatively healthy reaction of many countries in the region to those cataclysmic events has often been narrated: domestic manufactures and even primary products replaced many imports, and domestic savings financed nearly all capital formation (Díaz Alejandro, 1980a; 1981b). During the early years of the crisis most incumbent administrations were swept out of power; few other political generalisations seem possible. Import-substituting industrialisation proceeded under conservative regimes as in Argentina, as well as under reformist ones, as in Mexico. Changes in relative prices, generated in world markets or as a consequence of attempts to equilibrate the balance of payments, plus stop-gap measures to deal with depressed demand were observed in most countries with some degree of autonomy in economic policy, regardless of the precise colouration of governments.

These closings of the 1930s and early 1940s did stimulate inventiveness among public and private actors. New public agencies to promote development were created and new national entrepreneurs appear to have come to the fore. The economic and political power of export-oriented traditional landowners waned. By the end of the Second World War the relative position of Latin America in the world economy looked strong, and these nations had a modest but significant voice in the emerging Bretton Woods institutions and the United Nations.

But Latin America during the 1930s and 1940s appears healthy *relative* to the depths of depression and the destruction and political horrors elsewhere. It is doubtful that per capita incomes grew during 1929–45 faster than during earlier decades; available evidence shows that they grew less than in later years. Except for Brazil, manufacturing growth was lower during 1929–45 than in earlier or later years. The relatively good performance of countries with significant autonomy in economic policy, including not only large countries like Argentina and Brazil but also Chile and Uruguay, was to an important extent based on the economic and institutional infrastructure developed during the era of export-led growth. Large pre-1929 exports in those countries led to the high per capita imports reported in Table 2.1; those imports provided rich and obvious targets for entrepreneurs during 1929–45.

The immediate post-war years, say 1946–48, may have witnessed the peak of Latin America euphoria. In most countries, external demand for traditional exports boomed again, and the supply of capital goods and intermediate products still difficult to produce in the region was becoming more plentiful than in earlier years. Contrary to the gloomy views of some conservative observers, industrialisation not only maintained gains registered during the war but advanced further in the post-war world. It was during 1946–48 when value added in Latin American manufacturing surpassed that in rural activities. As late as 1953, when he should have known better, General Perón was telling General Ibáñez, then President of Chile, that there is nothing more elastic than the economy. As noted by Albert Hirschman the rapid industrialisation of the 1930s and 1940s (coupled with favourable terms of trade during the immediate post-war period) led to delusions of economic invulnerability among some policy makers (Hirschman, 1979, pp.61–68).

If import substitution, protection and rigorous exchange controls had done so well during the 1930s and 1940s, why not continue and strengthen those policies? The fierce protectionism and arrogant economic nationalism embraced by major industrialised countries since the late 1920s had scarred peripheral nations who prior to 1929 had allocated their meagre resources largely on the assumption that hegemonic powers were serious about free trade and convertibility. The Bretton Woods agreement and the International Trade Organisation (ITO) promised a partial return to freer trade and some convertibility, but the abortive British return to convertibility in 1947 and the 1950 death of ITO in the United States Congress were ominous signs. A sharp recession in the United States during 1948–49 and the difficulties experienced by European post-war reconstruction (before the Marshall Plan) revived fears of a new Great Depression. The coup d'état in Prague and the Berlin blockade in 1948, the victory of the Chinese communists in 1949 and the outbreak of the Korean war in 1950 made those forecasting an imminent world war worthy of at least a hearing. Even if a hot world war was avoided, a prolonged cold war between the two superpowers looked very likely, as evidenced by the signing of the North Atlantic Treaty Organisation (NATO) and the detonation of the first Soviet atomic bomb in 1949.

An economic opening under those circumstances seemed to imply for Latin American countries the abandonment of any pretensions to an independent foreign policy. Many pre-war European markets appeared lost or reduced; the old continent could not be counted on, as in the past, to act as an offsetting influence to that of the United States. Around 1950 'the Third Position' was the monopoly of Argentina, Spain, Sweden and Switzerland, neither a politically homogeneous group nor a formidable economic block. Naturally, those who had prospered in Latin America under the protective circumstances of the

1930s and 1940s made the most of the gloomy outlook for the international economy. Shortages of external supplies of steel, shipping and weapons during the early 1940s placed many a member of the Latin American armed forces in the post-war protectionist camp.

The 1950s mood of export pessimism, which nevertheless rejected autarky, predominating in Brazil and the Southern Cone countries well into the 1960s, was expressed in a 1953 report of the United Nations Economic Commission for Latin America. Discussing possible export incentives, the report noted the instability of foreign markets, adding:

> A sharp fall in prices, such as that which occurred a short time ago, while retaining some of the benefits from the increase preceding the Korean War, revives a series of previous vicissitudes which hardly encourage production for export. Although coffee prices are today relatively high, it should not be forgotten that Brazil was once obliged to destroy large unsaleable stocks of this commodity. For similar reasons, during the war, Argentina accumulated several grain harvests which had later to be wasted as emergency fuel. In contrast, the prospects on the domestic market are generally more stable, above all, in manufacturing activities. Industry, however, requires certain exports which provide it with essential goods (ECLA, 1953, p.xxii).

Some medium and large Latin American countries, such as Mexico and Peru, early in the post-war period phased out a good part of their depression and war-time policies, moving towards more even-handed incentives between exports and import substitution, while retaining non-trivial levels of protection. The Peruvian transition was managed by the dictatorship of General Odría; the Mexican one occurred under the administrations heir to the Mexican revolution. Central American countries, which had exercised little policy choice during 1929–45, on the whole continued to ride along with the impulses emanating from abroad, come what may. These small, open and mostly passive economies registered as a group impressive growth rates in exports and gross national product during the 1950s and 1960s. Those two decades also witnessed economic expansion in both Mexico and Peru. Curiously, the relatively open and fast-growing Central American and Peruvian economies moved toward greater protectionism during the early 1960s, perhaps under Southern Cone influences, but without reaching the extreme protectionism of that region.

Brazil and the Southern Cone, which so many social scientists seem to regard as the whole of Latin America, struggled along with stagnant exports and increasingly expensive import substitution until around the mid-1960s, when an opening trend, timid in some countries, became noticeable. The persistence of 1930s trade policies into the 1950s hurt Brazil less than Argentina, and hurt Uruguay more than Argentina, the reason being that in small markets and in the context of an expanding international economy the costs of protection, in terms of efficiency and growth, escalated sharply.

Table 2.2 compares the dollar value of Latin American exports during the five years 1961–65 with those registered during 1946–50, with all data at current prices. During an interval of fifteen years a variety of export records were achieved. Luck in the commodity lottery and other particular events and circumstances influenced the outcome, but a role for trade policies would be difficult to deny. (Those trade policies may have led to some Latin American countries gaining market shares at the expense of others). Compare the performance of Chile with that of Peru, those of Uruguay and Costa Rica, and those of Argentina and Mexico. The conjecture that feeble external demand during the 1950s induced the persistence of favourable incentives for import substitution is further weakened by the substantial export expansions of many countries, large and small. Somoza's Nicaragua heads the list, and the then democratic Uruguay is at the bottom, but no robust political generalisations emerge from Table 2.2. Costa Rica does somewhat better than Guatemala, while Paraguay and Haiti have export performances about as dismal as that of the then democratic Brazil.

When a longer retrospective look is taken at the evolution of Latin American foreign trade, the astonishing fact emerges that in most countries (or at least in countries where the largest share of Latin Americans live) per capita imports, measured at constant prices, were during the early 1960s below, in some cases substantially below, levels reached during the late 1920s. Table 2.3 lists countries for which such data are available. The growth in per capita gross national product which occurred during that interval clearly involved profound shifts in both production and consumption structures. The fine performance of El Salvador is a reminder, if one is needed, that a prosperous external sector need not eliminate all development problems. The similar performance of Mexico and Venezuela is also interesting; the latter underwent an oil boom during the period covered in Table 2.3, while the former saw its oil exports dwindle and vanish after the 1938 nationalisations.

*Openings in Latin America since the mid-1960s*

Having offered this brief overview of the history of openings and closings from the 1800s to the 1960s, and the perceptions regarding openness which these experiences helped to mould, we now turn to some of the salient features of the trade and financial openings

Table 2.2

Dollar values of Latin American merchandise exports
at current prices, 1961–65
(Values for 1946–50 equal 100)

| | |
|---|---|
| Nicaragua | 535 |
| Peru | 359 |
| El Salvador | 334 |
| Panama | 314 |
| Ecuador | 303 |
| Venezuela | 278 |
| Costa Rica | 258 |
| Mexico | 244 |
| Guatemala | 228 |
| Chile | 206 |
| Dominican Republic | 204 |
| Honduras | 184 |
| Colombia | 168 |
| Paraguay | 149 |
| Haiti | 121 |
| Brazil | 120 |
| Argentina | 99 |
| Bolivia | 96 |
| Cuba | 94 |
| Uruguay | 92 |

Source: Basic data obtained from Naciones Unidas, *America Latina: Relación de Precios del Intercambio* (Santiago de Chile, 1976). According to this source, for Latin America as a whole, import unit values in 1961–65 stood at 128, with 1946–50 equal to 100.

openings may be presented. The heterogeneous political circumstances surrounding the openings will also be noted.

Moves toward export promotion worked in the sense that the target of expanding exports was achieved. Export pessimists were simply wrong; when incentives were provided both domestic supply and external demand proved to be sufficiently elastic. While Brazilian and Colombian merchandise exports, measured at current dollar prices, expanded between 1970–71 and 1978–79 at an annual rate of 22 per cent, those for Peru grew at only 12 per cent. Fast export growth was accompanied by substantial commodity diversification; by 1981 coffee amounted to less than 15 per cent of Brazilian merchandise exports, a fact few would have forecasted in 1963. Fast export growth, it should be emphasised, need not be accompanied by laissez-faire policies, nor indeed by the elimination of all protection. Brazilian and Colombian export achievements have been registered while substantial (even excessive for many sectors) protection was maintained, and with the public sector actively intervening in the export drive. Such 'Japanese approach' toward export promotion seems to have been followed by some Asian super-exporters, e.g. South Korea and Taiwan, countries which have maintained non-trivial import restrictions and rigorous exchange controls, while relying on subsidised credit, public enterprises and managed exchange rates as parts of their policy package. These experiences suggest that in a dynamic context the best index of trade openness for industrialising countries may not be relative levels of effective rates of protection and subsidisation as between import substitution and exports, but actual export growth rates, particularly those for non-traditional exports. Imports, after all, are the tangible fruits of the gains from trade, and if exports grow at a high and sustained fashion, imports will follow suit sooner or later.

Export promotion does not, as is often portrayed, inevitably lead to greater dependence on 'the capitalist-imperialist' centre. This can be seen in Table 2.4 which shows the geographical destination of increases in merchandise exports for several Latin American countries between the averages for 1970–71 and 1978–79. The degree of diversification and the relatively modest share going to the United States, the traditionally hegemonic power of the region, are remarkable. It is noteworthy that the country whose exports grew least, Peru, shows the greatest concentration on two markets. Compare also Peruvian and Uruguayan trade with other Western Hemisphere countries in Table 2.4; interestingly, the former was a rhetorical champion of Latin American integration during the 1970s. Adding the figures for oil-exporting countries (which include Venezuela) plus other Western Hemisphere countries yields the highest percentages for Argentina, Chile and Uruguay, three countries that by the late 1970s were

Table 2.4

Geographical destination of increases in merchandise exports
between 1970–71 and 1978–79
(percentage of total increase)

| | Argentina | Brazil | Chile | Colombia | Peru | Uruguay |
|---|---|---|---|---|---|---|
| United States | 7 | 20 | 12 | 30 | 43 | 17 |
| Japan | 6 | 6 | 9 | 4 | 15 | 2 |
| European Economic Community | 31 | 29 | 28 | 30 | 6 | 28 |
| Oil-exporting countries | 5 | 7 | 5 | 13 | 2 | 2 |
| Other Western Hemisphere countries | 22 | 14 | 29 | 5 | 14 | 42 |
| USSR, Eastern Europe and China | 12 | 7 | 3 | 3 | 7 | 3 |
| Other countries | 17 | 17 | 13 | 15 | 13 | 6 |
| Memo: Average annual percentage growth rate of exports, at current dollar prices | 19 | 22 | 14 | 22 | 12 | 16 |

Sources: International Monetary Fund, *Direction of Trade Yearbook*, Washington D.C., several issues. 'Oil-exporting countries' includes Venezuela. 'Other Western Hemisphere' covers basically Latin America and the Caribbean, excluding Canada and Venezuela.

hardly champions of third world solidarity.

Behind the aggregate figures there is further evidence that the realities of a multipolar trading world seem to have been missed by the metaphysical categories of some 'delinkers', whose writings would not prepare their readers to expect massive trade between an Argentina ruled by conservative military and the USSR, nor significant Brazilian exports of weapons to the Middle East, nor active commercial links between post-1973 Chile and China.

The traditional primary products/manufactures dichotomy can also be misleading. Both economically and politically, in the world of the 1980s, exporters of wheat, soybeans and corn have better prospects than exporters of steel and petrochemicals. As an example, contrast the economic benefits and international autonomy the latter industries have brought Argentina, with those generated from Argentine sales of corn, sorghum and beef to the Soviets.

There is considerable evidence for the post-war years showing that in the medium and the long term, faster export growth has been associated with faster growth in gross domestic product, even leaving aside from the latter the value added by the export sector (Michaely, 1977, pp.49–54; 1979, pp.141–3). Faster growth also appears to have been associated with larger expansions of employment opportunities in modern sectors. Beyond that the claims for export-led growth achieved in Latin America become weaker. The effects on income distribution are complex but of unclear direction and strength, partly because the variety of non-traditional exports cannot be simply labelled 'labour-intensive' or 'land-intensive'.

Neither the effect of trade openings on political change, nor the effect of political regimes on trade policies are unambiguous. Since the mid-1960s, regimes moving in the direction of export promotion, albeit at different speeds and using different instruments, have included the Frei administration and Pinochet government in Chile, several constitutional Colombian governments, the second Belaúnde administration in Peru and the Cuban government led by Fidel Castro. Other countries have witnessed a steady concern for a healthy export sector, including Barbados, Costa Rica, Ecuador, Mexico, Paraguay, Trinidad-Tobago and Venezuela. Ecuador and Venezuela have mixed oil exports with democratic politics, with Venezuela since 1958 having an admirable record of constitutional government. Some might argue that oil makes Venezuela a special case, but they should then explain why Saudi Arabia has not surpassed Sweden in social democracy and constitutional liberty.

The open economies of Central America, while maintaining prosperous export sectors, experimented with moderate collective protection during the 1960s; in most countries the domestic beneficiaries of that common market appear to have been privileged social groups not too different from those benefiting from exports. Direct foreign investors, as elsewhere in Latin America, also benefited from such 'infant industry' protection: a combination of partial closing in trade and opening toward direct foreign investment seems both economically and politically dangerous, particularly for small economies, as foreign investment can magnify the distortive effects of excessive protection, while creating powerful vested interests for the maintenance of trade restrictions. Caribbean open economies flirted with the Central American approach during the 1970s, but on the whole have maintained great concern for dynamic exports of goods and services. In spite of adverse economic shocks and difficult social circumstances during the 1970s many of these island economies have maintained fairly open political regimes; examples include Barbados, the Dominican Republic and Jamaica.

Openings toward international financial flows have been more dramatic than those toward trade. Since the late 1960s a number of Latin American countries have borrowed extensively from private international banks; these flows have surpassed those for direct foreign investment and concessional finance. This vast topic can be discussed in great detail (Griffith-Jones in this volume; Bacha and Díaz Alejandro, 1981), but here only a few features will be highlighted, again pointing to the non-uniqueness of the openings-politics link. The list of borrowing countries includes Cuba, Chile, post-revolutionary Nicaragua and Guatemala. The management and instrumentation of borrowings have been highly diverse. For example, Brazil and Colombia have maintained exchange controls and have closely supervised regulated external borrowing. On the other hand, Argentina during 1978–81 moved close to a laissez-faire attitude toward connections between domestic and international financial markets. Controls over the direct presence of international banks in domestic economies have also varied. A look elsewhere confirms this heterogeneous picture: major borrowers also include Hungary and Poland, South Korea and the Phillippines.

The incentives and opportunities available in international financial markets interacting with domestic financial and exchange rate policies naturally affect domestic economic actors in different ways, and political implications may follow from changed international circumstances. It can be argued, for example, that the liquidity of the Euro-currency market during the 1970s allowed many Latin American public enterprises a degree of initiative and autonomy not available previously.[6] That market also strengthened the potential bargaining power of governments in negotiating with transnational enterprises as well as with the International Monetary Fund, the World Bank and countries dispensing either concessional finance or selling weapons. Financial pressures by the Carter administration against the Chilean government in an effort to gain human rights concessions were dulled by the Chilean ability to borrow in the Eurocurrency market, an expedient also used by the Cuban government during the 1970s. Of course, borrowing gives flexibility today, but if the funds are not managed wisely, or if one is just unlucky in the commodity lottery, it will decrease flexibility tomorrow, as both Peru and Poland found out.

Some types of 1970s openings toward capital flows have yielded new experiences and dilemmas. The great mobility of financial flows has raised the possibility that openings to capital may conflict with sustained trade openings. Consider the bizarre Argentine experience of 1978–81 where massive borrowing sustained an appreciation of the real exchange rate which clashed with export promotion efforts. That Argentine experience shows that, at least for some years, one can wreck both the import-competing and the export sectors, with the gainers from such policies including some bankers and a few other groups. Chilean and Uruguayan exporting efforts appear threatened by similar considerations.

Direct foreign investment has shown itself shier than financial capital in accepting the lure of more open doors. Regulations for transnational corporations have been relaxed in many Latin American countries, although the picture remains quite heterogeneous in this field also. Post-1973 Chile has been the clearest example of a drastic opening toward direct foreign investment. In spite of almost pathetic invitations from Chilean authorities, and in spite of the rhetoric of some business publications praising investment climates created by authoritarian regimes, the inflows of foreign investment into post-1973 Chile have been modest, and not obviously higher than those going into other economically comparable Latin American countries having stiffer regulations. It is one thing to lend other people's money and another to commit one's equity, especially when the stability of the rules of the game in the host country may depend on one person's caprice or heartbeat.

## Conclusions and doubts

Even a hasty review of Latin American economic history provides damaging counter-examples against simple generalisations about the openness-politics link, whether of the optimistic, classical economists' variety, or of the more recent delinkers' species. The degree of openness of an economy and its political system may be regarded as just two endogenous variables in a socio-economic general equilibrium system; partial correlations between those two variables in isolation are unlikely to yield robust or meaningful results. In an interesting pioneering study John F.O. Bilson has attempted to explain econometrically the degree of civil liberties in 55 developed and developing countries as a function of several economic variables, including openness to international trade, measured as the ratio of exports to gross national product. Population, per capita income, share of wages in aggregate income and other variables are included. The coefficient for openness indicates a positive link with civil liberties, but it is not statistically significant. The only economic indicator found to be a significant predictor of differences in the extent of civil liberties was the level of per capita income (Bilson, 1982).[7] These econometric results are compatible with our historical review for Latin America.

The non-uniqueness and looseness of the openness-politics link is confirmed by other regions and other times. Within the group of socialist countries, Albania, 1960s China, Pol Pot's Kampuchea and Romania on the whole minimised and scorned outside links. Cuba, Hungary, Poland and Yugoslavia have maintained extensive international commerce with anyone willing to trade with them. At first sight such a contrast within the socialist camp gives some (modest) support to the hypothesis of classical economists.

Over the last 60 years the Mediterranean world, always of interest to Latin America, has witnessed authoritarian regimes which sometimes favoured delinking (Mussolini during the 1930s and Franco during the 1940s and 1950s), while at other times followed orthodox outward-oriented trade policies (Mussolini during the 1920s, Franco during the 1960s, and the Greek colonels during the late 1960s and early 1970s).

As in the Mediterranean world, authoritarianism in Latin America has much to do with the armed forces. The nature and laws of motion of the collection of men in uniform are the darkest black boxes in Latin American social science, but one may conclude that the attitude of the armed forces toward economic openness has been neither unambiguous nor steady. The case of the Peruvian armed forces is particularly interesting: led by General Odría, they favoured across-the-board openness in trade and investment, but under General Velasco Alvarado they increased import barriers and neglected non-traditional exports, while trying to maintain traditional exports under state direction. Regarding capital flows the Velasco Alvarado administration borrowed substantially abroad but increased controls over direct foreign investment. The heterogeneity of economic views within the Argentine and Brazilian armed forces is well known (and arguments about economic policies between various factions have more alarming side effects than those between Samir Amin and Arnold Haberger). Armed forces, at least in South America, are unlikely to be great enthusiasts of free trade in goods and services, will be sceptical about direct foreign investment and financial flows, and will certainly be hostile to free migration with neighbouring countries. Argentine and Brazilian generals in charge of public enterprises are unlikely to accept tariff reductions increasing foreign competition to 'their' firms.

Other points noted in this essay may be worth stressing. It does appear possible to argue that the role of the foreign sector in Latin American development has been exaggerated and indeed mythologised. Of course policies towards international trade and capital play an important role in terms of efficiency and growth, and are more important the smaller a country is. Interaction with the rest of the world offers some potential gains; that is why most clever politicians firmly in control will try to take advantage of them. Those interactions will cause problems and set constraints, so clever politicians, uniformed or not, will keep an eye on those links and will select those with the highest benefit-cost ratios, at least to themselves. But even in a small country the foreign sector will influence only indirectly many key developmental variables, such as productivity in non-export agriculture, willingness to save and decisions to invest in human capital. Income distribution and political participation will be more influenced by these and other domestic variables than by whether effective rates of protection are 10 or 150 per cent.

The need for care in the definition of economic openness is another important point emerging from this chapter, even if no definitive formula has emerged. (Others will have to dwell on definitions of authoritarianism and liberty.) The literature is full of judgemental labels, such as 'outward-oriented' and 'inward-oriented' economies. The matter is not an easy one, even if one focuses just on international trade in goods and services. The problem lies in separating the effect of policy measures on observed trade from those generated by the natural endowment, population and per capita income of a country. Examining the balance between policy incentives for exporting versus import substitution is one approach, but it should be noted that such a balance may exist both at zero (or negative) incentives for both, or at high levels of incentives for both. Other policy variables such as the exchange and interest rate, are of critical importance in determining the size of the sector producing internationally traded goods and services. Clearly, trade may occur under a variety of institutional arrangements: Chile, Hungary, Japan, South Korea and Yugoslavia may be said to be economies fairly opened to trade, yet their policy instruments are far from identical. The nature of those instruments and institutions are important for determining the effect of openness to trade on other domestic variables, whether economic or political. Openness was once closely linked with policies of laissez-faire, laissez-passer, but such an association is no longer valid.

The workings of an economy, whether open or closed, imposes constraints on what political actors do. Is the open economy more of a 'delicate watch' than a closed economy? The point is debatable. In so far as certain types of openness increase the international mobility of some economic actors, such as financial capital and skilled labour, it augments their bargaining power vis-à-vis the less mobile factors (those whose wealth is tied up in land and unskilled labour with nowhere to go). Yet openness may also increase the flexibility of a political leader bent on neglecting one productive sector to benefit others; if you can import grains, you can neglect food production as long as you have something to export in exchange or somebody lends you money. However, on balance, it seems plausible that specialisation tends to increase vulnerability, and that the lower the international mobility of an economic agent, the greater its vulnerability will be. Trade unions of unskilled workers in activities producing exportable goods, whether in Sweden, Japan or Colombia, will have limits set on their wage aspirations by international conditions, yet their real incomes and welfare may be higher than under a closed economy perhaps giving them job security but neither gains from trade nor greater personal liberty. It should also be noted that any economy, whether open or closed, aiming at high rates of capital formation or defence expenditures, will have to limit consumption and real wages. Closedness did not generate much growth in real wages in the Soviet Union of the 1930s nor the Spain of the 1940s, while South Korean real wages appear to have risen faster than those of Burma during the last twenty years.

Examples of trade-offs between gains from trade and security are easily multiplied: oil importers prefer to trade with suppliers who cannot always guarantee deliveries to being self-sufficient in energy when only charcoal is available at home. Additional constraints imposed by openness can also be illustrated by international financial flows: clearly a country borrowing today commits itself to earn or save enough foreign exchange tomorrow to service the debt. This common-sensical reality may lead a country to conclude, like Polonius, that it is best to 'neither lender nor borrower be', but other nations with attractive investment projects will think otherwise.

Openness will set limits particularly on political actors seeking drastic and rapid transformations in their societies. Freedom to migrate presents obvious headaches; capital mobility may or may not work in their favour; trade in goods and services provides dangerous conduits to the enemy during revolutionary times. Revolutionaries, whether fascists, religious fundamentalists or leftists, will usually favour sharp degrees of delinking to establish their power and achieve a radical transformation in the economy and the polity. Once firmly in control, openings may follow.

The untangling of the economic and political consequences of a certain degree of openness maintained over many years from the effects of a transition toward another degree of openness (whether from openness to closeness or vice versa) is one of the most difficult questions raised by this essay.[8] Recorded Latin American economic history may be viewed as the result of long-term forces disturbed by frequent external shocks and often erratic changes in domestic policies; allocating observed phenomena to each of these causes is not a simple task. As noted in the review of what mainstream economics does and does not say regarding openness, there is a notorious lack of integration between the pure theory of international trade, which addresses long-run questions using the method of comparative statics (or comparative dynamics), and the theory of balance of payments adjustment mechanisms, which addresses short-run macroeconomic questions, sharing with modern macroeconomics a good deal of controversy and confusion. The study of Latin American openings and closings requires that attention be paid both to short- and long-run considerations, and seldom will both bring unambiguous gains or losses.

In an important paper John Sheahan has argued that at the start of the 1960s economic distortions of all sorts had accumulated to such a point in many Latin American countries that repression appeared to be, falsely but understandably, the necessary condition of economic policy (Sheahan, 1980, pp.267−91). The poor economic performance generated by the distortions, including those in the area of foreign trade, undermined support for open governments; those governments, Sheahan argues, which gave great emphasis to efficiency criteria were placed by the distorted structure of the economy in automatic alliance with the wealthy minority against organised urban labour.

Sheahan's article emphasises how transition problems may create a demand for authoritarian regimes; his article also covers broader economic policies, going beyond those related to the external sector, underlining the complexity of the transition process. Nevertheless, from the evidence provided by the overview of openings and closings in Latin American history, the argument being made in this chapter is that the demand for authoritarian regimes in the Southern Cone of Latin America mainly came not from poor long-run economic performance, but more immediately from unhinged macroeconomic conditions, including three-digit inflation and unsustainable balance-of-payments deficits. The chaotic climate created by those short-term circumstances opened the way for the men in uniform.

Did the poor long-term economic performance induced by sluggish exports lead to short-term macroeconomic disorder in the Southern Cone? Perhaps. Mediocre growth, under the 1960s political circumstances of Latin America (including the then-shining example of the Cuban revolution) increased the appeal of clashing authoritarian formulae, first from the left and then from the right, promising to break out of perceived economic and social miasmas, at the expense of previous democratic achievements. Populist regimes first rode the crest of demands for reform, but lost control of macroeconomic conditions unleashing hyper-inflations and balance of payments crises.

But poor long-term performance need not have led inevitably to chaotic populism nor to murderous authoritarianism. Consider a mental experiment: suppose a country had very stiff import restrictions, sluggish export growth and tight controls over capital flows, but inflation remained in single digits, the balance of payments was problematical but under control, and there was a low but reasonably steady growth. Under these circumstances it is difficult to imagine an abrupt authoritarian offensive to eliminate market distortions. And if it came about, the recessions, unemployment and real wage cuts associated with Southern Cone stabilisation plans would be much less likely to happen. The mental experiment has a fairly close real-world counterpart: to the exasperation of nearly all types of economists, for more than thirty years India has combined a mediocre economic performance with reasonably democratic political institutions.

Why Southern Cone authoritarian regimes chose certain economic policies, and why peculiar alliances were forged between rational economic technocrats and leading generals is a fascinating topic (not unlike the Speer–Hitler connection), but one from which few generalisations may be drawn, at least for the openness-authoritarianism link. The need to check hyper-inflation and quickly correct balance-of-payments deficits is one which naturally brings together those used to discipline, command and punishment with those emphasising order and soundness in budgetary and monetary policies, at least regarding civilian expenditures and credit. Anti-inflationary measures do require a degree of persistence that make authoritarian politics appealing to some economists (and businessmen). The need to check hyper-inflation may then provide a convenient cover to liquidate trade unions and political enemies. However, even within the Southern Cone the degree to which authoritarian regimes have moved toward free trade and free capital movements is far from uniform. As during the 1950s, some observers tend to generalise from the Chilean case to all of Latin America. Chilean tariff books in 1981 paradoxically looked more like those of Switzerland than those of Argentina, Brazil or Uruguay.

It is time to close by looking at the future. What was done in the Southern Cone during the 1970s was badly and brutally done. But it does not follow that those who will come after the authoritarians should undo everything which was done. The advantages of dynamic export growth was a lesson learned before Mr Pinochet became notorious, and should survive him. It would be foolish to rule out the use of exchange controls because they were used by Hitler; it would be silly to oppose lower tariffs because Pinochet liked them.

But what if the 1980s turn out to be more like the 1930s than the 1960s as far as external demand for exports? That possibility, although unlikely, cannot be ruled out. Private entrepreneurs deciding whether to produce for the foreign or the domestic markets are aware of these uncertainties, and it is debatable whether public policy should push them very far one way or another. The public sector in most countries still faces many spending and investment decisions for which expectations regarding the buoyancy and openness of external markets are important. It would be premature to adopt an expectation of external catastrophe in these decisions. While selling abroad during the 1980s may not be as easy as implied by the comfortable small country assumption, the likely effort appears to be worth a try in many activities. A country like Japan plans its exports come what may; circumstances may force changes in products and markets, but the decision to maintain a brisk export expansion is unquestioned. Whether because of the need for irreplaceable imports, such as oil, or because of commitments to service their debt (so long as there are no major changes in the working of international capital markets), or because of plausible opportunity cost calculations, Latin American countries may be wise to follow the Japanese example. If such an openness strategy is followed for trade, a more active participation in international rules would be desirable. But that is another matter (Díaz Alejandro, 1980a, pp.38–53; Camps and Gwin, 1981).[9]

Similar considerations apply to interactions with international capital markets. The favourable conditions which existed for some borrowers during the 1970s, such as plentiful credit at negative real interest rates, are unlikely to exist in the 1980s. Just as Brazil exhausted opportunities for easy import substitution in the 1930s and 1940s, it exhausted its easy borrowing phase in the 1970s. Yet the option to borrow abroad, for Brazil and the rest of Latin America, is likely to remain during the 1980s a profitable one for the careful investor and a dangerous one for the spendthrift.

One may note that southern delinkers have become 'objective

allies' of northern protectionists who cloud the outlook of the less developed countries for the 1980s. Many a northern observer expresses concern about southern despotism only after his or her profits or wages have been harmed by Brazilian or South Korean exports (if the exports were Indian, old concerns about the morality of neutralism may be voiced instead). The old 'pauper labour' argument for protection has become the 'repressed labour' argument for higher tariffs (D. Lal, 1981). The development strategies of Albania, Burma and Kampuchea have a powerful appeal to northern capitalists and workers battling against competition from Colombia and Taiwan. It is not so surprising then, that *Business Week* should refer to Samir Amin as one of the third world's best economists and expound his views (*Business Week*, 9 November 1981, p.29).[10] South-south trade and a basic-needs development strategy are also viewed with favour by many northern protectionists. One cannot easily reconcile criticisms of northern protectionism as unfair to the third world with proposals for southern delinking. Some northern academics, especially in Europe, who regard themselves as progressives and friends of the less developed countries appear to take the paternalistic view that if they do not delink on their own, northern progressives (those academics and their trade union allies) will do it for them, by erecting import controls.

In spite of the troubled and uncertain outlook, the 1980s could witness Latin American economies which are open to trade and finance, in a selective fashion not unlike that of smaller European countries, such as Denmark, Finland or Hungary, while Latin American polities either emerge from the nightmares of the 1970s or deepen their earlier democratic achievements. Surely the message of this essay is that there is nothing unscientific in such a vision.

# Notes

1  'The general result on gains from trade shows that, given the necessary redistributive tools, an autarkic economy *should* move to free trade, and a free-trading economy *should not* move to autarky. This is so irrespective of the comparison of the two steady-state consumption levels. Economies in the real world are clearly constrained by their historically determined initial conditions. The kind of ahistoric comparison made in the Golden Rule result, or the result of Steedman *et al*, is clearly of no practical relevance for accumulation or trade policy' (Dixit, 1981, p.288).

2  Professor Haberler has been consistent on this point. In 1943 he argued: 'In fact, the obstacles to free or freer migration are so formidable, so much greater than those to free or freer trade, that it may well be argued that the question should be dropped altogether or at least not linked with the question of freeing the movement of goods in order not to jeopardise the chances of achieving something in the trade field'.

In a footnote to this sentence he added: 'Just think of the chances of persuading the people of the United States, Australia or any other country with a high standard of living to permit the free immigration of Chinese (not to speak of Japanese) labour after the war! Also, from a selfish point of view of the country or of large groups (e.g. labour) in the country into which immigration is to take place, much more serious objections can be raised against free immigration than against the free importation of goods' (Harberler, 1943, pp.326–7).

3  This observation is based on the reactions of students to a course taught jointly by Hugh Patrick and myself at Yale University on the economic history of follower countries. The students have often remarked on the manner in which the Latin American section of the course spends much more time dealing with the external sector than does the Japanese half of the course; though, of course, this may be due to the idiosyncracies of the teachers involved.

4  For a discussion of the problems associated with growth based on oil exports and the *rentista* state that may develop, see Chapter 7 by G. Philip in this volume.

5  For an overview of Samir Amin's and other similar arguments extolling the virtues of withdrawal or 'delinking' from the international economy, see Carlos F. Díaz Alejandro (1978).

6  See Chapter 6 by P. Evans in this volume for a fuller discussion of this point.

7  Bilson writes that, '... there is no clear evidence that a gradual move towards greater government intervention in a democratic state will be associated with a decline in civil liberty. There is, however, a clear and predictable correlation between the concentration in the

political system and the extent of personal freedom. In other words, if an individual is told that a country is capitalist this information is not very informative with regard to the extent of civil liberty in that country. On the other hand, if the individual is told that the country has a multi-party political system, this information is valuable' (Bilson, 1982).

8   For an interpretation that emphasises openings as a condition for income redistribution see Chapter 5 by E.V.K. FitzGerald in this volume. Chapter 7 by G. Philip also exemplifies the viewpoint that authoritarianism was necessary to restore export growth.

9   Hungary and Poland applied during 1981 for admission to the International Monetary Fund and the World Bank; China joined those organisations earlier. It remains to be seen whether a similar trend toward globalisation will also occur in GATT.

10   Not all northern capitalists, of course, will fear southern export expansion. In terms of international trade models, attitudes will depend on the degree of mobility, domestic and international, of the different factors of production.

# 3 The growth of transnational finance: implications for national development*

STEPHANY GRIFFITH-JONES

International capital markets have shown an impressive growth in the last two decades. Since the early seventies an increasing proportion of lending has been oriented towards less developed countries with balance of payments deficits. Latin American countries have been especially prominent debtors, particularly to the private multinational banks. The Latin American non-oil exporters account for about half of the total debt of non-oil less developed countries, and have increased their borrowing more rapidly than others in recent years. As a result, Latin American debt service (defined as payments of amortisation of loans and interest divided by the value of its exports of goods and services) is much higher than that for the rest of the less developed countries. In this aspect, Mexico and Brazil not only lead the region, but the world as a whole; in 1979 Mexico's debt service (64.1 per cent) and Brazil's debt service (34.6 per cent) were the two highest in the world. In both cases the 1979 debt service ratio about tripled the 1970 level. In recent years other Latin American countries, such as Chile and Argentina, have been increasing their debt and debt service dramatically (World Bank, 1981, p.159).

* This chapter is based on work done under the Transnationalisation Project, directed by Professor Osvaldo Sunkel, and financed by SAREC. I wish to thank several colleagues at IDS for useful discussions on this subject. I am particularly grateful to Dudley Seers and Osvaldo Sunkel for very valuable discussions. I am also grateful to Mr Nimatalah for the valuable insights which I gained while working as his temporary technical assistant at the International Monetary Fund and to Diana Tussie for her detailed and very valuable comments on an earlier draft of this paper. The responsibility is, as always, mine alone.

Some academics and third world governments have expressed concern that increases in balance of payments deficits, leading to rapid inflow of external funds and growth of the external debt, imply a worsening of dependency. Amongst the first to pioneer this approach was Osvaldo Sunkel who wrote: 'It is in this aspect, ... the overbearing and implacable necessity to obtain external financing, ... which finally sums up the situation of dependency; this is the crucial mechanism of dependency' (1969, p.159).

With the recent upsurge of external indebtedness concern along these lines has grown. Some dependency scholars argue that a new set of international structural linkages has evolved leading to a new situation of conditioned development. An extension of this argument is Dudley Seers's contention that 'If there were massive resource transfers to the South, these would perpetuate a pattern of growth which is simultaneously oil-intensive and in general inegalitarian' (Seers, 1981, p.1060). The main argument is that growing integration into the world financial and economic system supports unjust and inefficient patterns of national development.

Other Latin American social scientists, whose thinking was originally influenced by the dependency school, have begun to argue that interdependence has become today a more valid concept, considering the greater autonomy of semi-industrialised countries. An important ingredient in this lessening of dependency is precisely the abundance of international liquidity in the seventies and the new financial options it has opened.[1]

This chapter examines the evolution of international financial flows to Latin America since the Second World War and their implications for national development. It attempts to show how past developments may illuminate future ones.

The first section summarises the main trends in external financial flows after the Second World War, stressing developments during the seventies. The analysis concentrates not only on the quantitative trends, but also describes the main forces which caused these flows. The second section analyses the effect which the changing magnitude and nature of the financial flows had on the development of Latin American countries. In a final section the main conclusions from the historical analysis are extracted, with particular reference to the problems of the eighties.

Although concentrating on Latin America, some reference is made to other less developed areas. Before beginning, it is necessary to distinguish clearly at least three categories within this group of countries: oil-exporters, middle-income countries (which include the semi-industrialised ones) and the poorest or low income countries. The nature of external financial needs and flows, as well as the issues of relative autonomy or dependency, vary widely for each of these categories.

## External financial flows after the Second World War

During each of the post-war decades a new actor arose, whose financial flows to Latin America played a major or dominant role in providing foreign exchange. In the fifties it was the foreign investors pursuing greater profits which provided the main source of finance. During the sixties official aid agencies played the most dynamic role as, in this decade, aid was perceived to be in the interests of industrial countries, particularly the US. During the seventies, the most dynamic actor was private bank credit, as at the time it was in the multinational banks' interests to rapidly expand their lending to several Latin American countries. Even though partly responding to the needs and pressures from Latin America, naturally the main motive for these flows was that they were perceived as serving best the interests of the agents carrying them out.

In each decade the flows were initiated mainly by institutions or enterprises based in the US, and then the process became 'multinationalised' as institutions or enterprises from other countries increased their share in international capital markets. In the sixties and the seventies the new flows helped service the outflows from the previous decade. This was particularly significant in the sixties, when in Latin America official flows could be said to have basically covered net outflows by foreign direct investors.

### The fifties and foreign direct investment

As the Second World War came to an end, two developments had an important influence on the future nature of international financial flows: the creation of the Bretton Woods institutions and the great weight of the US in the world economy. The 1944 conference of Bretton Woods had agreed on the need for international consultation and cooperation on monetary matters. The two Bretton Woods institutions, the International Monetary Fund (IMF) and the World Bank, were created to avoid the instability of exchange rates, the financial chaos that had accompanied the world depression of the 1930s and the protective controls and competitive devaluations of the inter-war period. Bretton Woods, and the institutions it created, represented the first coherent attempt at imposing order and stability on world monetary exchanges and preserving their unity as a single system. As Díaz Alejandro and Bacha (1981) have pointed out, the initial stages of the financial order emerging from Bretton Woods reflected the 1930s disenchantment with laissez-faire in financial transactions and Fabian/New Deal notions then dominant in the United Kingdom and the United States bore an important influence.

The attempt at control of the world monetary system by official international institutions was not accompanied in practice, however, by large financial flows from them, particularly to the developing countries. The main feature of international capital movements during the immediate post-war years was the large outflow of funds from the United States (Lamfalussy, 1981). During the late forties and fifties, the United States was clearly richer and stronger than ever before, and was the only country able to offer both economic aid and military protection. Yet, even though it controlled the Bretton Woods institutions, the United States preferred bilateral channels for its financial flows. More importantly, the original Fabian notions which were evident at Bretton Woods were increasingly pushed into the background once the war was over.

When Latin America appealed for a Marshall Plan of its own between 1945 and 1948 George Marshall replied that only private funds would be available. Obviously, the main reason was that Latin America played at the time a very secondary role in the cold war. Both the Truman and Eisenhower administrations recommended that Latin America concentrate on improving the political and material incentives for private foreign investment, and that foreign capital be given guarantees of 'just treatment'. Arthur Schlesinger (1975) has aptly defined this prescription as 'the theory of immaculate private conception'.

As a result both bilateral and multilateral official institutions played a negligible role. As can be seen in Table 3.1, financial flows were mainly in the form of private direct investment by multinational corporations. The import substitution policies of the Latin American countries provided them with profitable business. Investment was protected by high tariff barriers and credit was obtainable on favourable terms. Multinational corporations jumped the high tariff barriers in these countries by setting up or buying enterprises in the Latin American countries. This led to internationalisation of industrial production with important effects on the patterns of consumption in Latin America (Sunkel and Fuenzalida, 1979).

Table 3.1 also shows that during the whole period 1946–61, US net private capital flows to Latin America were much higher than official ones; this was even more marked in the first ten years of the post-war period, as during the second half of the fifties US official flows to Latin America began to increase.

In 1950 approximately half of US foreign direct investment was in the developed countries, and over 40 per cent was concentrated in Latin America. The share going to developing countries systematically declined between 1950 and 1979 mainly as a result of the fall in the share of investment in Latin America (see Table 3.2). This decline was more rapid during the late fifties and sixties.

American flows to Europe show the opposite trend of those to Latin America. During 1946–48 it was official flows, through the

## Table 3.1

### US capital movements 1946–61
### (in billions of US dollars)

| | 1946–48* | | | | 1949–55* | | | | 1956–61* | | | |
|---|---|---|---|---|---|---|---|---|---|---|---|---|
| | Total | Europe and Canada | Latin America | Other countries† | Total | Europe and Canada | Latin America | Other countries† | Total | Europe and Canada | Latin America | Other countries† |
| US Capital (net) | −3.52 | −2.54 | −0.38 | −0.60 | −1.30 | −0.60 | −0.33 | −0.38 | −4.12 | −1.65 | −0.99 | −1.47 |
| Private | −0.77 | −0.15 | −0.32 | −0.28 | −1.04 | −0.54 | −0.24 | −0.26 | −3.30 | −1.74 | −0.69 | −0.82 |
| Government | −2.75 | −2.38 | −0.06 | −0.32 | −0.26 | −0.05 | −0.09 | −0.12 | −0.82 | −0.09 | −0.30 | −0.61 |

\* Annual averages

† Including international institutions

Source: US Department of Commerce, *Balance of Payments Supplement* 1961.

Table 3.2

US direct investment position abroad
(percentage composition, by areas)

|                      | 1950   | 1957   | 1966   | 1979*  |
|----------------------|--------|--------|--------|--------|
| All areas            | 100.0  | 100.0  | 100.0  | 100.0  |
| Developed countries  | 48.0   | 55.1   | 68.1   | 71.6   |
| Developing countries | 48.0   | 40.5   | 26.8   | 24.8   |
| Latin America        | (40.6) | (31.4) | (18.9) | (19.1) |
| Others               | 4.0    | 3.4    | 5.1    | 4.6    |

* Choice of years is based on those for which the information reflects a benchmark survey, whereas intermediate years are only based
on sample information. For explanation, see O.G. Whichard 'Trends
in the US Direct Investment Position Abroad, 1950–79' in op cit.
below.

Source:   Data taken from *Survey of Current Business*, February 1981,
US Department of Commerce.

Marshall Plan, which predominated. Large American aid to help finance
the reconstruction of post-war Europe was a mixture of enlightenment
and foreign policy interests; of special political importance was the
American aim to stop the 'advance of Communism' in Western Europe.
Similar political motivation later led to substantial increases of US
aid to Latin America.

   Private American investment in Europe grew very rapidly during
the fifties and sixties. Once economic reconstruction was under way
the incentive to replace and expand pre-war investment increased.
Furthermore, moves toward currency convertibility in Europe assured
US investors that their income and capital could be largely or wholly
repatriated.

   The changing shares in the composition of American investment
occurred in the context of rapid growth of total US direct investment
abroad during the period 1950–79 (at an annual nominal rate of
10.1 per cent). Thus, although American foreign investment was growing very rapidly, the share going to less developed countries, and to

Latin America in particular, declined substantially as US multinational corporations found more profitable and/or more 'secure' investment opportunities in other industrial countries, particularly in Europe. US direct investment in less developed countries grew relatively more slowly during the sixties than in other decades due to conditions both in the industrialised and in the third world countries. In less developed countries the issue of foreign control became increasingly sensitive; this was reflected in expropriations and prohibitions of entry into sectors such as natural resources and telecommunications. On the other hand, the US government imposed both voluntary and mandatory controls on outflows of capital to protect the balance of payments. Such controls particularly affected inter-company outflows.

An important trend which emerged in the composition of US investment during the period 1950–79 was that reinvestment of earnings grew while equity and inter-company flows declined; in fact during five years of the period 1972–79 absolute declines in inter-company flows were registered (US Department of Commerce, 1981). It is, of course, only the inter-company outflows which imply a transfer of financial resources to other countries.

The relative decline in the proportion of total US investment which went to Latin America along with the diminishing importance of inter-company flows, as well as the rising level of profit remittances by US companies, implied that in the sixties the total net flow of direct private capital from the US into Latin America was already negative. Thus, between 1961 and 1968, net direct investment minus profit remittances of US companies in Latin America amounted to US$5.7 billion (Levinson and Onis, 1970, p.120).

In the late forties and in the fifties private flows predominantly took the form of direct investment. The international financial and money markets had not yet recovered from the shocks they had suffered during the great depression. Private credit flows were small and mainly the result of credit provided by suppliers for the purchase of equipment. Thus, in Latin America in 1960, of total debt to private creditors, 48 per cent was owed to suppliers (Inter-American Development Bank, 1979, table 59).

This flow of private credit was induced by companies exporting capital goods or carrying out related equity investment in developing countries. Due to this close relationship with the corporations it has recently been suggested that suppliers' credits should be considered as a variation of direct foreign investment (Billerback and Yasugi, 1977). But even if one disagrees with this categorisation, the fact remains that capital flows to Latin America until the sixties were mainly private investments by American corporations.

Towards the end of the fifties, the American attitude towards official aid began to change rapidly. As Christopher Prout (1976, p.361) points out:

> [the] motivation [for the increase in aid] was *unashamedly political*. Americans believed that contributing to the economic and social development of the uncommitted nations would lead to the growth of societies sympathetic to their way of life.

The turning point was the triumph of the Cuban Revolution in 1959 and the subsequent launching of a massive aid programme under the Alliance for Progress. The Kennedy administration believed that economic development and social reform, spurred by North American aid, could blunt the appeal of radicalism, which had been ignited by Cuba's example. This was explicitly recognised by US government officials involved in the inception of the Alliance programme, as well as in its subsequent evaluation.[2] Latin American underdevelopment, until then relegated to the hinterlands of American foreign policy-making, became a cold war issue.

However, the Alliance for Progress was not merely an American imposition. Its blueprint and its initial rhetoric were strongly influenced by Raul Prebisch and ECLA. Their policy prescriptions for Latin American development from the mid-1950s had stressed the merit, on the one hand, of structural transformations such as agrarian reform and, on the other, of increased foreign financial assistance.

The US government was not the only one to trace a direct causal relationship between underdevelopment and the advent of communism. For example, Brazil's foreign minister, H. Lafer, and Argentina's D. Taboada voiced their fears that underdevelopment 'facilitates in increasing measure the intervention of Communism in many of our countries' (Parkinson, 1974, p.81).

Certain segments of American big business, and particularly the multinationals with important interests in Latin America, joined in to support increases in US aid. One of the strongest defenders of the Alliance in the US Congress was the influential international banker, David Rockefeller. Particularly during the Johnson administration, the influence of multinationals on the implementation of the Alliance increased, while that of 'progressive' thinking both from Latin America and the US declined.

As can be seen in Table 3.3, the total level of gross US economic assistance to Latin America during the sixties was rather impressive, surpassing US$10 billion for the period 1961–69. However, net disbursements were substantially smaller. Over half of gross economic

assistance was devoted to repayments, amortisation of previous loans and interests. American official credits and aid were supposed to finance government investment programmes. However, if the total financial flows between the US and Latin America are considered, it becomes evident that the *net outflow* of US private investment funds from Latin America to the US (which includes net direct investment minus profit remittances) *exceeded the net inflow of US official funds*. It could therefore be said that the net inflows of official finance were used up entirely to pay for the net outflows of private direct investment. This trend is perhaps the main factor which explains the support of US multinationals for the Alliance for Progress.

As was the case of foreign direct investment, the initiative for the flow of official assistance came from the US. Table 3.4 shows that during the first half of the sixties, nearly all bilateral official flows to Latin America came from the US. At that time US bilateral aid was by far the main source of net external finance for Latin America. Gradually other industrial countries came into the scene, partly as a result of the American desire to persuade its affluent allies to share the financial burden of allegedly common foreign policy objectives more equitably. American attempts to persuade its allies were mainly carried out through the Organisation for Economic Co-operation and Development (OECD); the establishment of the Development Assistance Committee there in 1961 was tangible evidence of such American pressure. When American interest in their official bilateral aid declined in the mid-sixties, other industrial countries (particularly the smaller ones) were increasing their aid programmes. As is shown in Table 3.4, by the mid-seventies US net official flows to Latin America were smaller than those from other industrialised countries, which contrasts sharply with the relative shares in the early sixties.

Similarly, multilateral development official flows to Latin America began largely at the initiative of the US government. It had a leading role in the creation and establishment of initial finance for both the World Bank in 1945 and the Inter-American Development Bank in 1959. They, too, acquired a dynamic of their own. Thus, although during the seventies the contribution of net multilateral development official flows declined relatively as a source of finance, their decline was much less than that of US net bilateral public flows.

To summarise, official aid in the sixties was predominantly an American initiative; it responded fundamentally to foreign policy interests of the US, even though the financial needs of Latin American countries played a part in the determination of the magnitude and composition of aid. Aid, albeit unintentionally, compensated for the net outflow of foreign direct investment. Finally, the US initiative was later followed, and surpassed, by other industrial countries. Like foreign direct investment, aid became a 'transnational' initiative.

Table 3.4

Structure and level of net inflow of external resources to Latin America*

| % Structure | Annual averages | | | 1976 | 1977 | 1978 |
|---|---|---|---|---|---|---|
| | 1961–65 | 1966–70 | 1971–75 | | | |
| 1 Net public inflow | 60.2 | 40.1 | 25.2 | 19.6 | 12.0 | 7.3 |
| (a) multilateral | 19.5 | 15.7 | 13.4 | 14.4 | 7.4 | 3.1 |
|     development | 16.6 | 17.1 | 11.6 | 6.6 | 8.4 | 7.2 |
|     compensatory | 2.9 | – 1.4 | 1.8 | 7.8 | –1.0 | –4.1 |
| (b) bilateral | 40.7 | 24.4 | 11.8 | 5.2 | 4.6 | 4.2 |
|     US | 36.9 | 23.6 | 6.8 | 2.6 | 1.7 | 0.8 |
|     other countries† | 3.8 | 0.8 | 5.0 | 2.6 | 2.9 | 3.4 |
| 2 Net private inflow+ | 39.8 | 59.9 | 74.8 | 80.4 | 88.0 | 92.7 |
| (a) banks** | 2.1 | 9.3 | 43.8 | 61.0 | 48.3 | 56.6 |
| (b) suppliers | 7.7 | 13.8 | 2.3 | 3.7 | 5.8 | 9.8 |
| (c) bonds | 5.0 | 2.5 | 2.5 | 3.3 | 14.8 | 10.3 |
| (d) direct investment | 25.2 | 33.3 | 26.2 | 12.4 | 20.1 | 16.0 |
| 3 Total % | 100.0 | 100.0 | 100.0 | 100.0 | 100.0 | 100.0 |
| Total actual level (US$m) | 1,575.8 | 2,641.3 | 7,561.9 | 15,301.5 | 15,637.0 | 21,807.2 |

\*    Includes the member countries of the Inter-American Development Bank and the sub-regional agencies.
†    Includes the socialist countries and the OECD members except the US.
+    Includes credits for nationalisation.
\*\*  Includes financial institutions other than banks.

Source: Calculations based on data in Inter-American Development Bank, *Economic and Social Progress in Latin America 1979 Report*, Washington DC.

During the seventies four clear trends emerged in external financial flows to Latin America. As can be seen in Table 3.4, since the late sixties the proportion of external finance coming from private sources has increased dramatically from 39.8 per cent in 1961–65 to 92.7 per cent in 1978; this implies growth of private net flows from an annual average of US$627 million in the period 1961–65 to US$ 20,205 million in 1978.[3] The relative and absolute increase of private flows to Asia and Africa is also very great, though not as spectacular as the change for Latin America.

The second change is related to the composition of such private flows. Table 3.4 shows that during the 1960s private funds were predominantly direct investments, (though, as discussed above, the net flow of foreign investment was already negative due to the outflow of profits). Since the seventies, multinational banks have provided the main source of flows and they have surpassed both direct investment and public funds.

Net private credits from multinational banks have gone up from an annual average of US$246 million in 1966–70 to US$12,348 million in 1978, that is, an increase of *more than 50 times in a period of approximately ten years*. This feature follows the general trend for all less developed countries, but it is much more marked in Latin America where a very high proportion of total credits have been concentrated. In December 1980, of accumulated net total lending by multinational banks to non-OPEC less developed countries, over 80 per cent went to Latin America (BIS, 1981a). This rapidly growing proportion of net external finance arising from international banks has naturally led to the 'privatisation' of the debt structure of developing countries.

A third related trend is that during the seventies, and particularly since 1973, there was a sharp increase in the nominal and real level of total net financial flows to Latin America. Although partly boosting foreign exchange reserves, these loans were mainly used to cover the growing deficits in balance of payments current account. As a result of the rise in the price of oil and of other imported goods, coupled with reduced demand for their exports due to the recession in the industrialised countries, the current account deficits of Latin American countries (and particularly the oil-importing ones) increased substantially. Table 3.5 shows that the current account balance of Latin America grew from US$3.5 billion in 1973 to US$14 billion in 1975.

A fourth new feature of financial flows after 1973 was that members of OPEC began to replace the industrial countries as net suppliers of capital (Table 3.6). Thus, the shortfall of national savings over domestic investment in the oil-importing world was met by the savings surplus

## Table 3.5
### Current account balance of Latin America 1972–78
(US$million)

| 1972 | 1973 | 1974 | 1975 | 1976 | 1977 | 1978 |
|---|---|---|---|---|---|---|
| −4,375 | −3,492 | −7,206 | −14,058 | −11,075 | −11,209 | −16,372 |

Source: As Table 3.4

## Table 3.6
### The pattern of global capital flows†
(in billions of dollars)

| | 1967–73* | 1974–77* | 1978 | 1979 | 1980 |
|---|---|---|---|---|---|
| Group of ten countries and Switzerland | −8¼ | −¾ | −19½ | 23½ | 51½ |
| Smaller developed countries | 1½ | 17¾ | 10½ | 12 | 22 |
| Non-oil developing countries | 6 | 21 | 22½ | 36 | 51 |
| Oil-exporting countries | −1¼ | −38 | −4½ | −68 | −116 |

† Total capital flows including monetary movements, (i.e. current account positions with the sign reversed); minus signs indicate capital export.
* Annual averages.

Source: A. Lamfalussy, 'Changing attitudes towards capital movements', paper presented at the Conference on Changing Perceptions of Economic Policy, Oxford, 27–29 March 1981, based on IMF and OECD data.

of the oil exporters. The main conduit for 'recycling' this large volume of funds from surplus to deficit countries was the private multinational banking system.

Since the 1960s, most of the world's major banks have emulated other large corporations by 'going transnational', with the dollar as the international reserve currency base on which they could develop and expand their operations. The banks established branches and subsidiaries outside their national borders at an unprecedented rate. In 1960, only eight US banks had foreign branches; by 1975, 125 US banks had foreign branches. The main centres were situated in countries with few restrictions on banking operations and where favourable tax treatment was granted. Total assets of US overseas branches jumped from US$3.5 billion in 1960 to US$181 billion by June 1980 (Griffith-Jones, 1980, p.205). Banks from other countries began their expansion later than the US banks, but also at a very rapid rate.

What were the main reasons for private banking credits growing so rapidly that they became the most important single element in international capital movement? The recycling of petrodollars since 1974 is certainly one factor, but it is one which only accelerated an existing trend which started in the 1950s. What follows is an attempt to describe the other factors that contributed to this growth.

The rapid growth of transnational banking is to a great extent attributable to the asymmetry between the stringent regulations for residents operating their own national currencies and the freedom for non-residents to operate in foreign currencies from the same banking system. Moreover, it was natural for banks to expand their foreign business to follow and meet the needs of their transnational corporate customers who were investing and reinvesting their assets abroad. An additional demand factor was provided by the global expansion of trade after the war.

In the late 1950s two developments induced foreign banks to move into Europe. The first was the West European return to full current account convertibility, particularly for non-residents, in 1958. The second was the growth of Soviet trade with the West which generated dollars that the Soviet government preferred to deposit in Europe in order to avoid a possible freeze by the US government.

A far stronger impetus to transnational banking was given by several US government regulations which sought to stem foreign investment in an attempt to improve the balance of payments. By 1964 the persistent US balance of payments deficit was in danger of increasing even more as a result of the overheating of the American economy due to the tax cuts accompanied by increased military expenditure abroad, caused by the Vietnam War. The interest equalisation tax was introduced on foreign stocks or debt obligations acquired by US individuals and corporations. It stimulated US multinational corporations to deposit their earnings abroad instead of repatriating them and to finance new offshore investments through borrowing abroad by overseas affiliates; this trend was reinforced in 1968 by the introduction of mandatory controls on capital exports. The 1965 Voluntary Foreign Credit Restraint Program curtailed short-term lending to non-residents located in the US, exempting from these ceilings their foreign branches and subsidiaries. US banks responded by shifting transactions from their home office to branches and subsidiaries abroad.

Even though many of these controls were terminated or diminished by 1974, they undoubtedly did much to expand offshore US banking. Interestingly, the American attempt to stop the export of capital in the 1960s led to the export of the American banking system instead.

The main centre of transnational banking activity has been, and to a lesser extent still is, London. The main reason was that when transnational banking developed, London was one of the world's main financial centres. Its large size was linked basically to the absence of regulation over a long period; banks in the United Kingdom could accept deposits and make loans in any currency but sterling, completely free of regulatory restraint, as no interest ceilings or reserve requirements were imposed. Since 1979 restrictions on capital flows in sterling have also been eliminated. Other major centres are a rapidly growing number of 'offshore havens', offering not only the absence of practically any form of banking regulation or oversight, but also strict banking secrecy and no taxation of foreign banks.

The transnational banking market specialising in borrowing and lending of currencies outside the country of issue is commonly known as the 'eurodollar' market. Yet the term 'eurodollar' is not very accurate, as the market is no longer limited to Europe − the Far East and the Caribbean have a substantial share of operations. Neither does it deal only in dollars, even though this is still the major currency. In fact, a term such as 'transnational currency market' would be more precise.

Multinational corporations and public borrowers were the main borrowers in the 1960s. But hand in hand with the expansion of the eurocurrency market came the increase in loans to countries in the periphery. The larger Latin American countries began to obtain loans in the late 1960s and by the end of the 1970s approximately 50 per cent of euromarket loans went to less developed countries.

This rapid increase in lending to third world countries was a result of changed conditions in the eurocurrency markets. The credit demand of traditional clients had slowed down as a result of the recession, just at the same time that deposits from oil exporters were growing very rapidly. This inclined the banks to lend to borrowers previously considered as marginal. Furthermore, the search for new borrowers was also induced by the need to diversify portfolios and thus spread risks.

At the same time, there were factors which made both the public and the private sector in some of the less developed countries keen to borrow. Programmes of expanded public investment often contained a high proportion of imported capital goods and were difficult to finance with the country's own resources. This was accompanied by a relative stagnation in the net flow of official development assistance, as the industrial countries did not feel it was in their interests to continue increasing aid. The governments of the less developed countries may have preferred private to multilateral loans as they seemed to apply hardly any conditionality for disbursement. Loans could be made effective quickly and apparently had few strings attached as to how funds were to be employed or how the country's economy should be managed. New financial options seemed to provide an additional range of manoeuvre. Furthermore, some governments increased their restrictions on the flow of foreign direct investment and began to favour contractor, agency or joint ventures. This generally implied an increase in the demand for private foreign loans. Thus, governments seemed to prefer foreign private loans both to official credits and to direct investment, partly because the former were perceived as having fewer ties and thus allowing greater national government freedom of action.

A new phase of the eurocurrency market began after the price of oil increased at the end of 1973. The demand of less developed countries for finance increased sharply, as a result of their large current account deficits. Supply of funds to the eurocurrency markets increased rapidly as the OPEC countries, in their search for safe investment opportunities, turned primarily to the banking systems of the United States and the United Kingdom.

There are two main reasons why the euromarkets were the principal beneficiaries of 'petromoney recycling'. In the first place, they were the only international money markets already large enough and with sufficient links to absorb the vast sums being deposited by the oil producers. Second, whereas the oil surplus countries may have been willing to lend directly to safe borrowers like the US and Germany, they wanted to interpose commercial banks as a buffer between themselves and the 'high-risk borrowers', the less developed countries. Thus, the surplus countries shifted the risk involved in lending to the periphery to the private banks.

Initially, the private banks were unwilling to assume this role fully. Whilst surpluses of the oil-exporting countries were placed in short-term deposits, countries facing balance of payments deficits needed medium- and long-term loans. Furthermore, several bank failures (the main one being that of Herstatt) had led to a restriction of the inter-bank euromarket for a time during 1974.

Banks developed new operational techniques which diminished their risks for large loans with long maturities, that is, the type of credits required by less developed countries. Firstly, the roll-over credit was created, based on a floating interest rate that varies approximately with the cost of the money for the lender, who obtains his funds on the essentially short-term inter-bank market. Thus, although the loan may have a long maturity, i.e. ten years, the interest rate is changed every time the credit is rolled-over (usually every three or six months). This floating interest rate, as it is called, is crucial because it passes to the borrower one of the most important risks of the market; it is the borrower who must bear both the cyclical and the long-term changes of the interest rates.

Second, a very large part of the transactions on the eurocurrency markets by less developed countries have been through syndicated loans. Syndicated loans are credits shared by a large number of euro-banks. This mechanism has allowed the default risks of large loans to be spread over a great number of banks; it has also allowed smaller banks to participate in the eurocurrency market.

Despite the plethora of funds and the risk-minimising operational techniques, net private lending to the third world is extremely concentrated in a few countries, who either have relatively high GDP per capita, whose GDP per capita is growing very rapidly, or who fulfil both these conditions. Four countries, Mexico, Brazil, South Korea and the Philippines, were the largest borrowers, accounting for over 50 per cent of total accumulated debt to international banks in December 1980 (Bank for International Settlements, 1981b). A large number of less developed countries, the poorest ones, are not considered 'creditworthy' by the private bankers; these countries not only have very little access to private lending but are in many cases even net creditors with the international banks, as their reserves deposited with those banks exceed the loans received. Most of the poorest countries which are net creditors to the private international banks are in Africa or Asia; in Latin America Haiti, Guatemala, Paraguay and Surinam are also in this category (Bank for International Settlements, 1981b).

Here an important difference in the effects of private and official flows arises. A much higher proportion of public funds goes to the poorer countries. Thus, the swing towards private flows favours access to external finance by the middle-income, and relatively worsens the prospects of the poorest countries. As a result, the 'privatisation' of financial flows seems to have contributed towards greater disparities amongst countries in the periphery.

In the seventies the poorest countries were unable to follow the example of the middle-income countries and finance their increased balance of payments deficits by additional external flows; as a result their capacity to import declined. The World Bank *1981 World Development Report* (p.3) indicates that during the seventies growth in GDP per capita for the poorest countries declined substantially vis-à-vis their evolution in the sixties; most disturbing in this respect was the evolution in the poorest countries of Sub-Saharan Africa, where average GDP per capita actually declined by 0.4 per cent annually during the seventies. Whereas many factors may have contributed to this unsatisfactory evolution, constraints on their capacity to import played a major role, and larger external finance would have helped them to achieve a better performance.

Again, as in the case of direct investment and official flows, multinational bank lending on a large scale was initiated mainly by US institutions; after initial predominance by US banks, private lending has been increasingly 'transnationalised'. This trend became much more marked towards the end of the seventies; while in December 1977 US banks accounted for about 50 per cent of total outstanding claims on all third world countries, the share of US banks' lending between December 1977 and June 1979 was less than 10 per cent (Bacha and Diaz-Alejandro, 1981). As lending by US banks to the less developed countries started to dwindle, mainly because US banks were concerned at their high level of exposure, the initiative was taken by West European, Japanese and OPEC banks.

As discussed above, in Latin America net official inflows in the sixties financed net outflows of foreign direct investment (as the latter flows were higher than the former). In the seventies an important proportion of total private bank lending serviced payments of profit remittances by foreign investors, interest and amortisation of official debt and, increasingly, the private credits themselves. As shown in Table 3.7, the category of foreign investments' profits remained relatively constant as a proportion of exports and services while both interest payments and amortisation soared, particularly since the mid-seventies. This latter trend is due both to the 'privatisation' of the debt, which leads to shorter average maturities and an increase in the proportion of credits serviced on variable commercial interest rates, as well as to the dramatic rise of euromarket interest rates since 1978.

This has been the general trend for all borrowing countries; higher interest rates and shorter maturities meant that the growth in gross borrowing between 1970 and 1980 was not translated into comparable growth in net transfers. Net transfers of resources (gross borrowing minus amortisation and interest payments) equalled 43 per cent in 1970, increased to 50 per cent in 1975–76, but *fell to only 22 per cent in 1980* (World Bank, 1981, p.59).

Table 3.7

Net financial service charges of Latin America, excluding oil exporters, relative to exports of goods and services

(percentages)

| Period | Interests[a] | Profits[b] | Amortisation[c] | Capital service ratio[d] |
|---|---|---|---|---|
| 1950–54 | 1.3 | 5.9 | 2.8 | 10.0 |
| 1955–59 | 2.3 | 5.2 | 7.2 | 14.7 |
| 1960–64 | 4.0 | 6.5 | 10.9 | 21.4 |
| 1965–69 | 5.5 | 8.8 | 13.7 | 27.0 |
| 1970–73 | 7.4 | 7.1 | 17.2 | 31.9 |
| 1974–76 | 11.1 | 5.5 | 19.1 | 35.7 |
| 1977–79 | 12.0 | 6.8 | 28.1 | 47.0[e] |

a   Refers to net interest and profits (subtracting those received by Latin American residents).

b   This category overestimates the impact on balance of payments, as it includes earning of foreign direct investment, whether remitted abroad or reinvested domestically.

c   Amortisations cover those for both private and public debt of more than one year.

d   Capital service ratio adds the three former columns. The debt service ratio would add the first and the third columns.

e   Only 1977–78.

Source: C. Díaz Alejandro and E. Bacha, 'Financial Markets: a view from the semi-periphery', paper presented at international seminar on External Financial Relations, 19–21 March 1981, Santiago, Chile. Based on on ECLA data.

## The role of IMF credit

Part of this transnational system of net transfer of resources is the lending operations of the International Monetary Fund (IMF). Susan Strange has pointed out that IMF lending has tended to follow a selective pattern:

> A policy was slowly hammered out, which applied the Fund's resources in a highly political manner. Without its ever being stated in so many words, the Fund's operational decisions made its resources available neither to those in the greatest need nor to those with the best record of good behaviour in keeping to the rules, but paradoxically to those members whose financial difficulties were most likely to jeopardise the stability of the international monetary system (1973, p.277).

Latin America was on the whole not a significant borrower of IMF resources. The net contribution of IMF credit for current account deficit has been relatively very small, and occasionally even negative as reflected in the item of compensatory finance in Table 3.4.

Figure 3.1 shows that the increases in the level of use of IMF credit since the sixties were much smaller for the Western Hemisphere than for other oil-importing less developed countries and for industrial countries. Net IMF credit to the Western Hemisphere was only significant during the period 1975–76, when the oil facility (which operated only during those two years to compensate for the rise in the price of oil) and the compensatory financing facility (which compensates for declines in export prices) were widely used by Latin American countries.

Even though the net credit contribution of the Fund to Latin America has been quantitatively small its impact on economic policies has been significant. In fact, the practice of attaching economic policy conditions and performance criteria to the provision of Fund loans was gradually developed in the 1950s, mainly using Latin American economies as testing grounds for such techniques (Thorp and Whitehead, 1979, p.3). Access to Fund credit, particularly in the upper credit tranches, which implies stringent acceptance of Fund conditionality, usually has acted as a catalyst for increased inflows from other sources. In the sixties, US aid programmes were often conditional on the previous signing of an IMF standby agreement by the recipient country. This type of linkage was very common in the sixties in Latin America when disbursements of loans from the Agency for International Development (AID) were frequently conditioned by the fulfilment of narrowly defined fiscal, monetary and exchange rate targets previously determined in a standby agreement with the Fund; this was

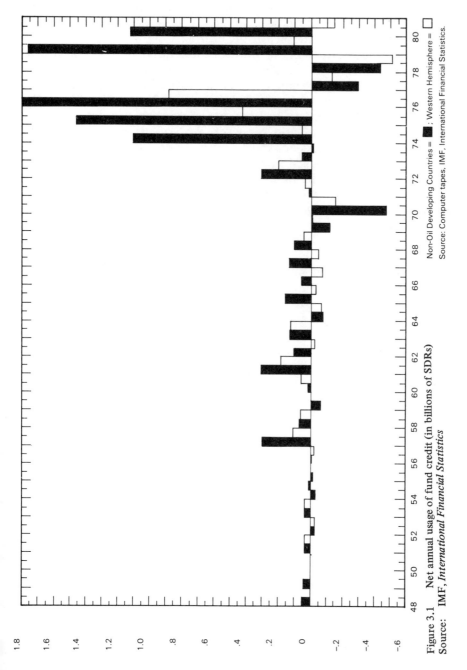

Figure 3.1   Net annual usage of fund credit (in billions of SDRs)
Source:   IMF, *International Financial Statistics*

Non-Oil Developing Countries = ■ ; Western Hemisphere = □
Source: Computer tapes. IMF, International Financial Statistics.

clearly illustrated by American aid to Chile in 1963–66 (Griffith-Jones, 1979, p.433). Similarly, in the seventies private banks frequently made it a precondition for granting a credit that the country previously agrees with the IMF on a 'stabilisation' programme. The role of the IMF is also crucial in the process of debt renegotiation, which augurs it an active role for the eighties.

Fund leverage to exercise influence on national policies and developments seems to be greater when there are few alternative sources of finance available, as happened in the case of Jamaica in 1978–79. This was the general case in the fifties when few alternatives to IMF finance existed at all, as both private and other multilateral official credit flows were at a very low level. That situation may arise in the eighties as private banks became reluctant to provide additional finance to third world borrowers. Fund leverage is also great when alternative finance requires its participation as a precondition. Such has been the case of private loans to very poor countries, e.g. Haiti and Mali, or to countries facing a situation of very serious financial disequilibrium, without a clear programme for a viable balance of payments in the near future. This was the case with Peru in 1978 and Costa Rica in 1981. The influence which the International Monetary Fund can exercise seems to be least when a country either has little need for external finance, e.g. major coffee exporters during the coffee boom of the 1970s, or can easily obtain external finance without IMF conditionality as a precondition. The latter has been best illustrated by the case of Brazil during the seventies, which was able to avoid Fund credit in the upper tranches, thus being able to preserve greater autonomy in economic policy making.[4] As Brazil's financial problems increased so did the pressures to go to the Fund.

*Fund conditionality*

As we have referred above to different types of IMF lending facilities with different levels of conditionality attached, it seems useful to describe these briefly here.[5] Currently, the only completely unconditional facility is the reserve tranche (i.e. purchase of a member's own quota subscription to the Fund) which is, in any case, part of a country's foreign exchange reserves. The facilities of low conditionality are not uniform in their terms. Under the buffer stock facility and the first 50 per cent of drawings under the compensatory financing facility (which compensates for temporary declines of a country's export earnings), there is virtually no conditionality once a balance of payments need has been demonstrated. For the second 50 per cent of drawings under the latter facility, a country must be 'co-operating with the Fund to solve its balance of payments difficulties. First credit tranche programmes are still of low conditionality in the sense that drawings are not normally conditional on performance, but they do contain objectives and performance targets which the borrower is expected to fulfil. The standby arrangement and the extended fund facility (EFF) in the upper credit tranche involve programmes of full conditionality, with access to periodic drawings, usually quarterly, dependent upon strict fulfilment of agreed perform-ance criteria. The standby arrangement is normally agreed for one year. The EFF introduced in 1974 envisages a three-year programme of lending and adjustment; currently it has a ten-year repayment period. The Fund's managing director recently pointed out that:

> in the period following the first wave of oil price increases approx-imately two-thirds of the resources were made available on terms involving a low degree of conditionality. At present, by contrast, some three-quarters of our new lending commitments involve 'upper credit tranche' programmes, that is, they require rigorous adjustment policies (IMF, 1981a, p.152).

The problems raised by IMF conditionality are being increasingly discussed.[6] We shall briefly outline here only the main issues. A general criticism is that the Fund's influence over the economic policies of member countries is concentrated on the deficit countries; this tends to impose a deflationary bias on the world economy as a whole, and in particular on those countries which need Fund assistance and/or its 'certificate of good behaviour' for obtaining other sources of fin-ance. Furthermore, the IMF has been criticised for laying too much emphasis on rapid moves towards balance in the external sector, at the cost of other important development objectives, such as invest-ment and growth. The Fund has also been criticised for failing to differentiate between the causes of balance of payments disequilibria, thus failing to address changes in its criteria that might contribute to successful adjustment in the new international environment. Further-more, even though the Fund claims that its recommendations are neutral as regards the burden of adjustment, its stress on measures such as reductions of state subsidies seem often to have negative effects on income distribution. Finally, the Fund admits to having a marked preference for orthodox market mechanisms and unrestricted flows of foreign investment, and a dislike for direct policy tools, such as price controls and restrictions on foreign exchange and trade.

## Effects of changes in the magnitude and composition of financial flows on national development

The new pattern of external financial flows coupled with an increase in volume entails the growing integration of Latin American economies into the world financial system. This evolution poses important questions. To what extent have larger financial flows, and their growing 'privatisation', augmented the options open to Latin American countries, and to what extent have they placed new constraints on policy making and on the nature of development? Has the relative degree of autonomy available to the national state on the whole tended to increase or decrease during the last decade?

Relatively little analysis has been done till now on the impact of rapidly changing financial flows on national development.[7] We shall attempt here some preliminary comments on this subject, looked at mainly from the perspective of the type of conditionality attached to different types of financial flows. As the analysis refers mainly to Latin America in general, less emphasis will be placed here on the specific national characteristics (political, social and economic) which, however, greatly influence the ultimate impact that external factors, including finance, have on national development.

Before analysing the impact of international financial flows on national development, it is necessary to clarify whether all countries are affected by this link. Is 'financial dependency' a valid concept for a particular category of countries? Does it refer only to less developed countries? Does it apply to all less developed countries? The answers seem to be found not in theoretical considerations, but in the realities of the international political and financial systems.

The reserve currency countries, particularly the United States after the Second World War, can finance their deficits with additional issues of their own currency; therefore they do not need to resort to institutions outside their own country for additional finance. Similarly, countries with large and relatively permanent surpluses in their balance of payments do not require external finance; on the contrary, they provide loans and aid to other countries and international financial institutions. Although in theory the Fund has power to influence policies of countries with balance of payments' surpluses, via the so-called 'scarce currency' clause, it has never used it. As a result the Fund only exacts adjustment from countries with deficits which ask it for assistance, thus introducing a deflationary bias in the world economy. This second category of surplus countries has in the past included industrial countries like Japan and West Germany. Particularly since late 1973, it has also included some less developed countries – the oil exporters with low absorptive capacity; Saudi Arabia and Kuwait are the two main cases.

Both categories of countries, the reserve currency countries and the surplus countries, can be considered basically as being financially independent; influence from abroad on their policies via financial mechanisms is very limited. Naturally, these countries may be 'dependent' in other dimensions; for example, the surplus oil exporters are technologically dependent on industrial countries.

Countries with large balance of payments deficits are not all equally 'dependent' on the wishes of their financiers. Affluent countries have recourse to diversity of sources. Thus, industrial countries, when in deficit, have access to special 'swap arrangements' amongst the Group of Ten or within the European Monetary System. This enables them to finance their deficits through credits from central banks of other industrial countries without needing to reduce their import bill or adhering to any explicit conditionality. Furthermore, they have easy access to private capital markets or even direct loans from oil exporters, e.g. Saudi loans to West Germany. Rarely do industrial countries go to the IMF. The last occasion in recent history was the UK in 1977.

In the case of the relatively higher income or semi-industrialised countries, their access to euroloans to finance their balance of payments deficits has also allowed them to avoid the explicit and detailed conditionality of the IMF. Furthermore, particular less developed countries have special access to regional financial institutions with less or different conditions, e.g. the Arab Monetary Fund.

It is normally the smaller, weaker countries which have fewer options for external finance, particularly when faced with a serious balance of payments crisis. They are therefore most often subjected to loans with more rigorous conditionality. The fact that IMF conditionality has affected poorer, smaller, weaker countries is not so much a reflection of the inadequacies of the Fund, but of the intrinsic inequities of the international financial system which the Fund was in charge of managing.

It can therefore be concluded that financial dependency *is* a relevant concept for some less developed countries, the poorest and weakest. Its relevance for industrial countries and large, semi-industrialised countries is relatively more limited. It becomes important in particular circumstances such as acute balance of payments crisis and/or in cases where high priority is given by a government to a strategy of opening up the economy.[8]

Not only does the impact of external finance on national development vary from country to country, one must also consider the different forms that financial flows have over time. On foreign direct investment several rich analyses can be found in the works of the dependency school.[9] These have argued that transnational corporations contribute to a net outflow of capital, displace local production, transfer little or inappropriate technology, encourage the transnationalisation of consumption patterns, widen inequalities and foster the development of particular class alliances.

Official loans and aid are granted mostly for specific projects particularly in the case of multilateral agencies, such as the World Bank and the Interamerican Development Bank. Their evaluation and surveillance are mainly in technical terms, but the use of funds is also closely monitored. Resources are allocated following sectoral priorities.

Increasingly, however, official flows (particularly of bilateral agencies, such as USAID) have established programme loans for general balance of payments support. Programme loans tend to concentrate on development strategies and general macroeconomic conditions. The criteria are very similar, and often in fact are directly linked to, IMF criteria. As mentioned above, disbursements of AID programme loans to Chile, which began operating in 1963, were linked to several narrowly-defined fiscal, monetary and exchange rate targets, which had been determined in the previously signed standby agreement with the IMF. Thus, aid through programme loans basically reinforced IMF criteria, even though also introducing others, such as structural reforms.

Both in project and in programme lending, the criteria for lending are basically influenced by the donor governments though the recipient countries intervene as well. The allocation criteria reflect prevalent trends in development thinking in the lending agencies, which in turn respond greatly to the socio-political model they advocate. Thus, during the initial stage of the Alliance for Progress, support was given to agrarian and taxation reforms, as well as to modernisation in agriculture. Much greater stress has been placed on financial criteria during the late sixties and seventies; during the seventies, great emphasis was placed on export promotion as the main engine for growth and development.

The type of financial flows dominant in the seventies, private credits from multinational banks, have a rather different impact. In practice funds are hardly ever tied to specific projects, and in those cases where they are, banks neither monitor actual expenditure nor carry out technical evaluation of the projects. Furthermore, there is no theoretical thinking on development or growth behind the lending policies of private banks. Banks seem to be less overtly political in their criteria than official institutions, as they do not serve so closely the political interests of their country or countries, nor are they influenced by their parliaments, but mainly pursue profitable business. As a result, banks are on the whole willing to lend to different types of political regimes, as long as they are 'firmly established'. The main criteria for lending decisions is the profitability and security of their loans; they prefer to lend to countries from whom they can obtain higher margins and/or to those which they perceive as more clearly committed to debt repayment and more able to do so. As a result their main emphasis is on short-term financial indicators. Great stress is placed on the balance of payments. Therefore, emphasis is put on variables such as the rate of inflation, the level of foreign exchange reserves and trade balances; it is noteworthy that the rate of investment to GDP (a rough indicator of medium-term economic prospects) is barely considered of importance to determine 'creditworthiness'. In critical situations the banks demand, as a precondition for granting further loans or restructuring existing ones, that the country sign a standby with the IMF, as was seen in 1982 with a score of countries.

While a country retains the 'confidence' of the transnational banks, that country or its enterprises have much greater freedom than in the case of aid to use the funds in whatsoever manner they think is best. In this sense, a greater degree of maneouvrability opened up in the seventies than existed in the sixties, particularly for the middle income countries, which the banks found more 'creditworthy'. Most importantly, those less developed countries that obtained such large volumes of credits on the private capital markets were able to sustain levels of imports well above those they could have afforded without such loans. Studies have shown that those countries that maintained or increased their imports also maintained high growth rates of both investment and total production (Dell and Lawrence, 1980). In Latin America, Brazil provided until 1982 a textbook example of a country which was able to continue its high growth rate through a strategy of 'debt-led growth'.[10] Brazil's ability and willingness to borrow in order to continue importing allowed it to maintain a positive growth rate despite the world recession. Finance thus had a counter-cyclical effect. Adjustment ceased to be the sole available option.

However, the availability of international liquidity without any technical or political surveillance may mean that many of these foreign resources are used up in excessive increases of consumption, much of it superfluous. As the market is the main 'allocator' of these financial resources it may not lead to either an efficient or a just development pattern. This is well illustrated by the Chilean case, where:

in the period 1970–78 there has been an important change in the composition of Chilean imports. The importation of non-essential goods expands very rapidly during this period, more than doubling, and its proportion relative to the total increases from a little more than 14 per cent in 1970 to more than 21 per cent in 1978. ... During the same period, imports of machinery and equipment, as a part of total imports went down from 20 per cent in 1970 to only 13 per cent in 1978 (Herrera and Morales, 1981, p.7).

Even if private credits are invested, there is the risk that unexpected changes in the international environment, such as increases in interest rates or declines in commodity prices, may mean that the foreign exchange required to service the loan will not be forthcoming in sufficient amounts or at an adequate pace. Thus, the risk of a balance of payments crisis is greater than with official loans; the risk seems even greater if governments exercise hardly any control over private inflows and their use, as in the case of Chile.

At the political level, the wish to attract foreign loans may encourage a policy model which over-emphasises financial equilibrium to the detriment of all other aspects of economic policy.[11] In the Southern Cone, the need to maintain or improve the country's 'creditworthiness' has been used to justify unpopular measures. A clear example is found in the following statement appearing in the main Chilean newspaper, *El Mercurio* (15 October 1978):

> Chile has recently obtained from the international banking community a treatment similar to that of serious and important countries. This asset of incalculable value must be maintained at all costs, and for this it is basic to sustain an economic policy of stabilisation, *which will reduce public expenditure and will moderate excessive increases in real wages.*

It is also maintained that structural changes such as 'freeing the magic of the market forces' and opening up the economy to trade and financial flows helps to improve the country's 'creditworthiness'. Certainly the large private international liquidity available during the seventies proved a powerful incentive for governments with different ideologies to 'open up' their countries more to foreign credits.

It can be concluded that the massive explosion of private bank lending opened new options of growth for some less developed countries, in principle implying greater autonomy than aid. It is to be feared, however, that the explicit conditionality of official loans may be replaced by a less clearly perceived implicit conditionality in private loans. Furthermore, as there is practically no accountability on the use of the private credits, either in the private bank or in the borrowing country, it is much more probable than in the case of aid, that vast sums of money may be used for consumption of luxury goods or investment in inefficient projects and even purchase of arms. It is amazing that those who vehemently attack aid as wasteful advocate private flows, which by their own uncontrolled nature must imply in many cases a level of waste inconceivable if some public control existed. Naturally, private international credit can be channelled into productive investment, provided there is systematic effort by the borrower, either private or public, to do so.

# Some conclusions for the eighties

The IMF *1981 World Economic Outlook* (p.129) points out that net long-term private lending to oil-importing less developed countries fell from US$33.1 billion in 1979 to US$27.2 billion in 1980; in 1981 it was estimated to have been (at US$31.0 billion) above the 1980 but still below the 1979 level. As the same source shows, this occurred during a period of rapidly rising current account deficits. It seems that the recycling role of transnational banks will become more limited. Many bankers wish to see their activities supplemented by official international institutions. They see their business as focusing mainly on project lending or to specific enterprises and would prefer that international institutions such as the Fund increased their role in financing balance of payments deficit.[1,2]

The managing director of the IMF, Jacques de Larosière, has repeatedly stressed the two main reasons for slow growth of Fund lending in the seventies. One was that total IMF quotas (which provide the Fund's capital base, on which the size of its loans are dependent) fell substantially in relation to the size of the payments deficits faced by member countries; in fact, the total of Fund quotas fell as a proportion of world imports, from 12 per cent in 1965 to only about 4 per cent in 1980. The second reason was that countries were increasingly reluctant in the seventies to enter into financial arrangements with the Fund due to the stringent conditionality attached to their loans (*IMF 1981 Survey*, p.152).

The IMF augmented the size of its operations under the policy of enlarged access, approved in early 1981. Countries may borrow up to 450 per cent of their quotas to support high conditionality programmes; this is an important increase relative to the situation during most of the seventies, when a country could usually purchase up to 165 per cent under an extended arrangement and previously up to 100 per cent under standby. The policies of increased access to resources are reflected in the sharp increase in financial commitments. In the first half of 1981, the Fund's new commitments doubled the amount for the same period in 1980 (Griffith-Jones, 1982). The loan made to India in late 1981 of SDR5 billion, the largest ever made by the Fund, illustrates the much greater scale of Fund lending.

The financial resources for these new operations come to a great extent from loans to the IMF. The central banks of thirteen industrial countries provided SDR1.1 billion. However, it is a loan from Saudi Arabia, made operational in May 1981 of SDR8 billion, that will be the major source of finance for the enlarged access facility. The US has refused to contribute to the enlarged access facility; in addition it has tried to toughen the conditionality for such credits and to curtail their expansion.

The issue of appropriate Fund conditionality will acquire increasing saliency in the eighties because the IMF will be playing a more active role in recycling as 1981 seemed to indicate. Moreover, a much greater proportion of Fund lending will tend to be in the upper credit tranches, which imply much more rigorous conditionality than that in lower tranches, as was underlined by Jacques de Larosiere (*IMF Survey*, 1981 p.152).

The growing disagreements on IMF conditionality clearly surfaced at the September 1981 IMF–World Bank annual meeting. While the less developed countries continue to press for some 'softening' of conditionality so as to make the twin targets of viable balance of payments and development more compatible and to overcome other inadequacies of Fund conditionality, the US government pressed for a reversal of recent trends demanding a 'toughening' of conditionality. The results of these international debates, as well as of specific negotiations between the Fund and deficit countries, will have an important effect on the economic and social development of many third world countries during the eighties.

The World Bank, like the IMF, is tending towards a more intimate relationship with less developed countries, particularly through its structural adjustment loans, which mean greater macro-economic conditionality than project loans. Structural adjustment loans require that:

> a country must be willing to adopt appropriate changes in its policies and programs to enable its economy to adapt over a reasonable period to changes in the international environment without sacrificing its long-term objectives (Wright, 1980, p.21).

A very probable important growth area for the World Bank will be co-financing, that is, joint financing with the private banks in which the bank will provide most of the technical expertise. Co-financing emphasises the trend towards privatisation of debt and higher, commercial, interest rates.

In public institutions, as in the private sector, there is an important expansion of financial flows via relatively new agencies, largely based on direct transfer of OPEC surpluses. The Opec Fund, the Kuwait Fund (the first bilateral development institution established in the third world), and the Saudi Fund provide three good examples of such institutions.

Social scientists formed in the dependency school as well as some policy-makers correctly fear that increased deficits and increased financial flows may lead to greater restrictions on their national autonomy. Taken to the ultimate extreme, supporters of this position would argue for complete de-linking from international capital flows. However, the failure of very extreme de-linking has been only too starkly illustrated by the Kampuchean régime under Pol Pot.

On the other side of the spectrum, others are concerned with the limitations of present recycling facilities, particularly for the poorest countries. Supporters of this position argue for increased 'transfer of resources' from North to South. The most ardent supporters of this view, the Brandt Commissioners, represent political groups, mainly Social Democrats, with strong Keynesian inclinations, who are out of power in their countries. The dominant Anglo-Saxon orthodoxy resists not only a high level of international recycling, but even a high level of national aggregate demand. If stringent monetarism rules in the US and the UK, what chance for international Keynesianism? In the 'monetarist' perception, increased recycling, like increased aggregate demand at home, will only augment pressure on commodity prices, particularly oil, and on real wages in their country, thus strengthening OPEC and their own trade unions, and reducing the possibility for an increase in the rate of profit. Therefore, their support for effective recycling is very limited; their perceived interests clearly differ from those of less developed countries, both oil exporters and importers.

From both these perspectives, the concern with dependency and the opposition of the British and American governments to recycling, greater hopes lie in initiatives taken in the 'South'. OPEC private banks have already begun to play a more active role. The volume of loans on the eurocurrency markets organised by syndications led by Arab banks grew from 10.3 per cent in 1980 to 26.5 per cent of total loans in 1981 (IMF, 1982, p.41). Approximately half of these loans went to less developed countries. OPEC funds may well continue to help finance increased loans by the Bretton Woods institutions, as the recent massive Saudi loan to the Fund did. It is also feasible that OPEC or other 'Southern' funds may expand or create new institutions more closely controlled by the less developed countries, for example, the OPEC Development Agency or a third world bank. Thus, the new dynamism for international flows will most probably not come from US actors as it did in the last three decades; the financial resources, and more importantly, the willingness and the motivation lies much more in the 'Southern' countries themselves; this refers mainly, but certainly not exclusively, to OPEC countries.

Greater dynamism by third world agencies, or by institutions where the third world has greater influence, could not only help to solve, at a more satisfactory level, the problem of 'recycling' to deficit countries. It might provide some answers to the 'dependency' theorists and policy makers critical of existent conditionality; alternative institutions could provide alternative conditionality, hopefully more adequate to the needs of third world development. Perhaps more importantly, diversification of international financial sources should reduce 'financial dependency' by increasing national options.

Two final caveats need to be made. First, if and when created, new agencies will be complementing and not replacing existing institutions. Second, further development of new financial agencies requires political agreement amongst third world countries, which may be difficult to obtain. Obstacles include both heterogeneity between third world countries as well as the fact that there is no dominant country in the third world which plays or could play a role comparable to US leadership after the Second World War.

# Notes

1   As an example of this trend, see Chapter 4 by A. Ferrer.

2   For example, Levinson and Onis (1970) wrote that 'the predominant objective of US policy in the Alliance for Progress was to prevent other Latin American countries from following the example of Cuba'. Senator Guering, in his report to the US Congress on the Alliance for Progress in Chile, could not be more explicit: 'The Alliance for Progress was designed as an alternative to Communist blandishment and chaos' (quoted in S. Griffith-Jones, 1979).

3   Even though part of this increase reflects US inflation, the growth in real terms of net private flows is quite dramatic.

4   See Chapter 6 by P. Evans.

5   See also P. Daniel, 1981, pp.29–31.

6   For valuable assessments see, for example, Brett, 1979; Dell and Lawrence, 1980; and Buira, 1981.

7   Amongst important exceptions are Chapter 4 by A. Ferrer and Chapter 5 by E.V.K. FitzGerald in this book, as well as articles by Seers (1981) and Diaz Alejandro and Bacha (1981).

8   See Chapter 5 by E.V.K. FitzGerald and Chapter 2 by C. Diaz Alejandro in this volume.

9   For a comprehensive overview of research on TNCs see P. Evans (1981, pp.199–223). See also Chapter 6 on the alliance between state, multinational and local capital in this volume.

10   For Brazil's development strategy, see Chapter 6.

11   For the use of economic theory as ideology, see Chapter 5.

12   See, for example, the Proceedings of the Financial Times *Conference on Euro-markets, 1981*, London, 21–22 January 1981, especially the inaugural speech by Mr Yassukovic.

# 4 Towards a theory of independence*

ALDO FERRER

Drawing on the historical experience of the region, Latin American economic thought has made a substantial contribution to the formulation of what is generally known as 'dependency theory'. This centre-periphery perspective has contributed greatly to an understanding of the relationships between Latin American underdevelopment and the international system. Recent changes in both the international system and the economic development of the region have given rise, however, to the hypothesis that centre-periphery relations, i.e. the ties of dependency, are rapidly being modified. These new trends include, in particular, the mounting internal tensions which industrial societies are now experiencing; the proliferation of economic power in the world economy; the change in the relative importance of the third world, especially Latin America, vis-à-vis the advanced countries; and the new conditions in which confrontation between the super-powers is taking pláce.

This chapter examines the possibility of formulating a 'theory of independence', i.e. an interpretation of the world economy which highlights the new options open to Latin American countries. It briefly reviews the main transformations in the world order mentioned above and then goes on to examine the factors which support the hypothesis that Latin America's freedom to manoeuvre within the international system is increasing.

* This chapter draws largely upon an article previously published in Spanish in *Comercio Exterior*, vol.29, no.8, August 1979. Thanks are due to the Banco Nacional de Comercio Exterior of Mexico for permission to reproduce parts of the article, to Susanna Davies for the translation and to Mary-Anne Thompson for additional research.

## Internal tensions within the industrial countries

From recent studies carried out by the OECD, the EEC Commission and the Trilateral Commission, a consensus is emerging that the present difficulties of the industrialised world are not rooted in passing insufficiencies of demand; surmountable short-term rigidities of supply; or circumstantial rises of certain prices or transitory problems of balance of payments adjustment. Studies available from these sources also suggest that, within the foreseeable future, there are limits to increases in the exploitation of non-renewable resources or the intolerable contaminating effects of development. For example, in the critical case of energy, it is argued that the possibility of exhausting hydrocarbon resources establishes the need to diversify sources of energy, but not to restrict energy supply in the long-term. As for the problem of polluting the environment, it has been shown that the economic and social costs of controlling pollutant factors are not very great. As far as technological change and its effect on the economic process is concerned, it is admitted that certain developments linked to the car industry and various branches of the chemical industry may have impaired the growth rates which had characterised these sectors and contributed to the economic expansion of the postwar period; but new frontiers in the fields of electronics, information and industrial applications of biology are opening up, which could be sources of increased economic growth and productivity. It would thus be seen that present versions of the Kondratieff cycle, based on the long-term comportment of technological change and capital accumulation, do not seem to reflect the actual nature of the deceleration of economic growth in the developed nations.

The OECD Interfutures report maintained that:

> the first challenge facing the advanced industrial societies is internal. How can these societies adapt to the pressures engendered in social, cultural and institutional changes that translate themselves into different demands about the distribution of the social product and individual participation in production and social decisions? How can these societies overcome these conflicts of value which make the elaboration of government policies so difficult? Are these societies capable of engendering the new values, the new comportments and institutions that will be capable of responding to the problems of tomorrow? (OECD, 1978, p.8).

These are the questions and conflicts that confront the advanced industrial societies today and they appear to originate from the same process of transformation that has been going on since the end of the

90

Second World War. According to a report from the EEC:

> every advance in material welfare and education reinforces the desire of people to participate in decisions that concern them. This urgent need is exacerbated by the simultaneous tendency for concentration, the enormity of economic power and the bureaucratization of political power. At the base of these conflicts is a more profound dissatisfaction, of a moral nature, which questions the results and significance of development, owing to its ecological effects, its human cost, its absence of a more profound meaning. This gives rise to a disorientation of conscience, a sense of inutility and inactivity — sources of frustration and violence (EEC, 1978, p.7).

The advanced industrial societies are undergoing a process of 'institutional sclerosis' which is linked to the formation of what could be described as 'social oligopolies', i.e. the concentration of economic power in large corporations, trade unions and the state. This situation has debilitated the capacity of these societies to adapt to change, a capacity they had exhibited during the entire period of postwar expansion.

> During the last quarter century, the advanced industrial societies have shown a marked structural ability to adapt to and confront the transformation of production; migration within sectors and between regions; the use of technology; the ties between groups; the internationalization of production and the characteristics of supply and demand for work (OECD, 1978, p.61).

This ability to adapt to change has been jeopardised by the 'institutional sclerosis', by the resistance of power groups to changes which affect them as well as by the questioning of values, held by broad sectors of the population, which have characterised this process of development from 1945 onwards.

Post-industrial society has engendered new values amongst which are demands for equality; the defence of the environment; preferences for individual security, hedonism and local traditions; the revalorisation of the family as a source of emotional support and the rejection of short-term decisions made by those in positions of power. These new values lead to a questioning of the legitimacy of a meritocracy founded on education, because it is based on an unjust social order, a 'genetic lottery' and the hereditary transmission of cultural patterns (OECD, 1977, p.3; and passim).

From this perspective, the inflation–unemployment problem is, in effect, the particular form that social conflict takes on the economic plane in a period of increasing rigidity of social structures (EEC, 1978, p.48). These phenomena help to explain the decline of private investment and the reluctance to increase productive capacity, to transform the composition of supply and generate new jobs. The corporations are faced with new investment demands to increase productive capacity, to substitute labour and to shift to energy-saving techniques that are geared to the preservation of the environment.[1] Yet, the permanent modification of relative prices and growing social pressures have altered the rules of the game under which private investment led the expansion of production and technological change in the last decades. The same may be said of the role of the state in the regulation of aggregate demand and in the expansion of investment and public expenditure. The state has been criticised as a source of concentration of bureaucratic power opposed to the new values, whilst at the same time mounting social demands inevitably impose an expansion in public sector borrowing. One of the central dilemmas confronting the advanced industrial societies today has its roots in the question of how to make these demands compatible with the growing resistance to tributary pressure. Everything seems to indicate that these societies are experiencing acute internal crises and that the solution to their economic problems will not be attained without profound politico-institutional changes.

This internal crisis of advanced societies is reflected in the management of their economic interdependence. Tensions in these relations in turn makes the internal contradictions of the developed countries more acute. For example, the instability of exchange rates of the principal currencies reflects imbalances in international payments and makes it more difficult to carry out domestic anti-inflationary policies and to control internal demand. In turn, the diversity in the rates of inflation and levels of economic growth, make the adjustment of international payments more difficult.

At the very least it may be said that the countries faced with these problems have not come up with clear answers to them. Growth is being questioned and restrained by conventional stabilisation policies. Yet at the same time, such a brake on further growth reduces the flexibility of the social structures to accept change. One of the great historical merits of capitalism in the centre countries is that by its very nature it is tied to growth. Its capacity to generate technology and savings leads to permanent expansion of supply and demand. If this is not achieved, internal tensions reach intolerable levels.

The political–social conflict in the advanced industrial societies inevitably expresses itself in terms of distinct economic strategies which fall into two broad categories. The first, which can be characterised as being 'defensive', seeks to accept a fall in the rate of growth in the long term and to accommodate the ensuing decline in the demand for labour by means of reducing the hours of work, and to compensate for sectoral and regional imbalances with ad hoc compensatory measures.[2] It seems unlikely that this line of thought will succeed in dispelling mounting tensions. One of its manifestations is protectionism against emerging competition from some third world countries as well as from Japan. Protectionism may postpone the need to readjust, but does not eliminate it. Moreover, it conflicts with the postwar process of the transnationalisation of production that has been carried out by the large corporations.

The second line of thought, which can be characterised as 'offensive', seeks to take on the challenge of change, to restore a strong rate of growth and to promote politico–institutional transformations which will free the forces of growth. Neither of these strategies fits into traditional categories of political thought of the left and right. In effect, these 'offensive' and 'defensive' strategies may well emerge in either camp of traditional policies.

The EEC and OECD reports point out that although 'new values' are not necessarily incompatible with further economic development, they do pose the need to draw up new rules of the game for capital accumulation, the assimilation of technological change and the distribution of the social product. The capacity of the advanced industrial societies to make these 'new values' compatible with development is a major question facing the international system today.

This central problem for the industrial countries — how to increase productivity while attaining sustained growth of demand with full employment and price stability — is in some senses, a vicious circle. Unemployment and inflation discourage the accumulation of capital, the penetration of technological change, the international division of labour and, consequently, the increase in productivity. In its turn, the slow growth of productivity, real income and demand increases the social tensions which fuel the struggle for distribution of income and inflation. These problems can only be solved from within the developed economies in which they occur. For example, the transfer of low technology industries to developing countries constitutes, from the perspective of the centre countries, a competent way of increasing productivity and real income. Yet, this requires that the developed economies recuperate satisfactory levels of growth, employment and demand to absorb the new production. Otherwise, as experience shows, protectionist pressures impose severe restrictions on the expansion of imports from developing countries.

## Proliferation of power in the world economy

Since the 1950s, the rapid economic expansion of Germany, Japan and other industrialised countries has contributed to eroding the hegemonic position of the United States within the world economy. In 1950, the United States' GNP represented 60 per cent of the industrialised world's total product. The rapid reconstruction of the belligerent European countries and Japan, and their subsequent rapid development, significantly modified the relative positions of the major countries. This led to what has been called a 'trilateral system', comprising the United States, Western Europe and Japan. By the 1970s, American participation in the gross product of the trilateral system had declined to 47 per cent, while three countries of the system (West Germany, Japan and France) represented 80 per cent of the United States' GNP (Ferrer, 1980, p.20, passim). The economic role of the United States has been further undermined by the rise of various developing countries which have achieved industrialisation, thereby increasing the number of national economies which are actively intervening in international economic relations.[3] In Latin America examples include the successful participation of Argentinian firms in large construction contracts in Middle Eastern oil states and Brazilian advances in the sales of engineering services and capital goods in Africa. The more active participation of the Soviet Union and the Eastern European economies in world markets has also contributed to the emergence of multipolarity.

The expansion of international liquidity, the development of eurocurrency markets and the internationalisation of banking in many countries, including some members of the third world, has debilitated the weight of traditional financial discipline imposed by the IMF.[4] The private banks' search for business is not attached to orthodox financial criteria and this had allowed numerous countries a greater, unconditional access to new sources of funds which can be used to finance balance of payments disequilibria. Public international financing with strings attached, such as IMF loans or credits tied to the purchase of goods, has lost importance in relation to free-market financing.

All these factors imply a dispersion of international economic power and a multiplication of the sources of supply of capital goods, technology and finance. The number of firms which participate in the principal markets has increased and the competition between them is greater than ever. The phenomenon of oligopolistic concentration in numerous industries in the United States and other industrial countries has been accompanied by an increase in the number of firms which participate in international operations. An important example is the automobile sector: approximately 90 per cent of automobile

94

production in each of the main industrial countries (United States, Canada, Japan, France, West Germany, Italy and the United Kingdom) is concentrated in three main firms. On a world scale, however, the sector is more competitive.

In this and other sectors, it is ironic that the American transnational, which typically works in highly concentrated industries, has been a principal factor in bringing about the decentralisation of foreign markets (Rose, 1977, p.113). With very few exceptions, a large number of firms compete in international markets for capital goods, technology and intermediate and finished goods. According to a study by the American Department of Commerce, which encompasses 56 industrial sectors, the number of American, European and Japanese transnational corporations which compete within the same industrial sector and in three or more foreign markets, quadrupled between 1950 and 1970. For example, in the case of corrugated cardboard for packaging, in 1950 there was only one transnational corporation that fulfilled these requirements; in 1970 there were eleven. In the same period, the number of beverage transnational corporations rose from four to eighteen and autopart transnational corporations for the car industry rose from five to thirty-six (Rose, 1977, p.112).

From 1945 onwards, the expansion of corporations from the United States and other industrial countries was favoured by a conjunction of factors. Economies of scale stimulated the process of concentration and agglomeration, as well as expansion on a world level. The concentration of expenditure on research and development in these corporations accentuated their technological lead even more. The organisational capacity required to operate in large markets and on the international level which the transnational corporations exhibit, also favoured their expansion. The control of information and the capacity to make use of a single decision-making structure which works on a transnational scale, was yet another strengthening factor for the development of the corporations and the process of transnationalisation. The potential for finance and accumulation for these firms contributed to an environment which was exceptionally favourable to their expansion from 1945 onwards. It is therefore not surprising that intra-industrial specialisation at the product level, which characterises the development of trade within the trilateral system, has relied largely on the transnational corporations. It is estimated that approximately 40 per cent of all international trade is carried out through intra-firm transfers of transnational corporations (UNCTAD, 1981, p.64).

Some prospective visions which conceived of the future organisation of the world economy as being reduced to a group of large transnational corporations were grounded in these developments. According to these perspectives, the concentration of economic power would constitute the base for the efficient organisation of the world system, over and above national sovereignty.

However, for a number of reasons the extremely favourable conjuncture for the expansion of transnational corporations began progressively to erode. The first of these is that the large size of transnational corporations tends to produce diseconomies of scale owing to the emergence of a bureaucratic 'sclerosis', typical of large organisations, which limits the adaptability of the firm to changes in technology and market conditions.

Second, there are warning signs of a shift from capital-intensive technologies to ones using more technical and skilled labour, especially in machinery and equipment production and in the electronics industry. This shift refers to what are known as 'light technologies' with an intensive use of skill especially suitable for application in small and medium-sized firms.

The third reason involves the development of new methods of communication and diffusion of information on a transnational scale which permits a greater monitoring of conditions of supply and demand in many markets, available technologies, financial conditions and other essential facts. This type of information, which was previously the preserve of the large corporations, is now available to many medium-sized and small parties interested in operating on a world scale. Thus, 'minitransnationals' have been acquiring an increasingly active role vis à vis the large transnationals.

The fourth is the multiplication and diversification of international sources of finance available to medium-sized and small firms. This increases their relative power with regard to the transnational corporations whose lead has also traditionally been based on access to international credit.[5]

Fifth, there has been the strengthening of the state in both the developed nations and those of the third world, with a view towards exercising more effective political control over the large transnationals, leading them to compromise in the light of social demands, consumer interests and preservation of the environment. In numerous third world countries the participation of transnational corporations in development, technology transfer and their relations vis-à-vis domestic public and private firms are now more closely scrutinised.[6]

Finally, in the case of American corporations, the devaluation of the dollar since the early 1970s has had a major effect in halting the expansion of purchasing activities abroad and production in third markets. It eliminated the stimulus that previous over-valuation had excercised as a substitute for the uncompetitive nature of exports from the United States.

These tendencies have induced significant changes in the organisation of production at the level of firms as well as in international economic relations. The small and medium-sized firms have become active participants in many markets, including high technology sectors. Examples include the American industrial complexes around Boston and California and the development of the Swedish machinery industry. In Germany, medium-sized firms constitute the 'nerve' of the national economy. The declining economic zones, like the Ruhr and the Rhine, are those in which large firms (*konzern*) are prevalent, whilst the medium-sized and small firms are concentrated in Bavaria and Baden-Wurtemberg, regions in full expansion. One out of every two German corporations abroad belongs to a medium-sized or small 'minitransnational' (*L'Express*, 1979, p.96). These firms are increasing their role in the international market of goods and services and have entered into joint ventures abroad.

Thus, it seems that the postwar period of expansion of transnational corporations may be coming to an end. Sales of transnational corporations' subsidiaries have increased significantly in recent years. United States' corporations sold 1,339 foreign subsidiaries between 1971 and 1975; equivalent to 10 per cent of the total number of American subsidiaries. In 1971, for every subsidiary sold, 3.3 new ones were established. The ratio fell to 1.4 in 1975. The process of disinvestment is concentrated in the more competitive low technology industries, such as textiles and clothing, leather, pneumatics, agrochemicals and beverages — though there are few disinvestments in the high technology sectors, such as pharmaceuticals, automobiles and office equipment (Rose, 1977, p.111).

## Transformations in the third world

*Relative position in the world economy*

Technological change and trends in international trade in the last thirty years have contributed to the marginalisation of countries involved in the production and export of primary products. With the exception of the oil-exporting countries, the rest of the third world has rapidly lost relative weight in international economic relations. Countries of Asia, Africa and Latin America generated 30.8 per cent of world exports at the end of the 1940s; at the beginning of the 1970s, the figure had dropped to 18.1 per cent (UNCTAD, 1981, p.116).

The feeble participation of the developing countries in the advance of technology and the process of industrialisation forcibly separated them from the most dynamic forces of the international economy. With the exception of the oil-exporting countries, these nations that were 'set aside' lost relative importance within the basic interests of the industrialised economies. These tendencies affect Latin America profoundly. On the one hand, the participation of the region in world trade and its importance as a recipient of foreign investment declined significantly. From the immediate postwar years to the end of the 1970s, the contribution of Latin American exports to the world economy declined from 11 per cent to 5 per cent. A notable example of this trend is the evolution of the region's relations with the United States. In 1950, 35 per cent of total United States' imports came from Latin America; in 1970, the proportion only amounted to 11 per cent (IMF, 1980). On the other hand, the same can be observed in relation to private direct investment. From 1962 to 1971, the participation of Latin America in total United States private direct investment declined from 26 per cent to 18 per cent.

Nevertheless, there has been a set of changes within the underdeveloped countries which has subsequently modified their traditional relations with the international centres of power. First, there was the dislocation of the colonial order. In 1938, 80 per cent of the land mass and 75 per cent of the world population was under the domination of the great western powers, primarily Great Britain. Decolonisation in Asia and Africa and economic development in these continents and Latin America, meant that new actors stepped into the international arena. These countries have raised their capacity to administer their own resources, to elaborate autonomous developmental strategies and to negotiate from an independent stance with the centres of world power. The decisions of OPEC probably constitute the most spectacular example of modification of traditional relations between the industrialised world and a group of peripheral

98

nations. Other notable examples include new régimes regulating foreign direct investment and technology transfer; policies to regain control of basic resources in numerous third world countries; and the recent United States/Mexico negotiations for the purchase of Mexican oil and gas.

However, the third world is far from being an homogenous group. The differences between developing countries are far greater than those which exist within the trilateral system. In the countries of the trilateral system, the ratio of highest to lowest per capita income is 1:3. In the third world it is 1:27.[7] The differences in terms of population, territorial dimension and endowment of natural resources are also wide. Cultural, racial and religious diversities contribute to the creation of an even more heterogeneous picture. Political and social systems, models of economic development and links with the centres of power also differ radically. The overall picture is so diverse that the category of 'third world' is losing its capacity to describe the roles played by the various countries included in it and in the international system.

These disparities will probably continue to increase. Recently industrialised economies, and another small group of countries in the process of industrialising, will probably overcome the barrier of underdevelopment before the end of the century and will be active participants in trade and other international transactions. These countries will be in positions to overcome the most acute problems of poverty, through appropriate domestic reform. Only political conflict over such reforms could frustrate the process of development and a change of role in the international system. The problem of extreme poverty will continue to be concentrated in various Asian countries (India, Pakistan, Bangladesh) and in sub-Saharan black Africa (World Bank, 1981). The dimension of backwardness in these countries is of such magnitude that it will be difficult for them to overcome their levels of underdevelopment in the future and the disparities of internal income distribution which characterise them. Furthermore, many small countries with scarce resources probably constitute examples of societies which are not viable within their own national limits. At the other end of the spectrum, the oil countries of the Middle East have become major centres of influence within the international system, as a result of their control of a strategic resource and strong financial surpluses that have resulted from it. Their role in the international economic order will depend in a large measure on the evolution of the world energy situation, including the development of other sources of energy; on their own capacity to reinvest oil surpluses and on their internal political development. China is evidently a separate case within the context of underdeveloped countries. Although the trend seems to point towards more active participation in international economic relations, it seems unlikely that its influence in the international system will be comparable to its relative weight in population terms. Available projections indicate that China's international transactions will not reach the equivalent relative importance of the industrialised countries by the end of this century (UNCTAD, 1981, pp.55–7).

Given these conditions, it is clear that the bases of third world solidarity will be more rhetorical than real. There is no doubt that horizontal co-operation within the third world could have a positive effect on the promotion of development in each country and on the transformation of the international economic order. In practice, however, horizontal co-operation implies a degree of interference with market forces and an orientation of economic agents which is difficult to arrange between developing countries, at least on a large scale. The difficulties faced by the Latin American countries in their attempts at regional co-operation, despite certain favourable initial conditions derived from a common historical and cultural tradition, is sufficiently illustrative in this respect. The relationships of under-developed countries to the rest of the world will probably be more influenced by the technological change and the internal transformation of their productive and socio-political structures, than by any plans for horizontal co-operation on an international or regional scale. Thus, the nation-state will continue to be the framework within which the course of events will be decided.

*The emergence of the newly industrialising countries*

The 'newly industrialising countries' encompass Brazil, Mexico, Argentina, South Korea and Taiwan.[8] It is likely that in the medium-term other countries will make important advances in industrialisation and achieve international competitiveness and join the group: in Latin America, Venezuela and Colombia; in Africa, Egypt, Nigeria and Algeria; and in Asia, Malaysia and the Philippines. This group of countries now plays a significant role in international economic relations.

They are active in the trade of semi-manufactures (textiles, iron and steel, pulp and paper); metal machine goods (cars, transport and telecommunications goods); and finished consumer goods (clothing, toys, shoes and other leather goods). They control about 10 per cent of global trade in manufactures.[9] Their new role is anchored to dynamic comparative advantages that spring from increased investment in capital equipment and human resources. It is interesting to note that the wide range of goods exported by these countries comes under the heading of 'intra-industrial specialisation', i.e. the exchange of products within the same industrial branches. Intra-industrial specialisation is the specific form of the international division of labour

100

which occurs within the trilateral system and which has led to the rapid expansion of trade coupled with the growing integration of the domestic industrial structures. For the newly industrialising countries, this type of international specialisation also enables the 'opening up' of the economy to the outside world without sacrificing an integrated, complex and technology-absorbing economic structure.

The newly industrialising countries also play an important role as markets for the developed countries. In the period 1955 to 1973, 30 per cent of the increase in manufacturing exports from countries of the trilateral system went to the rest of the world, above all to members of OPEC and the newly industrialising countries (Blackhurst et al., 1977, p.19).[10] Although the transnational corporations also play an important part in their industrialisation, principally in technologically advanced industries like electronics and metal machinery, the expansion of manufactured exports has been carried out largely by national firms. Examples of this are Argentinian exports of turnkey plants and machine tools.

These countries are the main borrowers in the international capital markets and it is through this conduit that they have become more closely integrated into the trilateral system. For the banks involved in these operations, loans to countries such as Brazil, Mexico and Argentina are far from marginal. Borrowers and lenders exhibit a mutual dependence from which a more symmetrical relationship has arisen.[11]

The growth of the external debt has brought numerous difficulties to countries such as Brazil, Argentina, Chile and Mexico. It is a good example of the contradictory nature of international relations at the present time. On the one hand, the expansion of international liquidity and sources of credit displaced the traditional 'discipline' of the adjustment process during the period when the IMF was the only remedy available to confront acute external balance of payments problems. In the management of current account deficits and for the financing of projects and investment programmes, freedom to manoeuvre has increased. On the other hand, the rise of indebtedness imposes new constraints on the formulation of economic policies. Yet these constraints are emerging in a more favourable international context and one in which the range of options is richer than in the past. Today the course of external adjustment depends mainly on national economic strategies and on internal bases of political support, rather than on impositions of international creditors.

Even the reversal to orthodox prescriptions in the Southern Cone of Latin America cannot be attributed to external conditioning. The policy options chosen by the political regimes that came to power in Argentina, Chile and Uruguay in the 1970s were made of their own accord. The Argentinian case is the most ironic in this sense.

Argentina is the only Latin American country (and probably the only one in the world) self-sufficient in energy, with a substantial food surplus and a low import coefficient (less than 10 per cent), that has more than trebled its external debt in a five-year period, while at the same time its per capita income has fallen by 10 per cent. The difficulties of administering the large external debt now imposed on the Argentinian economy, have been completely fabricated from within. In this case, a Latin American country has exercised its greater international freedom to manoeuvre by dismantling its industrial system and becoming severely indebted. A perverse example of greater external independence.

*The third world initiative and responses of the trilateral system*

Historically, peripheral countries have played a passive role in international events: they have been tied to the world order as a result of events that occurred in the centres of power. Since the end of the Second World War, this situation has changed profoundly. In fact, the changing relationship of developing countries with the rest of the world is the result of transformations in the periphery, rather than at the centre. The most glaring example is the influence of OPEC on the international economy since 1973. (Not as great as some spokesmen in the developed world claim, but an important one nonetheless.) The new prominence of the newly industrialising countries in international trade in manufactures, is another process that originates from the periphery and has an impact on the structure of international markets. Finally, the political tensions of some third world societies, such as the recent experience in Iran, also contribute to destabilising the old order of international relations.

The trilateral system has been slow to respond to these challenges. Foreign aid programmes, including tariff preferences, not only comprise a low proportion of centre countries' resources, but also have done very little to improve the condition of extreme poverty in which about 1,000 million people in the third world live. In the face of oil price rises and the radical change that these impose on the relative prices of energy, the developed nations have not been able to take concerted action to diversify into less oil-intensive forms of production. Moreover, owing to high unemployment and slow growth, the trilateral system has not demonstrated a flexibility to adapt to increased trade from the third world.[12] Rather than adapting to expansion which was the key to its success in the postwar period, it is reverting to protectionism. Lastly, political crises in various African countries, Iran and Nicaragua have revealed the ineptitude of interventionism and have exacerbated tensions amongst the central countries. In sum, the loss of cohesiveness is gradually transforming the trilateral system into an antiquated concept.

Turning to the third world, in as much as it is undergoing an accelerated process of differentiation, the concept of periphery also needs refining. Just as there is no longer a single periphery, several countries that could have been labelled as such in the past are now more closely integrated into the world economy. Thus, the explanatory power of the centre-periphery contradiction should be reassessed. International economic relations are becoming more differentiated and complex than that model assumes.

### Relations between the superpowers and the third world

In the past, questioning of military expenditure came mainly from the third world, above all for its part in inhibiting the formulation of concerted international action to solve the problems of under-development. The maintenance of military structures, which in the Soviet Union accounts for 13 per cent of GNP, and in the United States about 5 per cent, had a binding effect in domestic politics. All internal antagonisms were subsumed by the overbearing weight of foreign policy concerns. This broad consensus is coming under intense attack and criticisms of the arms race are also levied from within the superpowers.[13]

Not only are governments confronted with the loss of legitimacy of their military expenditure programmes, but military expenditures also limit their capacity to satisfy the social and economic demands of their constituencies; in turn, this accelerates the breakdown of the consensus on which their political strength was built.

In so far as the internal vulnerability of the superpowers increases, their ability to impose their interests in a closely-knit sphere of influence declines. The success of overt intervention in the third world now seems restricted to the smaller, less powerful countries such as El Salvador. In the larger countries of the third world, political conflicts cannot be simplistically attributed to foreign manipulators; they are the expression of the underlying contradictions of national societies. This does not mean that certain political forces will not seek affiliation with one of the superpowers. Even so, political struggles are the reflection of domestic cleavages. Foreign intervention may hope to feed on these divisions by supporting eligible factions and 'destabilising' unfriendly regimes; but the opportunities are provided by internal conflict which in the end will only be resolved within national boundaries.

## Prospects for the future

> Le présent n'est jamais notre fin: le passé et le présent sont nos moyens, le seul avenir est notre fin. Ainsi nous ne vivons jamais, mais nous espérons de vivre; et, nous disposant toujours à être heureux, il est inevitable que nous ne le soyons jamais.
>
> (Blas Pascal, *Pensées*)

Protectionism, balance of payments disequilibria, exchange rate fluctuations and inflation reflect the process of transformation of the world economy and they will probably continue to be the dominant problems in the foreseeable future. The fear of reactivating inflation prevents developed countries with favourable balance of payments from expanding internal demand to facilitate the adjustment of deficit countries. Neither Keynesians nor neo-classicists have found a way to combine full employment with price stability and policy makers are confronted with difficult options.

Despite these siren calls, the collapse of the international economic order as in 1929 is unlikely. Mechanisms of economic management have become sophisticated enough to prevent an abrupt fall in global production and the breakdown of the multilateral trade and payments system that has evolved over the last thirty-five years.

Latin America may be faced with a conflicting external environment but one that is, by the same token, more permissive. The greater freedom of manoeuvre does not mean that external factors will not influence internal developments, but in as much as Latin America becomes more closely integrated into an increasingly transnational system the asymmetry of dependency is weakened. Dependency will change its nature: from its simple form involving the control of natural resources and related activities, it has now become a much more complex set of relations which involve the transfer of technology; the co-existence of sectors of high productivity and capital intensity with other sectors of lower productivity; the tying of the domestic financial system to international centres. It could be said that dependency has been 'nationalised'; that is to say, a set of relations has evolved in which large social sectors participate in a type of development with the centres of international power.[14]

In sum, if 40 per cent of Latin America's population continue to live in extreme poverty, it is due to inequalities in the distribution of income rather than a lack of resources. Of Latin America's population 50 per cent receives 14 per cent of the total income and the top 10 per cent receives 44 per cent. The solutions to these problems do not depend on the advanced countries nor on international reform, but rather on internal structural changes.

The primary and inescapable responsibility lies within the internal confines of each country, within the framework of an international context which offers, never more so than now, such possibilities for independent development.

**Notes**

1    For an historical analysis of the growth of transnational corporations, see Aldo Ferrer, 1980, pp.20–26.
2    Real growth for all OECD countries in 1981 was only 1.25 per cent. It is estimated that it will continue at this rate in 1982 (see OECD, 1982, p.19).
3    For example, the capital goods industry in developing countries grew by 40 per cent during the 1970s (see UNCTAD, 1981, p.101).
4    See Chapter 3 by S. Griffith-Jones in this volume.
5    Ibid.
6    For example, the United Nations Centre on Transnational Corporations has made countries more aware of the activities and performance of transnational corporations.
7    For a country-by-country analysis, see World Bank, 1981, pp. 182–3.
8    The inclusion of Argentina requires a clarification. This country has, until recently, been the most industrialised and the one with the highest per capita income in the group. It has also been one of the main exporters of manufactures amongst the NICs. Yet, its reversal in the second half of the 1970s to an agro-export model has aggravated its slow development in the long term and introduces an unknown quantity with regard to its place in the international order. As for the exclusion of Hong Kong and Singapore, two economies which participate actively in world trade in manufactures, they are two city-states, which resemble the city-states of Italy and the North Sea in the Renaissance more than third world countries.
9    For further explanation see UNCTAD, 1981, pp.71–4.
10    In the same period, exchanges within North America (the US and Canada) and Western Europe represented 25 per cent of the increase, and trade between North America, Western Europe and Japan, 19 per cent. It is interesting to note that trade expansion within the trilateral system expresses itself fundamentally as starting from regional integration. However, relations between the three poles of the trilateral system are most intense in the sphere of foreign direct investment (for example, American corporations in Western Europe), in financial flows (eurocurrency markets) and technology. The interdependence within the trilateral system thus encompasses the entire economic relations of its members.
11    This type of situation is not new for Latin America, nor has it reached the significance of other times. Think, for example, of the flow of British loans to Argentina at the end of the nineteenth century and how the balance of payments crisis of Argentina in 1890 made the principal financial market of the time totter.
12    For further analyses on the topic of protectionism see *South,*

January 1982, p.21; February 1982, p.105.

13    For a similar view of the breakdown of the consensus on social and economic policy, see J.K. Galbraith, 1982, pp.1—14.

14    The apparent contradiction of this situation is developed in Chapter 6 by Peter Evans in this volume.

# Part II

# The State and the Domestic Structure

# 5 The state and the management of accumulation in the periphery*

E. V. K. FITZGERALD

## Introduction

Within economic debate there is a contemporary insistence that the periphery can only be analysed as a subordinate element of a world economy in which capital has become international and that changes in its production structure can only be regarded as an integral element of a new international division of labour.[1] This 'world system view' argues that the downturn in the long postwar boom that occurred towards the end of the 1960s was brought about by a crisis, either cyclical or more profound, at the centre of the system; changes in the Latin American political economy would follow logically from that crisis due to the subordinate role of accumulation on the periphery. Such an approach is clearly an advance upon the simple dependency model which not only virtually reduced imperialism to mercantilism but had also reduced the concept of exploitation to that of unequal exchange in circulation.

* My thanks are due to Diana Tussie for editorial discipline, to the participants of the Millennium Conference for comments on an earlier draft, to the late Oscar Braun for his inspiring work on the neo-Ricardian development of ECLA theory, and to John Wells for his patient insistence that macroeconomic management is as important as state accumulation.

However, in its improving upon the simple dependency model, which had been in any case long suspended in its original Latin American terrain, the new approach seems to have lost sight of the individual nature of peripheral economic formations; this point is frequently made in critiques of the world-system approach, as well as in attempts to revive a more classical Marxian analysis.[2] Critiques have tended, nonetheless, to be of a sociological nature, concentrating particularly upon its lack of class analysis rather than its economic analysis in general. Indeed, the critiques have tended to make a virtue of this fact, accusing the world-system approach of being too 'economistic' in basing its analysis only on the necessary logic of capital accumulation.

Nevertheless, the world-system view can also be shown to be in error in terms of its economic analysis, particularly with respect to the process of accumulation (the generation of surplus and its realisation) and the role of the state in this process. Amin's argument that peripheral accumulation is blocked by the 'draining of surplus' and Wallerstein's that the peripheral state is merely a neocolonial instrument seem to be gross over-simplifications. This chapter suggests the lines along which a rectification can be made of the world-system approach without, of course, returning to a simplistic view of self-contained economies. It may well be that the ECLA school of economics, against which dependency theory itself was to a great extent a reaction,[3] contained an insight to the functioning of the peripheral economy which was lost in the 'dependency debate'. In particular, the ECLA model offers a fruitful starting point for analysis of the realisation problem as expressed in foreign exchange shortages, fiscal crisis and the need for monetary stabilisation, all of which are primarily state responsibilities.

This chapter will first consider these somewhat neglected analytical points, and then relate them to the problem of relative state autonomy on the periphery. From this starting point it will make a tentative approach to differentiate the way in which the six major Latin American economies have adapted to the postwar world economic cycle, and then conclude with some observations on the relation between economic theories and the ideology of state managers in Latin America.

## The state and accumulation on the periphery

*Developing the ECLA model*

A good place to start a discussion of accumulation is the ECLA model, not only because it was constructed locally to correspond to the particular features of a semi-industrialised region of the world economy, but also, more generally because it forms part of what can be broadly defined as the 'post-Keynesian' attempt to reconstruct political economy (Kregel, 1973). It is not primarily a theory of exchange, as is commonly held, but one of production and growth; the focal point is not the terms of trade but rather the interaction of two accumulation cycles, one at the centre and another at the periphery.[4]

The peripheral cycle is not constrained by the rates of profit or ex ante savings as such, but rather due to the incompleteness of the economy by slow productivity growth (limited technology) and the realisation of the surplus (reliance on imported producer goods). The trade problem arises, similarly, because central economies retain productivity increases in the form of sustained export prices (either as wages or profits, depending on the circumstances), while peripheral ones tend to have less productivity increases (due to the presence of surplus labour) and those that do occur are dissipated in price competition between primary producers.

The ECLA model is, in effect, a simple world model anchored on an empirical observation of a basic though not immutable difference between centre and periphery. This difference results from and in turn perpetuates a specific relationship between different parts of the world economy characterised by capitalist competition between nation states. In particular, there exists a diversified and integrated economic structure at the centre, capable of reproducing itself, as opposed to a specialised and disintegrated structure on the periphery, which can only accumulate through exchange of gross and financial assets with the centre. This point, and not particular assumptions about demand elasticities for imports and exports, places ECLA trade theory firmly within the 'alternative approach' defined by Steedman as follows:

> whether the particular starting point chosen be the production oriented analysis of Adam Smith, or that of Ricardo, or of Marx, or von Neumann, or Joan Robinson, or any other writer, the general framework and emphasis of the analysis will inevitably lead to a trade theory which is more concerned with growth and with the role of capital goods than is a trade theory – such as the Hecksher–Ohlin–Samuelson theory – which starts from exchange and consumption (Steedman, 1979, p.7).

113

For ECLA, the accumulation problem was central to the tendency towards external disequilibrium, while income distribution, in terms of wage goods supply and domestic demand for manufacturers, was central to internal disequilibrium. In other words, external problems arose from difficulties with Department One (producer goods), while internal ones arose from Departments Two (capitalist consumer goods) and Three (wage goods). It was also clear that state intervention had been an integral part in the history of this economic structure[5] and would be equally central to its resolution. This structuralist approach can be reasonably defined as a theory of value based on cost of production, as opposed to the subjective utility basis of neoclassical economics or the strict labour theory of value involved in Marxism. As such it can be considered to be within the tradition of classical political economy which now includes both neo-Ricardian and post-Keynesian writers.

Braun develops ECLA trade theory explicitly within the neo-Ricardian framework by formalising it in terms of the more modern Sraffa-type system of price formation in long-run equilibrium, where the periphery is assumed not to produce capital goods. This enables him to define dependency in terms of

the difficulty of achieving expanded reproduction, or even the simple reproduction, of capital because at least part of the machines and inputs required for production are monopolized by the other country (Braun, 1973, p.106).[6]

Simple neo-Ricardian international trade models for only two products (Mainwaring, 1979) require four central variables for a framework with capital mobility and labour immobility; wage levels at the centre; wage levels at the periphery; the single rate of profit; and the terms of trade.[7] Braun, in the ECLA tradition, takes the rate of profit and the terms of trade as being determined outside the model. He also argues that although the presence of transnational firms strengthens the system of dependency, it is not a necessary part of it. Thus, there is a sharp contrast with the 'world-system' view of dependency on the one hand, and the 'unequal exchange' views of Emmanuel and Amin on the other. Both of these views take the peripheral wage as essentially exogenous, as determined by subsistence levels in the peasant sector; but while Emmanuel takes the wage at the centre as the independent variable, determined by the class struggle, Amin adopts the rate of profit in a more 'orthodox' fashion. However, as Braun points out, this leaves a number of problems unresolved: first, why capital does not move out to the periphery on a massive scale; second, why the periphery cannot simply raise its wages unilaterally; and third, why the periphery does not use its position in raw materials,

114

particularly food, to establish higher prices in a truly Ricardian fashion. Despite suggestions to the contrary, capital has not moved to Latin America primarily in order to exploit cheap labour, but rather to take advantage of local markets and gain access to natural resources, and in both cases extensive bargaining and alliances with the host state are involved. If the terms of trade are the operative variable – supported by metropolitan tariff policy, direct negotiation over natural resource prices, industrial price maintenance and government promotion of capital goods exports – then the metropolitan state in turn becomes a central element of the trade pattern.[8] On the food question, the extremely costly agricultural support schemes subsidised by the state in the USA, the EEC and Japan are clearly designed not only to placate farm lobbies but to prevent the periphery from using food supplies as a bargaining counter. Finally, the role of the Latin American states in securing external finance to sustain trade imbalances, either from metropolitan governments or their markets, permits accumulation to continue in Latin America.[9]

The ECLA approach to the theory of accumulation, although not as explicitly developed as their trade theory,[10] nonetheless contains some important points relating to Braun's questions about accumulation. In the first place, ECLA argued that there is no ex ante savings constraint on investment. The explanation for this does not lie in the traditional Keynesian income-adjustment mechanism, which hardly operates in a semi-industrialised economy constrained by both bottlenecks in primary-sector supply and foreign exchange for production inputs. In monopolised economies without significant capital markets there is no separation between savers and investors: most savings come directly from enterprise profits and rents. Large firms, not least the transnationals, rely on retained earnings for long-term finance, so that given investment plans and variations in profits result in changes in capitalist consumption along Kaleckian lines.[11] This is strengthened by the widespread system of organising domestic firms in *grupos* around banks which provide funds for investment and working capital.

Secondly, manufactured prices are generally formed as a mark-up on import and wage costs, so that expected profits, and thus investment, will depend on the expansion of the local market; while at the same time export sectors invest according to continuous profits, i.e. expected profit on world markets, not the past or present profit record. The ECLA took this argument further by suggesting that the local market for the consumer durables which provided the industrial dynamic would be strictly limited by the consumption of the middle and upper strata of the population, and thus progressively worse income distribution would be necessary in order to sustain accumulation. The argument[12] is essentially that not only are ex ante savings not a constraint in accumulation, but rather that profit consumption is necessary to sustain it. In other words, reductions in wages may increase money profits but will not lead to an increase in investment, since expected profit depends on market size. Moreover, real wages depend more on the supply of wage goods, which are generally provided by the petty commodity production sector (peasants, artisans) and the state itself (housing, education, food imports), than on variations in the money wage.

In consequence, the problem of realisation becomes central to accumulation; converting profits and rents into consumer goods only obtainable with foreign exchange, and converting wages onto wage goods largely obtained from the domestic petty commodity sector. Thus the problem of realisation involves management of the balance of payments and of the internal terms of trade which are responsibilities of the state not of the individual capitalists. The relation between investment and the distribution of income is through the balance of payments and the internal terms of trade rather than through the wage-profits split as a determinant of savings.[13]

Therefore, stabilisation policy in order to be effective should cut profit consumption due to its high import content. If it is based on wage depression it will either have to be far more severe due to the low import content of wage goods, or involve a halt to accumulation.

We have been considering semi-industrialised economies, where the heterogeneous nature of the production structure (lack of producer goods and peasant food supply) means that a large part of the economy is 'non-traded', being composed of non-exportables or protected branches. The process of import-substitution was designed to eliminate internal disarticulation, and through eventual export competitiveness, to turn the economy into an homogeneous 'traded' one. Once all industrial goods become traded, the realisation problem is eliminated for the small economy. There is, in principle at least, no constraint on output due to market size. Reinvested profits again become the constraint on accumulation. Despite the maintenance of low wages reinvestment may still be low because of high capitalist consumption, speculation or capital flight. The real value of profits is fundamentally determined by exports and to a much lesser degree by the wage rate. It follows that strategies for accumulation will be based either on increased exports or disproportionate wage reductions.[14] In those cases, e.g. Argentina or Chile, where wage goods are effectively traded goods, because they are either exported or imported beyond the margin, then (as Kregel, 1973, p.83, points out) workers may try to 'circumvent' the wage goods constraint, determined by past investment decisions (including the decision not to raise agrarian food productivity), by access to food imports. In which case full employment as a policy objective is abandoned in order to protect the balance of payments. The balance of payments then ceases to be a structural constraint on accumulation but rather a Robinsonian 'inflation barrier' and the allocation of foreign exchange the equivalent of a conflict theory of inflation.

An analytical extrapolation of the ECLA model, therefore, suggests that the accumulation problem at the semi-industrialised periphery is not simply one of the wage rate or of the proportion of the surplus that is not drained away to the centre of the world economy. This is in direct opposition to the world-system view, which relies to a great extent upon these propositions.[15] What is implicit in such an extrapolation, and in the ECLA theory itself, is the special role of the Latin American state in directly managing accumulation during this semi-industrialised stage so as to make the realisation of both profit and wages possible.

## Finance and relative autonomy

The state is clearly necessary for a capitalist economy to operate at all, in order to keep workers under control and to maintain market links. Following de Brunhoff's (1978) line of thought, the state is responsible for the management of the two 'special commodities' which capitalists cannot manage for themselves: money and labour. Ironically enough, this is implicit not only in ECLA and metropolitan Keynesian thought, but in 'liberal' monetarism as well. Moreover, the fact that the dynamics of Latin American economies have derived historically from their insertion into the international division of labour, means that nation-states have always played a crucial part in the negotiation of that insertion. This tradition stretches back to colonial times when the state granted land, labour and mineral rights, import licences and tariff protection to domestic and foreign entrepreneurs (Kaplan, 1960). In a system where most of the surplus took the form of such rents, this meant that accumulation was based on 'crown concessions' rather than on competition or technical innovation. More recently, the state has played a new role in the industrialisation process as a 'third partner' in the relationship between multinational firms and domestic capitalists; it is a financer and producer as well as 'matchmaker' in a more general sense.[16]

Evers (1979) has set out some building blocks for a theory of the state on the capitalist periphery with particular reference to Latin America. It is an explicit critique of the world-system position which maintains that the peripheral state is entirely subordinate and responds to the requirements of, and changes in, the logic of the international economy. He points out that there have been initial steps to build an alternative theory in response to such crude interpretations of the state as a mere instrument of domestic or foreign capital, but they tend to be only partial interpretations of political phenomena and do not contribute to a comprehensive understanding of the role of the state in guaranteeing accumulation in the periphery. Such is the case of Cardoso's (1975) use of an ad hoc sociological construct, 'bureaucratic rings', that only explain certain immediate aspects of the relationship between civil society and the state. In fact, such 'bureaucratic rings' are organised around high officials (cabinet ministers, generals etc.) with the purpose of articulating immediate interests of particular groups, such as enterprises, press, even trade unionists on a specific policy issue. These are semi-formal unstable instruments since the official can be dismissed and the ring thereby broken. On the other hand, O'Donnell's model of bureaucratic authoritarianism (Collier, 1979) is more concerned with régimes than states, and thus contributes to an interpretation of contemporary political phenomena more than to a comprehensive theory of the state.[17]

Evers argues that the nature of the state can only be derived from the 'organic necessities of capitalism', i.e. the imperatives of the economy. Nevertheless, the concept of relative autonomy is needed in order to explain state intervention:

> the relative autonomy of the Latin American state as to its socio-economic environment and also to the world market is a necessary premise for the fulfilment of its function of guaranteeing the insertion of the local economy into the world economy (Evers, 1979, p.107).

Except in colonies this guarantee is necessary because the economic and the political spheres are not socially identical, the insertion into the international division of labour is not complete and there does not exist a world state. The mediation between the domestic and the international economy necessarily involves a certain 'ambiguity' or autonomy if legitimacy is to be maintained both among national capitalists and with the international community.

Evers also argues that the backwardness of the peripheral economy requires the state to engage in instrumentalist tasks, the organisation of the labour supply and the direct production of commodities. These are the two points most stressed in the literature.[18] However, as Evers points out, although circulation is logically subordinate to production on a world scale, on the periphery the reverse is true with respect to foreign trade and finance, so that the state has a crucial role in circulation too. The need for relative autonomy in those 'macro-economic management' tasks is greater than in the two 'instrumental' tasks identified above. If this point is combined with the empirical problems of realisation and accumulation discussed in the preceding section, four points of interest are identified that can be derived from the ECLA model: (i) the integration of the state itself in the international division of labour; (ii) the responsibility of the state for the determination of the real wage; (iii) the fiscal implications of the support of domestic accumulation; and (iv) the consequent relationship between the state and finance capital.

*The integration of the state into the international division of labour*

The integration of the state into the international division of labour is evidenced in its increasing involvement in direct investment and production of essential inputs. This role, particularly as part of an import substitution process, has been widely discussed.[19] It is worth remembering that in all (non-socialist) cases this activity has always been regarded as a second-best substitute for private domestic investment and preferable to foreign investment only in strategic sectors.

119

The close relationship between the state and foreign banks which grew out of the bilateral or multilateral funding of public investment in the 1950s developed into a purely financial relationship by the 1970s. Governments and state banks borrowed from metropolitan banks in order to finance imports, and increasingly to service previous debts.[20] This financial integration of the state into the international division of labour has wide implications, of which the influence of the IMF in the implementation of stabilisation policies is probably the most visible but possibly not the most significant. The structural development has been the direct access of the Latin American state to private capital markets, e.g. euromarkets, on the one hand, and on the other, the increased importance of state development banks in the finance of the private sector, including multinational corporations. Thus the state becomes a financial intermediary in its own right, locked into the international system but at the same time gaining freedom to manoeuvre domestically and, in the case of larger borrowers, even internationally. Nonetheless, much of this finance has been for state corporations, particularly in the energy and transport fields where technological dependence upon foreign supplies, particularly of capital goods, is very high.[21] Indeed, when the capital goods imported by the public sector for itself, the finance of equipment for the private sector and the direct state production of producer goods (steel, roads, dams) are all taken into account, it is reasonable to argue that the state is the main capital goods supplier in Latin America.

Finally, it should be noted that state trading in exports, both of primary exports and 'promoted' manufactures, and in imports, particularly fuel, food and producer goods, has increased[22] as world commercial conditions have become more difficult. State intervention in commodity circulation, therefore, is as important as in commodity production, and possibly even more widespread. As in the case of infrastructural investment and production, the objective is the support of private profits and thus accumulation by reducing costs and by expanding markets. Beyond this, the state attempts to overcome the realisation crisis brought about by deteriorating external terms of trade and the metropolitan trade cycle via borrowing to increase the supply of usable money – foreign currency. This role becomes a contradictory one as the state itself is steadily enmeshed in the financial difficulties it is supposed to resolve for the private sector.

*The regulation of nominal wages*

The regulation of nominal wages is an important aspect of the role of the state in the organisation of labour. Even though rigorous adherence to minimum wages may be lacking, they nonetheless remain a significant element of nominal wage scales. The role of the state is not simply a matter of repressing money wages in order to improve profits and control inflation. Real wages, or at least the real wage bill, are determined to a great extent by the supply of wage goods and this is a function of the state. This is at the centre of the ECLA interpretation of the inflationary process itself[23] which combines a conflict theory of nominal wages – the struggle between nominal wages and profits through prices – with a structural interpretation of constraints on real wages and main industrial output resulting from 'bottlenecks' in the agrarian and foreign sectors respectively. The state plays a key part in the organisation of domestic food supplies throughout Latin America, through attempts to rationalise the agrarian sector (land reform), manipulation of the internal terms of trade, investment in marketing systems and if all else fails, by the importation of food. To the extent that food is supplied from outside the domestic capitalist sector, i.e. from the peasant sector or abroad, this does not impose a direct burden on profits, but the consequences – in terms of the need to supply eventually more capitalist-sector goods to the peasants, to invest directly in agriculture, or to obtain the foreign exchange – will rebound in the form of fiscal or payments difficulties, through the financial status of the state itself. In addition, components of the real wage such as housing, education, public transport and recreation are also seen as state responsibilities and thus not to be directly financed by capitalists. Finally, it could also be argued that much of military expenditure can be viewed as a cost of labour control. In other words, the nature of state intervention in the setting of real wages, only displaces the profit-wage contradiction from the private sector to the state, and from production relations to financial relations.

*Fiscal implications*

State intervention in support of accumulation, particularly in the period of semi-industrialisation commonly known as 'import substitution', has resulted in a steady increase in state expenditures as a proportion of national income.[23] Such expenditure is mainly concerned with the support of Departments One and Three (producer goods and wage goods) and is normally financed out of taxation, the special prerogative of the state itself (as the 'crown') and essen-

121

tially a non-market activity. Despite the fact that this expenditure is designed to support capital accumulation the state finds itself pulled between the need to give investment incentives to domestic and foreign capitalists on the one hand, and the capacity of monopoly sectors to resist tax burdens on the other. The result is a very narrow tax base, leading to the imposition of direct consumption taxes which depress real wage expenditure on manufactures. Thus a 'fiscal crisis of the state' results in serious consequences for the accumulation process by propagating domestic inflation or leading to excessive foreign borrowing; it reduces business confidence and induces depressive stabilisation programmes at periodic intervals. As we shall see, the resolution of this crisis requires either a further extension of state access to the surplus or a severe reduction in the very expenditures necessary to maintain investment. In this way, the macroeconomic management capacity of the state is reduced, and its capacity to sustain accumulation is undermined.[24]

*Relationships with finance capital*

The Latin American state has a special relationship with the domestic banking system as well as with the international banks. The state must rely on domestic banks to implement its credit policies in order to regulate the level and composition of aggregate demand in the private sector; to absorb its own domestic borrowing requirement in the form of treasury bills or money and thus channel some part of financial savings towards the *hacienda*; and to implement a considerable part of its foreign exchange allocation strategy, whether through direct import controls, distribution of import credits or exchange rate policy. As against this, the banks themselves need the state in order to regulate their activities as well as to guarantee their assets and liabilities on a continual basis. The reliance of the banks on the state is more pronounced than that of firms in the productive or commercial sectors. This special relationship is strengthened by the virtual absence of domestic capital markets on the one hand and the need for government underwriting to obtain access to foreign capital markets on the other. In the financial sphere, then, the need for relative state autonomy is particularly evident. Moreover, in Latin America it is also increasingly true that 'finance capital' in the sense of Hilferding [25] is the main form in which domestic capital is organised, both in terms of the financial and operational co-ordination of the *grupos* composed of industrial, agrarian, trading and construction firms and in terms of the local relationships of foreign firms.[26] This means not only that facile characterisations such as 'industrial bourgeoisie' are problematic, but also that the freedom of action for the state to pursue a strategy of national accumulation in the long run as opposed to immediate private profit, is jeopardised.

In sum, it has been argued that the state has a particular role to play in the accumulation of capital on the periphery; a role which derives from its intervention in circulation as much, or possibly more so, as in production. This role goes beyond macroeconomic management of aggregate demand and of the balance of payments, commonly characterised as 'stabilisation' policy, and the regulation of labour supply to an attempt to resolve through the state the realisation problems presented by the incomplete nature of the semi-industrialised economy. However, the way in which this contradiction is resolved also depends upon the position of the particular economy within the world economy.

So far, it has been argued as if the postwar experiences of the Latin American economies were essentially similar, which is clearly not so, even though the problems faced are to a great extent shared. Indeed it is central to this argument that peripheral responses to changes in the world economy, largely generated at the centre, depend on local circumstances; and that to a considerable degree accumulation responds to a local dynamic.

During the postwar period there was a shift in world production and trade patterns from a period of relatively steady expansion during 1945–65 to a period of apparent stagnation in 1965–80 on the one hand, and a shift in Latin American development patterns from a broadly common one of import-substitution industrialisation to diverse strategies of restructuring with roughly the same periodisation, on the other.

The world-system approach would seem to suggest that Latin American economics indulged in import-substitution during the first phase of the cycle, when export demand was high enough to finance it. In the second phase the world recession forced these economies to seek new export revenues by depressing wages, to reduce imports by de-industrialising (less producer goods) and reducing consumption (less consumer goods), and to incur enormous debts. It would also argue that the internationalisation of capital via the transnational corporations evolved from their initial interest in natural resources to a postwar interest in low wage rates on the periphery. Postwar direct foreign investment was first a cheaper means than imports of supplying Latin American markets and then a means to supply metropolitan markets, as wages at the centre rose and profit rates declined. But the connection between the accumulation cycles at centre and periphery is not nearly so simple.

A broad picture of the world cycle, upon which there is reasonable agreement,[27] would show a long boom between 1945 and 1965, fuelled by high investment in OECD countries and expanding world trade, a period during which many large firms became 'multinational', building up considerable manufacturing facilities on the periphery as well as increasing primary export capacity. It is commonly agreed that the boom was already slowing down during the late 1960s before the oil crisis in 1973 and that the decline of profitability at the centre of the world capitalist economy is the central phenomenon. The origins of this crisis are not however common ground. Opinions can be divided broadly into three categories: a belief in a profit squeeze from wages; a belief in over-investment in inappropriate production capacity; and a belief in ineffective international demand management.[28] The reaction has occurred on all those fronts: demand deflation and downward pressure on metropolitan wages, with some success; a slow process of restructuring metropolitan industry away from traditional branches such as textiles and steel towards more dynamic, high-technology sectors; and rather unsuccessful attempts to reorganise international monetary institutions and restore a certain level of international demand, although this is undermined in practice by the former two objectives. The central tendency, however, is towards increasing labour productivity at the centre rather than a large-scale shift of productive capital towards the periphery. A few tax-free export zones do not add up to a new strategy. Certainly the concentrated use of cheap labour for exports along the lines of the South-East Asian model is not a central characteristic of the Latin American economies; even in Mexico the 'border industries' are of relatively minor importance in output and exports. Moreover, new transnational investment appears to be directed once again towards primary products, especially food and minerals.

More to our point, the form that restructuring has taken in the Latin American economies themselves has been largely a response to domestic circumstances, albeit located in and heavily influenced by the world cycle. The six leading economies of the region, Argentina, Brazil, Chile, Colombia, Mexico and Peru, account for about four-fifths of output and three-quarters of the population of Latin America, so a brief discussion of these should serve to support this point.[29] Three of these, Argentina, Brazil and Mexico, are semi-industrialised, with a large manufacturing output already averaging US$900 billion by 1970, high shares of manufacturing in output — averaging 30 per cent of GDP in 1978, similar to that for industrialised countries, although for very different reasons — and with about one-quarter of exports being manufactured goods. The other three were much less developed in this sense, although manufacturing averaged 25 per cent of GDP and 10 per cent of exports were manufactured in 1978. The degree of foreign ownership in manufacturing is similar for all six with about half of large firms being controlled by transnationals; their exports are dominated by primary commodities, and they all have chronic balance of payments problems. Nevertheless their reaction to the world cycle has been quite different.

Brazil and Mexico have pursued a strong industrialisation drive right through the world cycle, maintaining high rates of accumulation, higher indeed than at the centre, and developed manufactured exports out of their existing industrial base. In both cases this strategy has involved considerable external indebtedness, mainly in the form of state borrowing from multinational banks. Both were able until 1982 to resist the attempts by the IMF to impose, on behalf of the OECD countries, an 'orthodox' stabilisation policy involving an opening of the economy and reduced state accumulation.[30] Both countries have relatively strong states in the sense of continuity of régime and cohesive bureaucracy and thus have been able to work out coherent arrangements with foreign capital and conduct macroeconomic management with some autonomy relative to domestic business. Nevertheless, the realisation problems discussed above have posed a constant threat to accumulation in the postwar period. Although money wages were held under fairly strict control, wage goods supply to support the real wage entailed continual efforts to capitalise agriculture and increasing expenditure on urban infrastructure. Both economies encountered fiscal crises which threatened to limit the industrialisation drive: domestic finance capital, potentially in alliance with the IMF, attempted to force an opening of the economy. The crisis was overcome by gaining greater access to the surplus; in the case of Brazil by tax reform and profitable public enterprise, in that of Mexico by high bank reserve requirements and state oil exports.[31] Although size may well be a contributory factor, it does seem that it is possible to overcome the effects of the world cycle and a limited wage goods supply and push forward towards full industrialisation, i.e. production of producer goods, through concerted state intervention.

Argentina and Chile followed, particularly in the last decade, an alternative course. The role of transnational corporations in supporting pro-business regimes and the geopolitical influence of the USA in the region cannot be denied; but it is difficult to see how the shift towards wage repression, opening of the economy and reliance on primary exports can be seen, as it would have to be in a world system view, as a direct result of changes at the centre of the system, presumably connected to the downturn in the metropolitan cycle in the 1970s. As far as US geopolitics and transnational corporations are concerned, it is far from clear that this model is 'better for business' than that of Mexico and Brazil. Moreover, in the case of Argentina, the weakness of the state was related to the acuteness of the domestic class struggle. External trade conditions were broadly favourable throughout the postwar period; the income terms of trade rose by 40 per cent between 1960 and 1970, and by 61 per cent between 1970 and 1978. In the case of Chile the problem of the terms of trade was more serious as the barter terms rose from 53 in 1960 to 100 in 1970 and fell to 50 in 1977 due to the connection of copper prices to metropolitan accumulation and military requirements. But the move towards socialism and its subsequent destruction cannot be explained as a result of the fluctuations in the metropolitan cycle. The determinant was the strength and organisation of the working class. Moreover, after the shift neither Argentina nor Chile have become attractive locations for direct foreign investment, despite low real wages and positive encouragement to overseas firms. Changes in external conditions do not provide sufficient support to explain changes in Argentina and Chile. A better interpretation might be framed in terms of the realisation problem itself. The semi-industrialised nature of these economies in the postwar period made it increasingly difficult to translate profits into capitalist goods through imports or industrial deepening without further state intervention. Meanwhile the maintenance of the real wage required, in the case of Argentina, the consumption of exports and, in the case of Chile, increasing imports due to structural constraints on agrarian expansion. At the government level, in sharp distinction to Mexico and Brazil, popular pressure had generated an expansion of welfare expenditure in the decades following the Great Depression. This implied either access to domestic profits or domestic inflation intensifying the wage-profit struggle as sufficient foreign finance was not readily available. The 'new model' adopted in these two cases in the mid-1970s was intended, at an economic level, on one hand to resolve the fiscal crisis (a central element in the monetarist analysis) by reducing expenditure and on the other, to resolve the realisation crisis by, in effect, making all goods traded, i.e. eliminating tariff barriers and adjusting domestic prices to the world price level, and thus allowing the nominal factor income distribution to be translated directly into real commodities. Far from redistribution of income being a condition for opening the economy, free trade is a condition for meaningful downward income redistribution. Far from being an adjustment to a new international division of labour based on fresh manufacturing capital moving out to the periphery in search of low wages, it is based on making remnants of existing industrial capacity profitable in real, i.e. realisable, terms. The strategy is centred upon a return to a primary-exporting model where the main source of surplus is rent and the real wage bill is minimised by lowering both wages and the necessary labour force. At a deeper level, this might well coincide with a tendency to 'deproletarianise' the labour force where it has proved politically impossible to control it. Finance capital, because of its intersectoral character, has had no real difficulty in moving from the secondary to the primary sector. With relatively less need for state management of realisation once the economy has been opened because money profits can be translated into commodities through foreign exchange without difficulty, it might be thought possible to dispense with state intervention. However, its active participation is still required in attempts to negotiate better external terms of trade, e.g. wheat and copper deals, underwrite international finance and regulate banks; apart from the security apparatus, the new model may involve a smaller state in terms of expenditure or employment but certainly not a weaker one. In Argentina and Chile the state still necessarily preserves, therefore, a considerable degree of autonomy relative to different fractions of capital, while pursuing a project every bit as coherent, even though based on rent and stability rather than profits and growth, as that of Brazil and Mexico.

Peru and Colombia do not present such a clearcut picture; at first sight they would appear to be intermediate cases between the other two models. It could be argued that these are typical cases of small economies 'forced back' from their industrialisation projects by the downturn of the world cycle and the pressure of the TNCs. We find, however, on closer examination that the time and form of the adjustment does not really coincide with the world cycle or correspond to the changes in the organisation of production at the centre. In the case of Colombia, the strategic shift was already under way in the late 1960s in response to a prolonged period of popular pressure on wages, on the one hand, and the reassertion of the primacy of the financial-agroexport oligarchy on the other. The much-vaunted cheap-labour exports were based on the use of existing manufacturing capacity at low marginal cost and supported by fiscal subsidies, but they did not become a motor of export-growth; this remained coffee and, apparently, narcotics. The TNCs certainly took advantage of this shift and supported the new role of the state, including repression of labour, but the reasons for it were essentially internal: the contradictions of the previous industrialisation model.

In Peru, the problem was a different one, and, in a sense, the opposite one. A late attempt was made to pursue import-substitution industrialisation through massive state investment in manufacturing as well as mineral exports. Deteriorating terms of trade as well as the inability of successive governments to achieve tax reforms and the consequent fiscal crisis forced a stabilisation programme based on drastic wage reductions and attempts to reopen the economy so that the latter could translate into real profits. The financial sector re-emerged as the dominant fraction of capital and the industrialisation strategy was effectively abandoned for a return to the traditional Peruvian model of capitalist consumption based on export rents. Again, the shift was supported by the international financial community. In an almost tautological sense it can be argued that if they had been prepared to go on financing forced industrialisation indefinitely there would have been no such pressing need for a shift, but it cannot be argued that the IMF engineered the original lending in order to contrive the eventual consequences.

In sum, it is obviously true that if an economy forms part of the international capitalist system, and particularly if it is on the periphery, then it must conform to the 'rules' of that system; this is most clear when an attempt is made to leave that system, but in none of our six cases was that in question. The need to achieve external equilibrium in the long run, i.e. to adjust to the law of value, if accumulation is to continue, inevitably conflicts with other objectives, particularly the income distribution resulting from the wage-profit struggle. It is this subordination to a wider logic, and the role of the state in the adjustment mechanism, that is the major explanatory factor not the activities of TNCs taken in isolation.

## ECLA and CEMLA as economic ideology: some concluding remarks

At the outset of this chapter it was indicated that an analysis of accumulation based on the ECLA approach remained relevant. However, ECLA has had more than academic relevance; it has also influenced state managers themselves, in particular, the 'economic segment of the bureaucracy' which required a macroeconomic ideology – a scheme for the reproduction of peripheral capital distinct from the microeconomic profit-seeking ideology of individual businessmen.[32] In the postwar period, such a macroeconomic ideology was admirably supplied by ECLA, and reinforced by its advisory work to governments and training projects for planners. It provided a logical scheme for industrialisation that would maintain private profits and establish a basis for negotiation with TNCs. It also argued for raising real wages and agrarian reform in order to maintain social stability and stimulate domestic industrial demand; this would involve higher taxes, less capitalist consumption and state programming of investment. This is not the ideology of industrialists as such nor that of populism[33] but rather that of state managers, themselves corresponding to the need for an overall economic discipline and a longer-run 'developmental' view.[34] Clearly, the implied role for the state is objectively in the interest of these managers themselves (Dorfman, 1979). If it were carried too far, however, the interests of the bureaucracy would predominate which helps to explain why there is so much political resistance from the élite to state intervention even if it does support profits.

The parallel between this sort of ideology and Keynesianism is close. This is not because of theoretical influences, but rather that ECLA thought, like that of Keynes, was born from the need to manage the economy out of the metropolitan trade cycle, although in Prebisch's case the relevant problem was the balance of payments constraint on growth rather than unemployment as such (Love, 1980). Keynesianism too, corresponded to the outlook of the senior permanent civil service, regarding them as 'above' the direct pressures of the class struggle and responsible for the survival of capitalism in the long run (Skidelsky, 1979).

However, ECLA ideology was, and is, strongest among the state managers concerned with production and planning offices, ministries of industry and public enterprises. It never had the same acceptance in ministries of finance and central banks, nor did it have the support of any international force stronger than the UN system itself. The first reactions of what might be termed the 'financial fraction' of the state managers in Latin America to ECLA ideology were based on the traditional prewar concepts of monetary stability and currency convertibility as self-evident conditions for business confidence. This was to some extent supported by the more neoclassical pressure, from international institutions such as the World Bank, for reliance on low wages and the principles of comparative advantage as the basis for accumulation. By the early 1960s, however, monetarism had begun to appear, not merely as an analytical approach to inflation or at most a technique for post-Keynesian demand management (as it still was at the time in OECD countries), but rather as an alternative accumulation strategy.

The Centro de Estudios Monetarios Latino Americanos (CEMLA)[34] is essentially an organisation co-ordinating Latin American central banks, and thus the 'financial fraction' of the respective state bureaucracies. This fraction played an important part in exercising internal leverage for the application of 'IMF type' stabilisation policies. It can be argued that the modern monetary approach to the balance of payments is to a considerable extent derived from the Latin American experience of small open economies attempting fixed exchange rate policies. This approach represents, in effect, a return not merely to pre-ECLA times, but rather to the reigning orthodoxy in Latin America before the Great Depression, a period in which most Latin American economies left the gold standard and established national monetary control as a prelude to forced industrialisation. The monetary approach, with its 'law of one price' and effective subordination of national to international money, can be seen as a return to a somewhat tarnished gold standard half a century later, and a renewal of belief in the cleansing and invigorating effects of the trade cycle. But the 'CEMLA approach' goes beyond short-term macroeconomic management to the analysis of accumulation — what might be called 'structuralist monetarism' of the Stanford as opposed to the Chicago type, e.g. McKinnon as opposed to Friedman. The central propositions are: the development of domestic capital markets, i.e. the strengthening of finance capital and its articulation with international banks; the opening of the economy so as to stabilise prices and make all commodities tradeable, thus holding down real wages; the balancing of the government budget, at a low tax/expenditure level so as to sustain profits; and the abandonment of industrialisation as an aim in itself in place of maximising profitability based on comparative advantage potentially anchored on cheap labour but more realistically on primary exports.

The most relevant point for our discussion, however, is that the CEMLA approach implies considerable state-imposed discipline not only on workers but capitalists too — after all, no industrialist wants import tariffs reduced indiscriminately, with the *técnicos of the Banco Central* playing a central part (Canitrot, 1980; IDS, 1981). In other words, the ideology of CEMLA just as of ECLA requires a relatively autonomous state and powerful state managers.

In sum, this chapter has tried to suggest that accumulation on the periphery depends on a specific form of state intervention due to the incomplete nature of the economy; that this macroeconomic management requires a relatively autonomous state and a special role for state managers; that the differences in the models of accumulation correspond at least as much to the domestic class struggle as to the logic of the international division of labour; and that economic ideology has a significant role in those models. These points seem to offer the possibility of correcting some of the misconceptions of the world-system view of accumulation in Latin America.

**Notes**

1   Amin (1974) and Wallerstein (1979) give a representative cover-age of this broadly based but commonly held view of a single 'world system' as opposed to a world of competitive economies or classes. For a perceptive critique in the Latin American context, see Jenkins (1982).

2   See Brenner (1977) on the error of confusing exchange with production relations as defining characteristics of capitalism. Worsley (1980) extends the critique of the world-system view to cover its views on the central control of production. The nature of exploitation through trade (merchant capital) is better argued in Kay (1975).

3   Cardoso (1977) and Palma (1978) give good accounts of this.

4   This refers to the 1948–63 period, when ECLA thought was at its most coherent and influential, see Rodriguez (1980). The limita-tions of this thought are those of structuralism (or 'post-Keynesian' analysis) generally; however, the frequent criticism of ECLA for ig-noring foreign ownership is misplaced, at least by the 1960s.

5   This point is developed in Sunkel and Paz (1970).

6   My translation.

7   In the simplest form, with only two goods produced at the centre (1) and the periphery (2) respectively, the prices ($P$) are made up from the costs of production based on the unit import content ($m$), the unit labour current ($l$), the nominal wage ($w$) and the profit margin ($g$):

$$P_1 = (l + g_1) \ (w_1 L_1 + m_1 P_2)$$

$$P_2 = (l + g_2) \ (w_2 L_2 + m_2 P_2)$$

If $m, L$ can be taken as parameters (in fact later, the state plays an important part in their determination) and we set the metropolitan price as the numeraire ($P_1 = 1$), then we have six variables and only three equations to solve them. We need three more. The next step in this debate for Emmanuel, Amin and Braun is to take the profit margin as equalised ($g_1 = g_2$) by the international mobility of capital, or at least brought to some stable relationship (a rate of profitability, possi-bly). From here on, the authors diverge in their choice of which of the remaining variables to determine exogeneously. For some further analytics along these lines, see D. Evans (1981).

8   The cases of tariff barriers and international commodity agree-ments are clear enough, as is that of export promotion from the per-iphery; on US government involvement in capital goods exports, see Feinberg (1982).

133

9   See FitzGerald (1982) for a discussion and bibliography.
10   For some first theoretical steps in the right direction, see Parrinello (1979).
11   Flores de la Peña (1976); for references to the empirical evidence, see FitzGerald (1982).
12   Lustig (1980) gives a good critique of this 'under-consumptionist' view on both theoretical and empirical grounds.
13   Although this is not a central point in our argument, it is worth pointing out that the relationship between real wages, profits and peasant incomes depends on the internal terms of trade. Suppose an economy where manufacturing prices $(P_m)$ are given by a mark-up $(g)$ on unit labour costs, given by the nominal wage $(w)$ and unit labour requirements $(1)$:

$$P_1 = (l + g)\, wL$$

For a given marketed food supply (A) constrained by prevailing social institutions, the price of food $(P_2)$ will depend on the proportion (a) of the nominal wage bill (wL) spent on food, where employment (L) depends on manufacturing output (Q):

$$A \cdot P_2 = a \cdot w \cdot L$$

$$= a \cdot w \cdot L \cdot Q$$

so that the internal terms of trade are given by:

$$P_2/P_1 = \frac{a\, w\, L\, Q/A}{(l+g)\, wL}$$

$$= \frac{Q}{A} \cdot \frac{a}{l+g}$$

In other words, the internal terms of trade depend on the profit rate rather than the wage rate; or, if the state intervenes to keep the internal terms of trade down, the beneficiary is the capitalist.
14   These points can be seen by simply supposing that fixed proportion $(a)$ wages are spent on wagegoods $(A)$ and the rest on manufacturers. This gives us a manufacturing demand $(Q)$ of:

$$Q = (l - a)\, W\, L + (l - \lambda)\, \pi$$

where the ratio of retention $(I)$ of profits $(F)$ is given by the investment function

$$\pi = I$$

where

$$I = F(Q)$$

Imports ($M$) are given by

$$M = m\,Q + I$$

and constrained by

$$M < X$$

where exports are supply constrained (external terms of trade are exogenously determined as in note 10), but could be supplemented by an exogenously determined amount of foreign funds. To maximise $Q$ would require:

$$X = m\,Q + I$$

$$= [\,(1-a)\;wL + (1-\lambda)\,\pi\,]\;m + \lambda\pi$$

so that:

$$= \frac{X - (1-a)\;w\,L\,M}{(1-\lambda)\,m + \lambda}$$

and at equilibrium:

$$\partial\pi/\partial X \,\rangle\; 0 \;;\; \partial\pi/\partial\lambda \,\rangle\; 0$$

but

$$\partial\pi/\partial w = -(1-a)\;m$$

Empirically this real wage-profit coefficient will be very small: for example, if $a = 0.5$ and $m = 0.1$, then

$$\partial\pi/\partial w = -0.05$$

15  A point often misunderstood by those who in correctly attacking dependency writers tar ECLA with the same brush, e.g. Palma (1978).
16  See Chapter 6 in this volume by Evans for the Brazilian case; on Peru and Mexico as two further examples see Thorp and Bertram (1978) and Fragoso (1979) respectively.
17  The term 'régime' refers to the rules that impose social and political order while the concept of 'state', both on a concrete and abstract level, refers to the larger, more permanent system of economic and

political organisation (Collier, 1979). Thus a capitalist 'state' may fulfil its function with different forms or 'regimes' (authoritarian, democratic etc.).

18   See, for example, the papers in FitzGerald, Floto and Lehmann (1977). See also Evans (below).

19   This point was undoubtedly over-stressed in FitzGerald (1977), where it was suggested that production and investment themselves were the central state role in the development of the Latin American economies.

20   See Chapter 3 by Griffith-Jones in this volume.

21   For the example of the oil companies, see Philip (1982).

22   Sanchez (1980) gives empirical evidence of this.

23   This paragraph is based on FitzGerald (1978).

24   For a more detailed discussion of this point see FitzGerald (1982).

25   The main characteristics identified in Hilferding (1980) are: fusion of financial and industrial capital; central role of banks in the formation of monopolies; pooling of funds and the formation of cartels; and state support for tariffs and colonies. Except for colonisation, although Brazil might well turn out that way, the rest of the criteria fit Latin America very well indeed.

26   See FitzGerald (1982) for an expansion of this point.

27   Ranging from OECD (1979) to Mandel (1978).

28   There are, of course, the only logical alternatives if the profitability is defined as the project margin multiplied by the volume of production divided by the capital stock. See Weisskopf (1979) for a survey of these three views.

29   All data in this section is from World Bank (1981).

30   The purpose of this section is to give some background to the argument, not to make a detailed case, so no references are given; for a more detailed treatment, see Thorp and Whitehead (1979).

31   For a description of the manoeuvring of the Mexican state between its fiscal gap and its oil revenues see Chapter 7 in this volume by Philip.

32   What sort of economics, and specifically macroeconomics, ordinary businessmen do believe in, is a fascinating but unexplored subject; Keynes (in Chapter 23 of the *General Theory*) implies that it is still some form of mercantilism, which may well be true.

33   O'Brien (1975) and Rodriguez (1980), respectively suggest these bases.

34   The concept of 'state managers' is used here in the sense discussed by Block (1981); they are historical subjects and an essential characteristic of relative state autonomy. This term should be distinguished from 'state bourgeoisie' which refers to the social sector in *direct* relation to capital in the public sector — the officeholders of capital. State bourgeoisie is a distinct feature of a form of capitalism,

i.e. state capitalism, as discussed in Chapter 6.

35 Founded in 1963 with the support of the Rockefeller Foundation, and with its headquarters in Mexico City, it has nothing like the fame of the ECLA, nor its independent staff, but has played a quiet yet important role in the dissemination of Latin American monetarist thought.

# 6 State, local and multinational capital in Brazil: prospects for the stability of the 'triple alliance' in the eighties*

PETER B. EVANS

In August 1981 the political problems encapsulated in Brazil's current economic difficulties were violently dramatised. The people of Salvador, Bahia, enraged by a 60 per cent increase in bus fares, exploded against the buses themselves. Seven hundred and fifty buses were destroyed. At the same time, Brazil's political and economic problems were also being dramatised in São Paulo where the buses were made. Five hundred workers invaded the factory yard of Mercedes-Benz, manufacturer of the bulk of Brazil's buses and trucks, in response to the announcement of the company's plans to lay off over 5,000 workers (see *Veja*, vol. 8, no. 19, 1981, pp.84–90; vol. 8, no. 26, 1981, pp.20–22).

From the industrial centre south to the still backward north-east, the 'Brazilian model of development' seemed to be entering a new phase, a most problematic one as far as the ruling military regime[1] was concerned. Appropriately enough, the auto industry which had been the centrepiece of the initial stages of the 'Brazilian miracle' was also at the centre of the new problems. Volkswagen do Brasil, perennially profitable for a quarter of a centruy, recorded its first annual loss in 1980 and dismissed over 3,000 workers at the beginning of 1981. By the end of 1981 the Volkswagen situation had worsened

* I would like to thank Diana Tussie and the several discussants who commented on an earlier version of this Chapter at the Fourth Millennium Conference for their useful suggestions and encouragement.

139

substantially. Domestic sales for the year appeared likely to be less than one-third of 1979 sales and the parent company in Germany characterised the situation in Brazil as 'catastrophic' (*Veja*, vol. 9, no. 23, 1981, p.92).

Against the background of these economic difficulties Brazil was engaged in the most serious attempt since 1964 to move in the direction of real parliamentary rule. Whether the elections scheduled for the autumn of 1982 would actually take place was as important a question for most Brazilians as whether the inflation rate would come down or whether unemployment would go up. The sudden resignation of General Golbery de Couto y Silva, a persistent 'power behind the throne' throughout the post-1964 period, was as important to creating a climate of uncertainty as the collapse of local demand for automobiles.

Current uncertainties could resolve themselves in a range of ways. It is possible, though it seems unlikely, that the present combination of accumulation and exclusion can be preserved. More optimistically, there are grounds for arguing that resolution of current contradictions could take the form of movement toward a less exclusionary model of dependent development. Pessimistic scenarios are no less plausible. Some groups now in power may find change so threatening that they are willing to stop worrying about progress and focus on preserving order. While the combination of demobilisation and de-industrialisation that the Southern Cone suffered during the seventies would be difficult to reproduce in Brazil, movement in a regressive direction cannot be ruled out. Before indulging in speculation about the future, however, a more sustained discussion of past trends and existing structures is in order.

The anlaysis that follows will try to show how the interaction of external and internal contradictions has made the rule of the 'triple alliance' of state, multinational and local capital increasingly problematic. It will also try to show how tensions among the partners were intensified by the internal logic of dependent capitalist industrialisation, by the simultaneous pursuit of essentially contradictory goals. But, the chapter also argues that internal tensions were exacerbated by changes in the international system over which neither the Brazilian élite nor their transnational partners had control. Even in the absence of external pressure the Brazilian class structure as it stood at the beginning of the seventies could not have been preserved indefinitely. Moreover, a less beneficient external environment reduced the manoeuvring room available to the state, reduced the set of policies consistent with the continued profitability of both transnational corporations (TNCs) and local capital, and brought the contradictory nature of dependent development to the fore much more quickly than might otherwise have been the case.

Dependent development is contradictory even conceptually (see Evans, 1979; Gereffi and Evans, 1981). Development implies the accumulation of capital in the context of an increasingly differentiated internal division of labour, an expansion of the variety of goods that may be produced locally, more flexibility as to the goods that can be offered on international markets and therefore less vulnerability to the international system. In this sense, development is the opposite of dependence. Yet in Brazil and other countries of the capitalist 'semi-periphery'[2] development has been linked to continued reliance on capital housed in core countries. The local productive apparatus continues to be tied hierarchically to decision makers who are located in the core and whose decisions are aimed at the global maximisation of private profit. Thus, development has been united with its opposite.

The implicit collaborative pact which makes the historical process of dependent development possible and is its social structural counterpart is a 'triple alliance'. This pact binds together transnational capital, local capital and the entrepreneurial fraction of the state apparatus and involves a complex division of labour among the three kinds of capital. The calculus of the costs and benefits that accrue to each of the partners as a result of their collaboration is as complex as the division of labour.

For TNCs the attraction was quite obvious. Brazil was not only the seventh largest capitalist market in the world, it was also a very profitable one, in part because of the institutional framework which was maintained by the post-1964 Brazilian state. Strict controls on labour, generous subsidies to investors, protection of those willing to produce locally from competitors producing elsewhere and regulation of entry into important domestic industries all helped produce profit rates substantially higher than those that prevailed in the TNCs' home countries. In return for enjoying the fruits of operating in this profitable market, TNCs had to moderate the degree to which they gave global accumulation priority over local accumulation. Investment had to reflect at least occasionally the priorities of Brazilian state planners rather than flowing directly from a global analysis of the comparative advantage of different production sites. In some cases, legal ownership and managerial control of important investments had to be shared with local partners, strengthening the degree to which decisions were aimed at local rather than global maximisation.

Local private capital benefited from the same institutional arrangements that made Brazil profitable for the TNCs. It was also the beneficiary of certain extra privileges, such as special access to low interest (often negative in real terms) loans channelled through the state. Certain niches, e.g. insurance and commercial banking, were reserved for local capital. The requirement that TNCs take on local partners enabled local capital to enter industries where the advantages of the

141

TNCs would have otherwise made it impossible for them to compete. On the other hand, the triple alliance encouraged powerful transnational competitors to produce and sell in the local market and limited the extent to which the state could use legal mechanisms to restrain them. The implicit pact with the TNCs required that the rules of oligopolistic competition not be abrogated even if they were working to the disadvantage of local capital. TNCs might be denied subsidies for endeavours deemed too threatening to local capital, and in a few industries prohibited from entering at all, but the degree to which local capital could be protected from TNC competition was limited. The denationalisation of certain industries and the destruction of certain local capital groups was the price that local capital as a whole paid for what was otherwise a very profitable arrangement.

For the entrepreneurially-oriented segment of the state apparatus, the 'state bourgeoisie',[3] the triple alliance was an ideal vehicle for capital accumulation. Operating in collaboration with private capital enhanced their legitimacy both in the eyes of local supporters of 'free enterprise' and in the eyes of the international business community. Ties with TNCs provided technology, marketing expertise and better access to foreign financing. In addition, the 'good business climate' that attracted private capital also provided state-owned enterprises with opportunities for corporate aggrandisement. Accepting the triple alliance did, of course, place certain limits on the strategies open to managers in the state sector. The ideological pre-eminence of private capital remained unchallenged and consequently state-owned enterprises had to take care not to appear to be encroaching on space that could be filled by private capital, especially local private capital.

While the triple alliance was mutually beneficial for all three types of capital, mutual benefit did not erase internal conflict. The partners were also competitors. Their shared interest in a 'good business climate' coexisted with a number of specifically divergent interests. Both the state bourgeoisie and local capitalists were aware that TNCs continued to look for ways to use their operations in Brazil as a means of increasing the return on assets held elsewhere. They were aware, in addition, that if Brazil should cease to be defined as having a 'good investment climate' the TNCs would shift the focus of their expansion to other areas, abandoning their commitment to local capital accumulation. Both local partners had therefore to be wary of allowing the TNCs to gain too much leverage over the course of local accumulation.

For local private capital, tensions created by immediate competitive conflicts with TNCs were compounded by the possibility that state enterprises might use their legal and financial advantages to encroach on the industrial territory of private capital. Since local capital's greatest strength lay in its unique ideological claim to being both national and private, it also had a very different relation to the restriction of the political process from the other two partners.

Even the TNCs felt a certain trepidation in the face of the differing interests of their partners. The substantial assets that they had chosen to locate in Brazil, often embodying important proprietary technology, were at risk. They would be the most vulnerable of the three partners in the event that currently excluded groups were in a position to demand a change in the rules. The TNCs knew that the preservation of the normal rules of oligopolistic competition were essential to the benefits they were accruing. They were also aware that a variety of Brazilians, both inside and outside the alliance, see themselves as suffering under these rules and would like to modify them.

Like most political pacts, the triple alliance was an uneasy partnership, but the tensions that pervaded did not prevent its being the social structural base of very impressive economic accomplishments. The outlines of Brazil's performance are well known. Its GDP grew at about 10 per cent per year in the late sixties and early seventies. Production of capital goods and consumer durables grew at rates of over 20 per cent per annum and manufactured exports increased by almost 30 per cent per annum (Serra, 1979; pp.119, 121, 135; see also Baer, 1979). Nor was this simply quantitative expansion. As the economy grew industrialisation deepened. By 1970 the value added in manufacturing in Brazil exceeded that of all other developing countries as well as several of the smaller developed capitalist economies (World Bank, 1980, p.121).

This impressive record of growth was not, of course, simply the result of either the ability of different types of capital to work together or the special expertise of those managing the economy. On the one hand, the growth depended on sacrificing the interests of a large portion of the Brazilian population. On the other hand it was substantially aided by the international climate in which it took place. In so far as it depended on these things, the triple alliance was vulnerable to forces that it could not in the long run control.

The sacrifices of the Brazilian population did not take the form of consumption forgone so that investment could take place. Gross fixed capital formation as a percentage of GNP was lower during most of the 'Brazilian miracle' than it had been during the chaotic days of the early sixties. Instead, as José Serra puts it,

> the popular sectors seem to have provided resources for the more affluent classes in society, in part for their consumption and in part so that they could finance the purchase of consumer durables by the better paid sectors of the middle-class and working class (Serra, 1979, p.158).

While the GNP rose at record rates, the real incomes of Brazil's poorest paid workers fell. While the production of colour TVs was initiated, infant mortality rates remained at levels double those of countries with comparable per capita incomes (World Bank, 1980; Knight, 1981). The tensions created by one of the most inequitable income distributions of any country in the world (World Bank, 1981, p.183) did not threaten the stability of the triple alliance as long as all three partners were united. It did mean that any dissident member of the alliance who could make even the most feeble claim to being somehow 'on the side' of the excluded could count on evoking a powerful political response.

The extent to which it had benefited from a very favourable external conjuncture made the triple alliance vulnerable in a different way. In so far as favourable external parameters were built into the *modus operandi* of policy makers, their evaporation would require readjustments in strategy which would in turn have ramifications for the relative positions of the three partners. Negative shifts in external conditions increased the possibility of élite disaffection. In so far as élite disaffection opened the possibility of political links that tapped into the discontent of the excluded mass, the potential for disruption was considerable.

Preoccupation with tensions internal to the triple alliance was reserved for Cassandras in the early seventies. Even the oil crisis of 1973 did not shake the confidence with which Brazil's rulers viewed the future. General Geisel, inaugurated in 1974, sent the Second National Development Plan (II PND) to Congress with a message expressing confidence that Brazil could look forward in the near future to 'crossing the frontier to full development', primarily because ten years of 'renovating revolution' had produced

> an elevated coefficient of rationality, acceptance of even difficult truths and a serene and responsible pragmatism, all of which are spreading through all levels of the population, from the top to bottom of the social structure of this renewed Brazil (Federative Government of Brazil, 1974, p.6; hereinafter, II PND, 1974).

In order to understand the transition from the confidence of the Geisel regime on entering office in 1974 to the uncertainty of the Figueiredo regime in 1981, it makes sense to start with the shift in the external environment. This is not to argue that the external environment was determinative. On the contrary, internal contradictions probably played a more fundamental role. The shift in the external environment provided, however, a clearly exogenous nudge which helped set a variety of internal economic and political dynamics into motion.

## The external environment

Two elements of the international environment that characterised the late sixties and early seventies were particularly crucial to the success of dependent development. First, the period was marked by unusual growth in international liquidity. World reserves, which had grown at 2.8 per cent per annum from 1949 to 1969 grew at 22.7 per cent per annum between 1969 and 1974 (Malan and Bonelli, 1977, p.23). For Brazil this translated into the possibility of running perennial deficits in its current balance of payments account and still being able to borrow funds externally in such amounts that foreign reserves increased rather than decreased. The possibility of relying on external funds instead of increasing domestic savings was also important in allowing for the simultaneous growth of capital goods production and demand for consumer durables.

A second important factor was the existence of a buoyant market for exports. Annual rates of growth in world trade were three times higher in the late sixties and early seventies than they had been in the early sixties. The expansion of Brazil's exports, without which the current account deficit would have ballooned out of control, depended in part on the internal structural changes fostered by the triple alliance, but it was substantially facilitated by the expansion of world markets.

The general buoyancy in the world economic outlook during the late sixties was also important, at least indirectly, to explain the re-actions of TNCs to the prospect of making the kinds of investments in Brazil that were called for under dependent development. Many of these investments involved substantial periods between the commitment of funds and the expected returns and also relied on a rapidly expanding future market to absorb their projected capacity. Optimistic expectations for economic growth internationally helped legitimate even more optimistic predictions for Brazil in particular.

The worldwide recession of 1974–75, changed both the buoyant nature of the credit and capital markets and the long-term optimism of investors. As the external environment changed, so did the nature of capital flows to Brazil. In 1973 inflows of direct investment were two and a half times larger than outflows of profit. In the late seventies, profit outflows climbed to double or triple their earlier levels. Investment inflows grew but they did not keep pace. Thus, as Table 6.1 indicates, profit outflows came to represent an increasing proportion of capital inflows and the role of direct foreign investment in alleviating balance of payments problems declined.

The shift in TNCs preference for Brazil as a locus of accumulation can be seen in Figure 6.1, which charts this preference in terms of the ratio between local investment by US TNCs (inflows plus reinvest-

Table 6.1

Investments and the balance of payments: flows of capital and profits 1969–79
(in millions of current US$)

|  | 1973 | 1974 | 1975 | 1976 | 1977 | 1978 | 1979 |
|---|---|---|---|---|---|---|---|
| 1  Inflows of direct investment | 1,341 | 1,327 | 1,202 | 1,394 | 1,824 | 2,011 | 2,262 |
| 2  Payments of profits on foreign capital | 531 | 554 | 532 | 790 | 1,330 | 1,538 | 1,390 |
| 2 as a percentage of 1 | 39.6 | 41.7 | 44.2 | 56.7 | 72.9 | 76.5 | 61.5 |

Source: ECLA, *Economic Survey of Latin America*, 1980, p.117; 1981, p.122.

ment) and outflows from their Brazilian subsidiaries. Between 1969 and 1974 the ratio rose dramatically. At the peak of the charisma of the 'Brazilian miracle' TNCs were investing ten dollars locally for every dollar they brought home. By the end of the seventies, their relative preference for reinvestment in Brazil had dropped below what it had been at the beginning of the period. This shift in preferences away from local accumulation is also reflected in the 'S' shape of the curve representing growth in total book value of US direct investment in Brazil. Growth accelerated rapidly in the early seventies but had flattened out by the end of the decade. By that time inflows of capital from the US parent companies to Brazil were less than the flows in the other direction (see notes to Figure 6.1) and US direct investment was becoming part of the balance of payments problem rather than part of the solution.

The role of loan capital followed a similar shift (see Table 6.2). From the beginning of the decade until 1974, Brazil's ability to acquire new loan capital grew more rapidly than its interest and amortisation obligations. From 1974 onwards an increasing proportion of new financing went simply to make debt service payments. By 1979 debt service payments amounted to 95.5 per cent of the new financing obtained. The increasing burden of accumulated debt (estimated at US$65 billion at the end of 1981) was compounded by interest rates that had risen sharply and seemed likely to remain high in real terms.

Exports were the only bright spot in external economic relations. Despite the slowdown in the growth of the industrial economies, Brazil managed to find markets for an increasing volume of exports. Exports were expanded almost fast enough to keep pace with the growth of imports and the trade balance was kept within manageable proportions. The primary reason for this was the expansion of manufactured exports which came to represent over 40 per cent of total exports by the end of the decade (ECLA, 1981, p.123).

Shifts in the external environment did not in themselves make the model of dependent development untenable. The more hostile external environment did, however, force the Brazilian regime to design economic policy with a continual eye to the external account. Continuing pressure from the balance of payments first reduced their flexibility in dealing with conflicts among the partners in the triple alliance and limited their ability to respond to increasing pressure for redistribution. Perhaps most important, the unfavourable external environment limited the regime's ability to use growth as a solvent for internal tensions. With an elasticity of demand for imports two (Malan and Bonelli, 1977, p.24; ECLA, 1976, p.223) policies designed to stimulate growth were in direct contradiction to attempts to control the balance of payments. By the end of the decade even

Amount of US DFI in Brazil = Book value of US direct investors equity in or loans to their foreign affiliates or 'US direct investment position, year end'

Relative preference of US for Brazil as a location for accumulation:

(1) New capital transferred to Brazil + (2) Income reinvested in Brazil by subsidiaries

(3) Income transfer to parent from Brazil

Correspondence with US, *Survey of Current Business* categories:

1 'Net capital outflows' (from the US) or later 'Equity and intercompany account outflows' (from the US).
2 'Reinvested earnings of incorporated affiliates'.
3 'Balance of payments income' or later 'interest, dividends and earnings of unincorporated affiliates' or later 'income' 'Reinvested earnings'.

| Date | Current (in millions of US$) | | | Year end | |
|------|------|------|------|------------|------------|
| | (1) | (2) | (3) | Preference | Book value |
| 1968 | 80 | 73 | 75 | 2.0 | 1,484 |
| 1969 | 64 | 83 | 66 | 2.2 | 1,633 |
| 1970 | 102 | 106 | 92 | 2.5 | 1,847 |
| 1971 | 63 | 132 | 73 | 2.5 | 2,045 |
| 1972 | 194 | 238 | 77 | 5.6 | 2,505 |
| 1973 | 346 | 356 | 70 | 10.2 | 2,885 |
| 1974 | 462 | 304 | 97 | 7.9 | 3,658 |
| 1975 | 332 | 505 | 152 | 5.5 | 4,579 |
| 1976 | 347 | 491 | 240 | 3.5 | 5,416 |
| 1977 | − 13 | 409 | 250 | 1.6 | 5,930 |
| 1978 | 557 | 634 | 288 | 4.1 | 7,175 |
| 1979 | 326 | − 89 | 336 | 0.7 | 7,186 |
| 1980 | − 56 | 347 | 167 | 1.7 | 7,546 |

Delfim Neto, the most unabashed apostle of growth as a solution to Brazil's problems at the beginning of the decade, had been forced to introduce policies designed to cut back the rate of growth.

Table 6.2

Loan capital and the balance of payment 1970–79
(in millions of current US$)

| | 1970 | 1971 | 1972 | 1973 | 1974 | 1975 | 1976 | 1977 | 1978 | 1979 |
|---|---|---|---|---|---|---|---|---|---|---|
| 1 Loans and financing | 1,494 | 2,109 | 4,621 | 4,754 | 7,052 | 7,242 | 10,093 | 8,345 | 12,765 | 11,208 |
| 2 Debt service (amortisation and interest) | 1,072 | 1,217 | 1,630 | 2,306 | 2,606 | 4,050 | 4,648 | 6,300 | 8,013 | 10,700 |
| 2 as a percentage of 1 | 71.8 | 57.7 | 35.3 | 48.5 | 36.9 | 55.9 | 46.0 | 75.5 | 62.8 | 95.5 |
| Debt service as a percentage of exports | 37.2 | 39.4 | 37.3 | 34.4 | 30.1 | 42.1 | 42.7 | 48.0 | 63.3 | 70.2 |

Source: *Economic Survey of Latin America* (CEPAL, 1978, p.125; 1979, p.127).

## Growing internal contradictions

The internal problems of the triple alliance are best illustrated by a look at what happened to General Geisel's II PND (2nd National Development Plan).[4] Purely in terms of economic growth, performance during the period covered by the plan, 1975–79, was more than respectable. Brazil grew faster than all but a few countries in the world. Growth dropped below 5 per cent in only one year of the five (1977) and averaged over 6 per cent (ECLA, 1980, p.108; 1981, p.114). In terms of maintaining solidarity within the triple alliance, however, the plan was a failure. It contained promises to the national bourgeoisie which the regime could not deliver. Its ineffectiveness in this regard convinced an important segment of the local bourgeoisie that only a change in the nature of the regime would produce a state able and willing to protect their interests.

When the II PND was promulgated in 1974, its major promise to the local bourgeoisie was in the capital goods sector. The overall growth of industry was projected at about 12 per cent over the period and capital goods were specially favoured by emphasis on a 'new phase of import substitution' (II PND, 1974, p.37). The central role of local capital in meeting this increased demand was to be insured by a variety of mechanisms. First, low interest financing was available to manufacturers who purchased locally produced goods. Second, and even more important, the government's ambitious programme of capital expenditures made it a major source of the increased demand in the industry (see Suzigan, 1976, pp.117–8). Local capital was to be given first priority on government bids and 'special help' to insure their participation in major public projects (II PND, 1974, p.38). Finally, in order to enable local capitalists to expand their capacity sufficiently to meet this demand, the BNDE (National Development Bank) would provide loans. Firms unwilling to increase their debt could expand their equity capital through the purchase of non-voting preferential shares by EMBRAMEC (a subsidiary of the BNDE).

The expectation was that a strong local capital goods industry would develop under the plan and that in the process local capital would come into its own. With the assistance of the state, 'strong entrepreneurial structures' that could hold their own in a modern industrial economy would be created (II PND, 1974, p.51). The results were quite different. Output of machinery increased in 1975 and 1976, but rising rates of inflation (see Table 6.3) and a deteriorating balance of payments situation forced the Geisel regime to focus its attention more and more on maintaining its basic financial parameters at internationally acceptable levels. The budgets of state enterprises were substantially cut back and the state's demand for capital goods fell accordingly (see Lessa, 1979, pp.152, 159–63).[5]

The drop in government demand was compounded by weakness in the economy overall. Local capital goods producers who had heeded the government's invitation to expand found themselves in trouble. The orders they had counted on were not there. Even at concessionary interest rates, the loans they had taken out were a burden. And, to make matters worse, the government's optimistic predictions had attracted additional TNC competition (see Lessa, 1979, pp.138–9). The increase in the number of producers in the industry gave purchasing firms the possibility of solving their own budgetary problems by forcing capital goods producers to lower their prices. 'Excessive' competition combined with excess capacity was devastating to the local bourgeoisie and a major share of the responsibility seemed to lie with the state apparatus.

The expansionary opportunity promised by II PND had turned into its opposite. The incentives, exhortations and subsidies offered by the regime seemed in retrospect like an elaborate trap. Claudio Bardella, a leader of local entrepreneurs in the capital goods sector summed up the feelings of his *confrères* when he said: 'No artifice created by the government, and I consider all these measures artificial, is going to resolve the issue. Our problem is profits' (quoted in Lessa, 1979, p.139). For some local firms, the problem of profits proved fatal. Sanvas SA Industrias Metal Mecanica is one celebrated case (*LAER*, 1979, p.172). David Sanson, head of Sanvas, was a prominent figure among local industrialists and a vice-president of ABDIB, (the association of local capital goods producers). As early as 1975, Sanson began suggesting that the BNDE would have to offer even easier terms in loans to local capital if it wanted to ensure their survival. By 1979, Sanvas had succumbed. Sanson, an ardent nationalist, was forced to sell to the German firm, Linde. On selling, he denounced the 'lack of official assistance in the face of a growing threat of denationalisation' (*Gazeta Mercantil*, 25 April 1979, p.6). The accusation of 'lack of assistance' did not refer only to the BNDE. The proximate cause of the firm's demise was a drop in orders from its principal customer, Petrobrás, whose own budgets had suffered under the planning minister's cuts. Having set itself up as the promoter of the national bourgeoisie, the Geisel regime had also set itself up to take the blame for the problems of local capital. The prestigious *Gazeta Mercantil* echoed Sanson's discontent with the state apparatus:

It is necessary that those responsible for the industrial policy of government make an effort to avoid letting denationalisation become, due to circumstantial problems, generalised, an outcome which could have unfortunate results for the future of the Nation (2 May 1981, p.4).

The economic problems of the late seventies and the extent to which the state was implicated in them, made the politically closed nature of the Brazilian state much less tolerable to the national bourgeoisie. Discontent with the state's economic role became generalised into what Carlos Lessa (1979, p.129) has called 'the entrepreneurial rebellion', public opposition to the political structure of the state as it had evolved since 1964. The state's general commitment to the interests of capital and the possibility of individual ties with the bureaucracy (cf. Cardoso, 1975, pp.201–9) no longer seemed sufficient insurance of accountability to the local bourgeoisie. 'The President has absorbed all the decision-making power', members of the bourgeoisie complained '. . . (Y)ou can discuss with everybody, but the decision is closed' (Diniz and Boschi, 1977, p.172; see also Abranches, 1978; Diniz and Boschi, 1978). As the 'entrepreneurial rebellion' developed the local bourgeoisie became prominent in the struggle for 'redemocratisation'. By 1978, Claudio Bardella was advocating not just a more representative government but also a free trade union movement and the legalisation of socialist parties (Lessa, 1979, p.131).

Disillusionment caused by the apparent inability of the state to support them in hard times and increasing frustrations caused by the closed nature of decision making within the state apparatus were not the only sources of local capital's concern. Fears that the government's attempts to resolve external imbalances would lead it toward policies which favoured international capital at the expense of the local bourgeoisie were also important. Indeed, such fears were not unreasonable.

As dealing with the external account becomes more difficult,[6] the state needs more co-operation from international capital, both in the form of external financing and in the form of increased exports by TNC subsidiaries. Inducing TNCs to orient their output more to the export market has been central to the expansion of manufactured exports. Transportation equipment, produced almost exclusively by TNCs, is a good example. From 1973 to 1979 exports of transportation equipment rose from less than $100 million to over $1 billion to become the largest single component of Brazil's manufactured exports (ECLA, 1976, p.59; 1981, p.123). The leverage that accrues to TNCs as a result of their exports is increased by the fact that they also control the markets. More than three-fifths of the exports from Brazilian subsidiaries of US TNCs go to parts of the same corporate empire in other countries (Newfarmer and Mueller, 1975, pp.181–6). Finally, as Helleiner's analysis of the Tokyo Round shows (see Helleiner, 1979, p.389), the best defence against protectionism in developed country markets is to have one of that country's TNCs doing your exporting.

There is an obvious temptation to grant concessions to TNCs in

154

order to gain their co-operation on the export front, but such concessions are likely to strain relations with local capital. The potential for conflict is nicely illustrated by a recent case involving Dow Chemical. In contrast to most TNCs involved in basic petrochemicals, Dow has not brought local capital into its basic operations (see Evans, 1979, pp.210–11); 1981). In part because of this, Dow has been frustrated in its attempts to get state support for plans to produce ethylene and VCM (vinyl chloride monomer) at its complex in Aratu, Bahia. In 1980 it seemed that Dow would finally get its chance (*BLA*, 1980, pp.209–10). Dow had submitted to the government a proposal that involved producing ethylene and VCM, and then exporting all of the VCM plus a major part of the rest of the output to generate a total of US$500–US$800 million in export sales over a ten-year period. State planners, attracted by the export possibilities, gave Dow the tentative go-ahead and agreed to grant subsidies worth about US$173 million.

For local capitalists involved in the petrochemical industry, the proposal was an anathema. It would have given Dow a vertically integrated empire in ethylene-based products that was unique in Brazil. Given the prospects of over-capacity that already hung over the industry, the possibility that Dow might later try to shift some of its output onto the domestic market was particularly threatening. Paulo A.G. Cunha, president of the Association of Chemical Manufacturers (ABIQUIM) and leader of one of Brazil's most powerful locally-owned chemical firms (the Grupo Ultra – see Evans, 1979, pp.242–5; 1981), threatened to withdraw his participation from the third petrochemical pole unless the government rescinded its support for the Dow projects. In the end the government found the lure of increased exports less compelling than the strength of the nationalist opposition and Dow lost. Nonetheless, the fact that the proposal got as far as it did is testimony to the way in which the ability of TNCs to produce exports strengthens their negotiating hand.

The struggle to increase the supply of foreign loans also tends to shift power within the triple alliance toward the TNCs. A case from the aluminium industry provides a good example. During a generally unsuccessful tour of the citadels of international finance in 1980, one of Delfim Neto's most successful stops was in Japan. He was able to secure agreement on almost US$2 billion in loans. His success was not, however, applauded by Antonio Ermírio de Moraes, one of the acknowledged leaders of the local entrepreneurial class. A major portion of the loans was finance for an aluminium project in which several Japanese companies are involved. The project will produce aluminium for export to Japan. In order to secure the loans, Delfim had to make substantial concessions on the price at which the aluminium would be sold. As far as Ermírio de Moraes was concerned the

Japanese had the 'deal of the century'. As head of Brazil's only major locally-owned aluminium company, he was particularly irritated by the subsidised rates at which the Japanese firms would be allowed to buy electricity from the Brazilian state. The low rates amounted to a subsidy of US$400 per ton, which Ermírio de Moraes described as a gift from Brazil to the Japanese (*Estado de São Paulo*, 20 May 1979, p.12).

The influence of external financing on the internal bargaining power of TNCs can also be seen in a recent case in the petrochemical industry. Isocianatos, one of the '*tri-pé*' partnerships of state, local and TNC capital in the north-east petrochemical pole (Evans, 1981), had succeeded in putting together a proposal to produce methyl di-isocyanate (MDI). BASF joined the project as a minority shareholder and the supplier of the technology. Bayer also wanted to produce MDI, but it wanted to do so in a wholly-owned venture without local partners. Given Brazil's emphasis on the '*tri-pé*' form in the petrochemical industry (see Evans, 1979, pp.228–49; 1981), Bayer's proposal seemed almost certain to be refused approval by the CDI (Conselho de Desenvolvimento Industrial). However, Delfim Neto was engaged at the time in discussions with West German bankers. He assured them that there would be no problem with the approval of the Bayer proposal (*LAWR*, 19 June 1981, p.3). In the end, the CDI broke precedent and approved the proposal. BASF then withdrew from the now clearly less desirable joint venture project (*LAWR*, 26 June 1981, p.3), leaving local capital the loser. In this case good relations with external capital appears to have taken precedent over the support for local capital, exactly as local entrepreneurs have feared it might.

If it appears that the state is not just ineffective in supporting local capital but is actively favouring international capital, problems of legitimacy multiply. As O'Donnell has pointed out, even an authoritarian state like Brazil needs to 'present itself as the incarnation, as the political and ideological expression of the general interests of the nation' (O'Donnell, 1978, p.20). Given the blatant distributional inequities produced by dependent development, legitimacy cannot be based on any popular definition of the 'general interests of the nation'. It must be based on the support of local capital. Given the disillusionment generated among the leadership of the local bourgeoisie by the failure of the II PND to 're-equilibrate the *tri-pé*', the regime at the end of the seventies was ill able to afford actions which strengthened its relations with the international capital at the expense of its nationalist credentials.

The delicacy of the regime's position was starkly underlined by the appearance at the end of 1980 of a manifesto entitled 'In defense of a nation under threat'. The most prominent signatories of the manifesto were not left-wing politicians, but industrialists and generals.

Antonio Ermírio de Moraes and Claudio Bardella along with General Euler Bentes Monteiro, General Antonio Carlos de Andrada Serpa, an admiral and an air force brigadier, went on record as accusing the regime of having entertained proposals by foreign investors 'harmful to the Brazilian economy' and as having exhibited 'excessive tolerance' toward international firms (*BLA*, 1981, p.13; *LAWR*, 16 January 1981, p.7).

The combination of industrial and military signers represents the most potentially damaging combination possible as far as ruling military circles are concerned. Given the historically close ties that exist between military and civilian élites (cf. Stepan, 1971; Feichter, 1975; Dreifuss, 1981), and given the ideological attractiveness of nationalist formulations for a large component of the military élite, the choice between supporting a 'nationalist bourgeoisie' opposition or a regime which is military but apparently selling out to foreign interests would have the maximum possibility of dividing the military. Since preserving the integrity of the military as an institution is the *sine qua non* of military rule, the regime simply cannot afford to allow its nationalist credentials to deteriorate beyond a certain point.[7]

Faced with the possible erosion of unity within the military, the regime must obviously be tempted to move in a more nationalist direction. As should already be clear, however, its manoeuvring room in this direction is very restricted. Strong ties to international capital are essential to dependent development, without billions of dollars of new loans and without strong linkages to the international markets that are dominated by transnational firms, the profitable growth that has held the triple alliance together would be a thing of the past. As Delfim Neto is well aware, the alternative to maintaining good relations with Japanese and West German bankers is relying on the IMF, a strategy which would make it even more difficult for the regime to develop a nationalist economic programme.[8]

Independently of its external ramifications, a more nationalist economic direction would jeopardise relations with the TNCs internally. It is important to remember that the trend in direct foreign investment shown in Figure 6.1, is not simply a reflection of changes in the external environment. It also reflects doubts regarding the future 'investment climate' in Brazil. The spectre of TNC defection was raised dramatically in 1980 when Rhodia (a subsidiary of the French chemical giant, Rhone Poulenc) published its 1979 annual report. Rhodia is the archetypal TNC member of the triple alliance. Operating in Brazil for 60 years, it dominates the synthetic fibres industry and is a major force throughout the chemical industry. Its annual report placed the blame for 'the lowest profits in our 60-year history' squarely in the lap of the government (*BLA*, 1980, p.169).

Rhodia had not done badly in 1979 compared to TNCs like GM,

Dow, Ciba-Geigy and Goodyear, all of which lost substantial amounts of money. In fact, it had made a profit amounting to 14 per cent on capital and reserves (*BLA*, 1980, p.347). But relative to its expectations for its Brazilian operations, its profits were low. More important, Rhodia saw its profit levels as directly prejudiced by the fiscal and regulatory policies of the regime. Specific attention was focused on what it saw as discriminatory application of price controls by the Interministerial Commission on Prices. According to Rhodia its supplier's prices were allowed to rise, resulting in a 79 per cent increase in its costs, while its own price increases were held to only 42 per cent, squeezing its profits (*BLA*, 1980, p.169).

Unless policies changed, Rhodia announced, it would cut down on the amount of foreign loans it brought into the country, suspend its plans for new investment and reduce its attempts to expand exports (*BLA*, 1980, pp.169–70). The report amounted to a declaration that, as far as Rhodia was concerned, the implicit rules of the triple alliance had been abrogated by the state and that consequently Rhodia did not feel bound by its side of the bargain – a commitment to the promotion of local accumulation. Given Rhodia's key position in the triple alliance, such an open break was clearly a threat to the regime's ability to sustain the process of dependent development.[9]

For both external and internal reasons, the Brazilian regime cannot embark on nationalist policies that appear to prejudice the profits of TNCs. Yet the regime badly needs to impress its nationalist credentials by improving its relations with local capital. One answer to this dilemma is to subsidise the profits of both local and TNC capital, and to some degree this has been the regime's strategy all along. Trying to support the profits of both kinds of capital is, however, a demanding project. Support for local capital may backfire politically as in the case of the II PND and capital goods or, it may result in squandering the state's resources on economically unjustified bailouts. When support for local capital is combined with subsidies for TNCs the result is a very expensive package, one that has proved costly in macroeconomic terms as well as in terms of the fiscal resources required.[10]

The current plight of the BNDE exemplifies the problems of trying to succour local capital. The BNDE has continually been pulled in to support local firms that are beyond help. In some cases, like Fiação Lutfalla (*LAWR*, 6 March 1981, p.7) local owners seem to have used the bank as a means of extracting personal gain rather than as a means of reviving their firms. The difficult position of the BNDE was illustrated most recently by the case of Matarazzo. Having first refused to become mired in Matarazzo's problems (*LAWR*, 6 February 1981, p.6), the BNDE was later forced to contract a US$40 million loan on the company's behalf because the bankruptcy that seemed like the alternative was considered unacceptable by the local financial community (*LAWR*, 17 July 1981, p.6).

The most important subsidies involving TNCs have been those designed to promote exports. According to ECLA estimates for 1975 (1980, pp.119–20) companies were granted US$71 million dollars in subsidies for every US$100 million in textiles that they exported from Brazil. In the automobile industry, the corresponding figure was US$66 million. When such subsidies, most of which take the form of credit at below market rates, are combined with other similar subsidies, a major effect on resource allocation is the result. According to Peter Knight (1981, p.42): 'Credit subsidies have assumed truly macro-economic proportions – roughly equivalent of 5 per cent of GDP in 1977 and 1978 and perhaps as high as 10 per cent in 1979'.[11]

Since a substantial part of the resources which make such subsidies possible are generated by forced savings extracted from working-class Brazilians (Wells, 1977, p.327), subsidies are an important part of the regressive redistribution from poor to rich which has characterised dependent development. In addition, as Knight points out (1981, p.42), subsidies 'make rational economic calculation extremely difficult' and are 'one of the major mechanisms propagating inflation'. This last is particularly important since high levels of inflation undercut the predictability that O'Donnell (1973) suggests is one of the prime positive features of an authoritarian regime from the point of international capital. Comparing the spiraling inflation of the late seventies with the relative containment of the early seventies (see Table 6.3), it is not surprising that TNC managers have shifted from praising the efficiency of the military regime to complaining that 'any type of long-term planning is almost impossible under these circumstances' (*Wall Street Journal*, 7 April 1981, p.39).

The problem is not simply one of subsidies. In a highly oligopolised economy such as Brazil, market pressures are insufficient to prevent large firms from raising prices. As Rhodia's 1979 report demonstrates, the state cannot replace market discipline with administrative discipline without invoking the wrath of the members of the triple alliance. Price controls could not be imposed with sufficient stringency to prevent inflation from rising and have since been abandoned. Even less amenable to discipline is the financial sector which became increasingly powerful and profitable during the late seventies. Authoritarian as the regime was in some respects, it could not discipline the appetites of the members of the triple alliance.

To some degree it is, of course, no more reasonable to blame the problems of the late seventies on the regime's poor management of the economy than it was reasonable to credit the regime's 'high coefficient of rationality' with having produced the high growth rates of the late sixties and early seventies. Not only has the external situation changed, but important internal factors which contributed to Brazil's earlier performance have also been exhausted. From 1965 to 1973 Brazil was able to take advantage of a decline in the capital/output ratio based on higher rates of capacity utilisation. Growth was 'cheap' in terms of the investment required (Malan and Bonelli, 1977, p.29). By the mid-seventies the phase of easy expansion was over. During the latter half of the decade the capital/output ratio was rising and growth was becoming increasingly 'expensive' (Knight, 1981, p.21). Having taken the credit for the earlier expansion, however, the regime is hardly in a position to excuse itself by pointing to the importance of cyclical and external factors.

The dilemma of the regime is indeed a difficult one. It must support local capital or risk political opposition that threatens to penetrate the military apparatus itself. It cannot afford nationalist policies that will risk the disaffection of international financial capital or its local TNC allies. Yet, by trying to support both TNCs and local capital it undermines the overall efficiency and rationality of the process of accumulation itself. Just how intractable these problems are is indicated by the fact that the rate of inflation in 1980 matched the worst days of what the military considered the hopelessly corrupt and anarchic regime of João Goulart.

There does remain one rather curious possibility for uniting local capital and the TNCs without diverting additional resources in their direction. The central state apparatus may turn on state capital itself. State enterprises have enjoyed, on the whole, a high degree of 'relative autonomy' vis-à-vis the central state apparatus (Martins, 1977; Baer, Newfarmer and Trebatt, 1977). Indeed this is one of the reasons for their entrepreneurial effectiveness (cf. Tendler, 1968; Evans, 1981). But the division between state capital in its entrepreneurial guise and the central bureaucratic apparatus also opens the possibility that the latter could turn against the former. Furthermore, it has become increasingly clear in recent years that trimming the wings of state enterprises could be an attractive project for a regime anxious to build support simultaneously among both local capital and the TNCs.

'Anti-statism' was the first rallying cry of the 'entrepreneurial rebellion'. As early as 1975, a systematic campaign was mounted by a portion of the local bourgeoisie in opposition to the expansion of state enterprises (Evans, 1979, p.268; Lessa, 1979, p.131; Knight, 1981, pp.23–4). State enterprises are attacked not only for taking over economic territory that might be serviced profitably by private capital but also for allying with TNCs. The vulnerability of state enterprises to 'nationalist' attacks is nowhere better illustrated than in the charge by opposition congressional representative João Cunha in 1978 that the north-east petrochemical pole was 'in the service of foreign interests' (*Estado de São Paulo*, 22 August 1978, p.29).

Despite the benefits that had accrued to local capital in the formation of the pole (Araújo and Dick, 1974; Evans, 1981), and despite the fact that the deals which were negotiated represented a strong advance in the struggle to get TNCs to share their technology (Sercovich, 1980), Petroquisa, the state enterprise that had taken the lead in negotiating the deals was in effect being accused of 'selling out' to TNCs.

TNCs obviously have no quarrel with state enterprises making deals with foreign capital, but their underlying animosity toward state enterprises is probably greater than that of local capital. As tensions between the regime and the TNCs have increased, their opposition to the expansion of the state sector has become more open. Rhodia, for example, followed up its 1979 annual report with a 1980 report attacking 'increasingly tyrannical state enterprises', which, it claimed, are responsible for 'monopolizing credit and driving small companies out of the market'. The expansion of state enterprises amounted to 'creeping socialism', said Rhodia and constituted the 'posthumous revenge of Karl Marx' (*LAWR*, 15 May 1981, p.6).[12]

The Figueiredo regime seemed to be hoping to capitalise on anti-state enterprise sentiment when it announced in mid-1981 the formation of a commission composed of planning minister Delfim Neto, finance minister Ernane Galveas and minister (without portfolio) for 'debureaucratisation' Helio Beltrão, which would decide on a list of state enterprises to be 'privatised', that is sold to the private sector (*BLA*, 1981, p.236; *LAWR*, 24 July 1981, p.2). The beauty of this strategy is that it is not only ideologically attractive to both local and TNC capital, but also requires no expenditure of resources on the part of the state. Like any of the regime's other options, however, turning on the third partner in the triple alliance is problematic in a number of respects.

To be politically successful 'privatisation' must mean the sale of state enterprises to locally owned firms. Sale to TNCs would raise cries of '*entreguismo*' (selling out) and turn the programme into a political liability. Yet finding local buyers for any but a few state enterprises will be very difficult. Most of those that can be absorbed by local capital will be firms that were originally private to begin with, but fell under the control of the BNDE because of their inability to survive independently. Their transfer back to the private sector will hardly be seen as a great victory over statism.

Even if it were possible to transfer a number of significant state-owned enterprises to private owners, privatisation would remain fundamentally problematic as a solution to the regime's problems. Weakening the state enterprise sector, whether by sale of enterprises or more traditional means such as cutting their budgets or cutting their internal rate of accumulation through price controls, will weaken the state's ability to support the local bourgeoisie. The squeeze on state enterprise budgets was, after all, a major factor in the failure of the II PND to support local capital goods producers (Lessa, 1979, pp.152, 159–63). Orders from the state sector have also been an important element in creating pressure on TNCs to enter into joint ventures. In the electrical industry, for example, the government persuaded Standard Electric (an ITT subsidiary), Ericsson (a subsidiary of Swedish Ericsson) and NEC (a subsidiary of Nippon Electric), to allow local partners to gain majority ownership of their equity by requiring that the state-owned telecommunications sector make purchases only from firms which were majority locally-owned.

If the 'privatisation' campaign succeeds in cutting back the role of state enterprises it will have the effect of jeopardising the regime's capacity to secure its nationalist aims. Even the regime's capacity to promote accumulation could be jeopardised. State-owned enterprises have provided flexible, but aggressive instruments for the promotion of projects that neither TNCs nor local capital were willing to undertake. State-owned firms have also played an important role in the local absorption of advanced technology (Sercovich, 1980; 1981). Weakening the state enterprise sector would undermine an important element in the entrepreneurial dynamism of capital accumulation in Brazil. Privatisation is, therefore, a no more likely panacea than the other strategies that the regime has used to keep the solidarity of the triple alliance intact.

There is, of course, another quite different aspect to which the evolution of dependent development that the manoeuvres discussed so far do not address. Despite successive waves of repression, opposition to the military regime from below has continued throughout the post-1964 period. At the end of the seventies this opposition had become much more powerful. In 1978, over half a million workers joined an unprecedented wave of strikes (Moreira Alves, 1981, p.23). Most disturbing from the point of view of the regime was the fact that this strike wave was concentrated in São Paulo, Brazil's industrial heartland. The metal workers of São Paulo accounted for 350,000 of those on strike and established themselves as Brazil's most powerful union. In 1979, the strike wave broadened in scope. While São Paulo remained the most crucial arena of confrontation, over three million workers in at least fourteen different states were involved.

The workers involved were not 'junior partners' in the 'entrepreneurial rebellion'. They had spent fifteen years watching Brazil's productivity and the affluence of the upper class grow without seeing any indication that their turn was coming. As inflation grew more virulent and key industries, such as the automotive sector, began to stagnate, Brazil's working class had good reasons of its own to move into more active opposition to the regime. While recognising the very

162

different character of opposition from below and opposition from within the triple alliance it is, however, important to recognise that the growth of opposition from below is connected in a number of ways to the growth of opposition within the local bourgeoisie.

The local bourgeoisie needed an *abertura*, an opening to democracy, in order to have the political space necessary to press its grievances. Such an *abertura* required in turn some protection of basic civil rights. Repression must be limited and some freedom of speech and assembly allowed before even the bourgeoisie can engage in politics. There are limits on the extent to which such civil rights can be guaranteed for the bourgeoisie without being extended at least partially to non-bourgeois groups. The rules of *abertura* created then a partial umbrella from repression which facilitated the political organisation of working-class opposition. Support for political change among local entrepreneurs also helped to legitimate both the participation of a broad range of political figures who had been exiled and increased political involvement on the part of the church.

The political environment in which the triple alliance must currently operate is even more different from that of the late sixties and early seventies than is the case with economic environment. A half dozen political parties, including three labour parties contested the 1982 elections held as scheduled. Trade unionists are increasingly engaged in the struggle to create union structures responsive to their membership, both on the shopfloor and at the national level. The Catholic church has become deeply involved in both community-organising efforts in working-class communities (see Singer and Brant, 1980; Moreira Alves, 1981, p.29; Knight, 1981, p.24) and in the support of strikes.

In the current political environment there will be pressure for redistribution in a progressive direction. An increase in the share of state expenditures for the majority of the population is likely to be on the agenda. An increase in labour's share of the returns from industrial and agricultural activities almost certainly is on the agenda as well. Even if no redistribution in a progressive direction actually occurs, it will be much more difficult to use the forced savings of workers as a means of subsidising the profits of TNCs and local capital. Just as cyclical and external sources of increased profitability seem to be exhausted, the option of imposing further sacrifices on the excluded majority of the population is also being taken away from the regime.

## Prospects for the future

Hemmed in by the international environment and having exhausted the internal conditions that facilitated their earlier cycle of growth, the country's military leadership cannot reproduce the buoyant conditions of the late sixties and early seventies. Consequently, they cannot offer either local or transnational capital the same prospects of profitability and they cannot provide state enterprises with the same opportunities for expansion. The legitimacy of the regime has deteriorated severely in the eyes of the local bourgeoisie while serious challenges are being mounted from below.

The future of the triple alliance seems most precarious. A pessimistic scenario of the regime's future is not hard to construct. Faltering inflows of foreign direct investments are coupled with an increasing reluctance of local capitalists to risk investments in productive ventures. State enterprises are crippled by anti-inflationary fiscal policies and 'privatisation' programmes designed to appease private capital, while inflation continues to be fuelled by the state's inability to discipline private capital. At the same time the expansion of exports is being stymied by lagging growth and burgeoning protectionism in the world economy as a whole and the OECD countries in particular. The final blow is delivered by the captains of international finance who demand even more extreme fiscal retrenchment as the condition of supplying the foreign exchange that the economy must have, to continue functioning at all.

In so far as this projection is seen as transpiring in a relatively brief space of time, it must be considered as pessimistic even from the point of view of those who would see the collapse of Brazilian capitalism as the opportunity for the construction of a more equitable socialist order. Neither the trade union movement nor the newly reconstructed progressive political parties have the political strength to manage the transformation of Brazil under desperate economic conditions. If the pessimistic scenario is borne out economically, civilian politicians could come to power just in time to be forced to take responsibility for a period of stagnation combined with IMF imposed regressive austerity.

Plausible as the pessimistic scenario may seem, it is not the only projection possible. Peter Knight (1981), for example, suggests that current difficulties could push Brazil in the direction of 'redistribution with growth' and that such a direction is already prefigured in the Third National Development Plan. 'The essence of the strategy', according to Knight (1981, p.30), 'is to invest in basic public services (through the state sector) and in basic wage goods (through the private sector)'. He points out that basic public services and consumer goods are likely to be more labour and less energy-intensive than the mix of goods produced under the current strategy. Consequently, a more 'needs-oriented' strategy would have favourable implications for balance of payments problems.

Investment in basic services is not only attractive from an equity point of view, it is also likely to increase worker productivity and therefore contribute to lowering costs and increasing profits. More labour-intensive orientation of production could be stimulated by withdrawing subsidies to capital and reducing the indirect charges that increase the cost of labour, e.g. by subsidisation of social security charges. Furthermore, increased emphasis on wage goods would be a boon to local capital, since local capital is much stronger in basic wage goods sectors than in consumer durables and intermediary products.

Knight's projection is an attractive one because it suggests that the more equitable strategy is also the more economically rational. The reorientation it implies would, however, be resisted by powerful firms whose production is geared to the current profile of demand. Even if the reorientation was reasonable from the point of view of capital collectively, individual firms and entrepreneurs would be vehement in blaming the regime if their profits seemed to be suffering. As Knight himself admits, the transition would be slow unless incremental shifts are combined with redistributive reforms which 'take from the rich and give to the poor' (1981, p.29). Without such reforms it may be difficult to convince the poor that more than the rhetoric has changed. At the same time the opposition of both the local bourgeoisie and the TNCs will increase. Since any reorientation will have to be accomplished in the same difficult international environment and the same inflationary internal environment that the military faces currently, the possibility of quickly establishing legitimacy on the basis of economic performance is small. All of which suggests that, even if the optimistic scenario is economically impeccable, the transition will be politically problematic.

In the end, the political legacy of dependent development may prove more difficult to shed than the distortions that have been created by the pattern of economic growth. In order to prevent the emergence of active and widespread opposition during the past seventeen years of inequitable growth, the military constructed not only an authoritarian decision-making apparatus but also a complex and very powerful repressive apparatus. Just as state enterprises acquired a certain 'relative autonomy' vis-à-vis the central state machinery, so did this repressive apparatus. The prospect of 'redemocratisation' is more threatening to the repressive apparatus than to any other element in the dominant elite. Its raison d'être, after all, is preserving power in the absence of a legitimating political process.

The ominous potential of the security apparatus was dramatically

165

demonstrated in the spring of 1981 when two of its members were blown up, apparently by the premature explosion of a bomb of their own making, intended for a May Day rally. What was ominous about this event was not so much that it occurred, but that President Figueiredo was subsequently unable to force a full investigation of why and how it had occurred (Moreira Alves, 1981, p.11). By mid-summer General Golbery Couto y Silva, who some consider the most influential political figure of the post-1964 period, resigned as the head of Figueiredo's civilian cabinet. The problem of the security apparatus was clearly an important element in his decision to leave. In the process of leaving the government, Golbery, who was the creator and first head of the National Intelligence Service (SNI), said: 'I created a monster' (*Veja*, 14 October 1981, p.27).

Should hardline factions of the military linked to the security apparatus decide that the current process of redemocratisation is too threatening, it is by no means outside the realm of possibility that they would have the power to shut down the electoral process, impose their own candidate for the Presidency, and assume power. The more negative the evolution of the economy in the short term, the more likely such a mission to 'save Brazil once again' would become. Rule by such a group would portend a grim period, lacking even the commitment to economic growth that characterised the post-1964 regime and focusing almost exclusively on the preservation of the existing structure of power and privilege by whatever means necessary.

Such apocalyptic possibilities cannot be ruled out. Nonetheless, pragmatic and partial solutions have been more characteristic of past Brazilian regimes (even the current military one) and a future based on 'muddling through' current difficulties somehow seems more probable. Economically, ingenious and unexpected ways of coping with an unfriendly international environment are constantly reappearing. Take, for example, the recent success of a local entrepreneur in building out of nothing a US$250 million dollar a year export market for frozen Brazilian chickens in the Middle East (*New York Times*, 27 April 1981, p.5), surely an unexpected contribution to the expansion of exports. Or, take the US$5 billion dollar trade agreement recently negotiated with the Soviet Union, which included among other things a subcontract for a private Brazilian construction firm to help the USSR build a hydroelectric project in Peru (*LAWR*, 12 June 1981, p.8; *BLA*, 1981, p.239), another unexpected combination of projects and partners. Politically, the careful ballet that has been danced by opposition and regime over the past year has demonstrated the same kind of flexibility and pragmatism. Whether ingenuity will suffice remains to be seen, but it must certainly be an important factor in any equation that attempts to predict Brazil's future.

166

The conditions which enabled Brazil to consolidate the triple alliance and undertake a project of dependent development in the late sixties and early seventies have changed and the course of dependent development and the structure of the triple alliance must be also modified. Grim outcomes of the kind that have occurred in other countries of the Southern Cone cannot be ruled out, but neither can more positive changes. If the 1980s seem particularly crucial for Brazil's future, it is also worth keeping in mind the epigram with which a Brazilian friend used to respond to apocalyptic analyses: 'Brazil is balanced on the end of a precipice . . . and has been there for 500 years'.

# Notes

1   For the distinction between 'regime' and 'state', see Chapter 5, note 17.

2   In the sense used by the world-system approach. See Introduction.

3   This class concept is an integral part of the involvement of the state in production and refers to the social agents *directly* involved in accumulation in public enterprises. It differs from the concept of state managers used by FitzGerald, Chapter 5, which emphasises the regulative role of the state and refers to the overall state apparatus, not only to its entrepreneurial segment.

4   I would like to thank Mario Presser for drawing my attention to the pivotal role of the II PND in the evolution of the triple alliance.

5   The discussion of the II PND and the capital goods industry represented here is based principally on the excellent analysis provided by Carlos Lessa (1979).

6   For a discussion of this issue see FitzGerald, Chapter 5.

7   As O'Donnell (1978) points out, the state does not need to legitimate itself as the defender of the local bourgeoisie against the TNCs, as long as the threat that the entire structure of power and privilege may be overturned from below remains credible. It is only when the local bourgeoisie is convinced that anarchy or socialist revolution are not the only alternatives to military rule that nationalist credentials become essential.

8   For an expansion of this point see Griffith-Jones, Chapter 3.

9   Rhodia was not alone in these accusations. Gessy-Lever's 1979 annual report also suggested that its plans for expansion would be cut unless government regulatory policies changed (*LAWR*, 18 July 1980, p.5). Bayer and Nestle both decided to stretch out their investment plans (*BLA*, 1980, p.253).

10   See Chapter 5 for further elaboration.

11   Knight cites the World Bank as the source of this data.

12   This particular company's opposition to state firms has, of course, been made moot by the fact that its French parent was nationalised.

# 7 Dependency and the oil-exporting countries: has the system been broken?*

G. PHILIP

Latin American export economies have seldom achieved lasting economic progress, at any rate without years of intervening crisis. The strategy of export-led growth through mineral or raw material exports, in at least the largest Latin American countries, first became discredited as long ago as the 1930s. After the Second World War there came to exist a broad consensus based on ECLA[1] around the pursuit of domestic industrialisation fostered deliberately by government policies which aimed to reduce Latin American dependence on export markets. Between 1945 and 1960, Latin America's share of world trade fell significantly while substantial progress was made in the direction of domestic industrialisation.

The dependency school which became prominent in the late 1960s and early 1970s radically criticised this form of import-substituting industrialisation. This criticism, which at its worst became dogmatic and crudely determinist, focused on the extent to which even significantly industrialised Latin American economies remained dependent on the international system — mainly, if not exclusively, through the agency of multinational corporations. Some authors argued that this dependence doomed Latin America to perpetual stagnation and underdevelopment unless a clean break could be made through socialist revolution (Frank, 1967; Dos Santos, 1970). As such a view became increasingly implausible, so scholars came to concern themselves less with apocalyptic predictions and more with the subtleties of dependent relationships, including the balance of interests between state, local private and international capital in Latin American coun-

169

tries (Evans, 1979, and Chapter 6).

The most important change to have taken place in international economic relationships during the 1970s has had little to do with the themes directly explored by the dependency school. This change was a vast increase in the internationally traded price of crude oil, coupled with an irretrievable loss of market power by the international oil companies and a massive transfer of financial resources to a small number of oil-exporting countries. As pointed out in Chapter 3, these developments have also led to a significant change in international financial arrangements.

Several Latin American countries are net exporters of hydrocarbons, but only Mexico and Venezuela are producers of genuine world importance. At first glance, the success óf these countries, and OPEC as a whole, might seem to show that ECLA, and *a fortiori* the dependency school, were wrong to dismiss so easily any possibility of successful development based on the export of raw materials. Canada and Australia have successfully pursued such a path, so why — it may be asked — should those members of OPEC not embroiled in political turmoil not also do so? It is perhaps obvious that matters are not quite so simple as this and clear that successful development of this kind, even on the basis of vast export revenues, is fraught with problems. Nevertheless, this is a point worth considering and it provides the main question in this chapter: how far can a raw material bonanza contribute to economic development? It will be useful to begin the discussion by returning to some of the earlier literature on the subject in order to consider again the main objections that were made by *Cepalistas*[2] and some dependency writers to strategies of raw material and mineral export-led growth.

## Some weaknesses of export economies

It is obvious that export economies depend on export markets. The classic argument to which this relates is the Prebisch hypothesis which states that there is a general tendency for the price of raw materials, including minerals, to fall relative to that of manufactured goods (Prebisch, 1950). A vast amount of econometric work has been done on this question but it has not shown a conclusive general trend of the kind described. Nevertheless there can be no doubt of three main disadvantages facing raw material exporters. First, raw material prices have fluctuated far more than those of other goods. Second, as a consequence of this, prices are highly sensitive to rates of economic growth in the main consuming countries which, since 1973, have been low and show no immediate sign of increasing. Finally, whatever may be the trend for raw material prices as a whole, particular raw materials and minerals are always vulnerable to substitution either by a competing product, as aluminium has competed with copper, or by the development of lower-cost supplies in other parts of the world. Attempts to set up producers' cartels in order to limit the possible scope of such substitution have rarely been successful; the only really important example has been that of oil which will be discussed in more detail below.

The Prebisch hypothesis, and the other points made above, do not amount to a demonstration that raw material-exporting countries will never enjoy significant returned value from their products over and above the actual cost of production. Particularly rich mineral deposits or attractive arable land may always earn a 'rent' of some kind which may, under certain circumstances, be very considerable. The point is, however, that this kind of income is always precarious and subject to fluctuation; a producer who comes to depend on a monopoly price for his product under such circumstances is likely to suffer seriously in the long run.

This line of argument leads to another. Historically, almost all large mining and oil ventures in Latin America have involved foreign capital. When this has taken the form of the multinational corporation, a substantial share of the resulting income has been repatriated, in the form of profit, to the parent company. When foreign capital has been borrowed, debt repayments have been scarcely less burdensome. Empirical research has not generally borne out the extreme case, sometimes put forward, that returned value is generally insignificant. On the contrary, while there is a good deal of variation between industries, countries and periods, there have been cases in which governments have been able to bargain effectively with multinationals in order to secure a very considerable share of the surplus through taxation; such bargaining has been particularly successful in the oil industry

171

(Mikesell, 1971; Tugwell, 1975; Philip, 1982). Nevertheless, even if the argument is sometimes exaggerated, it remains true that debt repayment and profit repatriation further reduce a country's potential earnings from oil and raw material ventures.

The question of returned value, although important, is not the whole of the matter. There are also socioeconomic questions. Capital within any country tends to gravitate to the main centres of profitability and social structures develop around patterns of capital formation. Export economies are likely to develop a distinctive type of social structure which will influence politics and thus tie economic policy making into a particular pattern which may, in the long term, prove costly and damaging (Baran, 1957; Cardoso and Faletto, 1969; Thorp and Bertram, 1978). Moreover, whereas all economies are to some degree inflexible, mineral and raw material-exporting economies are likely to be both more inflexible and inflexible in more damaging ways than the others. Specifically, the entry or perceived availability of foreign capital in such export economies is likely to take the edge off such domestic entrepreneurship as may exist by making it easy for potential entrepreneurs to live as compradors or state bureaucrats. The state apparatus may become particularly central to the economy; this is less likely to lead to a 'strong' state (in the sense of being autonomous enough to be able to carry out a long-term development plan) than to a weak state which spends indiscriminately rather than strategically, with the aim of co-opting potential opposition through clientelistic mechanisms rather than developing the economy (Mouzelis, 1975). A comfortable but undynamic social structure may come into being with corruption providing easy fortunes at the top and government spending co-opting potential radicals further down.

Roughly at this point, there is a difficulty with arguments of this kind presented within a dependency framework; the description and analysis presented above are hard to fault, but reformist and radical writers have not generally been convincing in tackling the question of what should be done to avoid this outcome. Partially successful industrialisation and an increase in social welfare spending financed by an export commodity, the policies historically pursued by much of the moderate left, are actually likely to worsen the situation. In a 'pure' export economy, any reduction in export income will be felt almost exclusively on consumption, and particularly the consumption of the wealthy who will consequently be able to afford fewer luxury imports. However, once capital and intermediate goods need to be imported to sustain a protected consumer goods sector, as typically happens during the intermediate stage of import-substituting industrialisation, a fall in export income will have a considerable cumulative effect on employment and economic activity in general.

Moreover, once the state comes to provide considerable welfare and developmental services from tax revenue provided by the export commodity, any enforced cutbacks due to poor export performance will have serious political effects. Such fluctuations in government spending (and, thus indirectly, the export industry), providing con-politicisation among groups likely to be affected. Politics is then likely to divide around the distribution of benefit from government spending (and thus indirectly, the export industry), providing con-siderable further stimulus to popular mobilisation. Under these cir-cumstances political antagonisms are likely to sharpen, particularly if successive governments are driven by the pressure placed upon them to increase taxation upon the export sectors until these weaken or go into decline. At this point a zero-sum game must be played out.

There are, therefore, good reasons for making a general statement that a protectionist semi-industrialised economy which still relies on primary exports (of the kind existing until the mid-1970s in Argen-tina, Chile and Uruguay) is prone to periodic balance of payments crises which tend to lead to accelerating rates of inflation and an erosion of political institutions as conflict over resources becomes increasingly bitter. How should these crises be resolved? The view-point of the political right is clear enough; what is needed, in their view, is the restoration of the primacy of the export economy. This must be done by sharply reducing government spending, to divert resources into investment and exports, and reducing tariffs on im-ports to put an end to the bias against exports. When such policies are pursued, the consequences for the poor are tragic. Many com-panies, which are uncompetitive internationally, are liquidated with a major loss of employment, while those which survive can only afford to pay wage rates far below the previously established level. Wage reductions are often then facilitated by government coercion, liquida-tion of independent trade unions etc. Real reductions in public spend-ing are similarly achieved partly by dismissals and partly by increasing the price of wage goods which are provided or subsidised by the gov-ernment. Even if, as is by no means always certain, such measures bring about a restoration of competitiveness to the economy, the social cost is immense. Moreover, the political dimension must also be considered. It is likely that an urban economy built on tariff pro-tection and high government spending will acquire strong trade unions and interest groups liable to resist an abrupt worsening in their stand-ard of living. It is therefore likely that half-hearted attempts to adjust prices or to impose austerity will result in militant political resistance and prove unfeasible. At first, therefore, such efforts will fail and an inflationary bias will instead become built into government policy. The cost of breaking this may then be a harsh military dictatorship whose repressiveness, and lavish military spending, will further increase the already horrendous social and economic costs of this kind of economic 'rationalisation'.[3]

Dependency school writers have generally done more to show how this state of affairs might arise than how it may be averted. Indeed, right-wing critics might legitimately point out that some of the most intractable features of post-Peronist Argentina, for example, stemmed from the consequences of too much government welfare spending and too indiscriminate domestic industrialisation. Nevertheless, neo-liberal remedies for this kind of situation are often implausible, or brutal, or both. It would be absurd to argue that host governments should minimise returned value from export industries as a matter of policy but, once returned value becomes considerable, a degree of dependence upon it is inevitable. Some attempt to foment domestic industrialisation and to increase welfare spending is surely desirable even though such spending is notoriously easier to increase than to cut. However, once there has evolved a state apparatus devoted to redistribution and development spending, and once urban society has come to expect the standard of living which this permits, what is to be done if and when the export economy becomes incapable of sustaining it?

## Three crucial variables

At this stage it may be useful to introduce questions relating to the situation in which the main oil-exporting countries of Latin America, Mexico and Venezuela, find themselves. It is important to determine how likely these countries are to find at least one of three possible ways in which the potentially disastrous situation referred to above may be averted. The simplest way of averting crisis is the indefinite expansion of export revenue. If export income continues to increase without a serious reverse, a government will not face the harsh choices imposed by zero-sum politics. It will instead be possible to reconcile some degree of economic growth with some measure of welfare spending. Since it is most unlikely that any country can indefinitely increase the real price of its main export product, increased revenue will at some point need to come mainly, if not exclusively, from export volume. A second avenue lies in the achievement of a high degree of domestic industrialisation. In all but very small countries, there comes a point when home markets, previously too small to permit low-cost production, become large enough to permit economies of scale in a number of key industrial processes. Once this point is reached, unit costs fall and the industry in question can survive with a much lower degree of protection. The largest Latin American countries are already able to enjoy significant economies of scale in such industries as automobiles, steel and petrochemicals. If a country can generate enough returned value from its export sector, domestic purchasing power may help bring about a qualitative change in industrial capacity which will greatly facilitate the necessary structural adjustment when the export sector falters. Finally, there is the government sector itself. Government revenue is often wasted but it may, under certain conditions, be used to bring about a permanent increase in the productive capacity of the country in question, whether by direct enterprise investment, infrastructural projects, or by intervening to raise productivity in sectors which it does not itself control.

*Export revenues*

When we look at export revenues, an immediate problem appears. Oil exports now fetch a monopoly price, but do so at the price of encouraging considerable substitution and conservation in importing countries. For oil-producing countries as a group, real prices must fall if output is to be increased, or perhaps even maintained. For an individual country, it may be possible to secure an increase in export volume at the price of some reduction in per barrel take; the larger the producer, the greater the required reduction. At the extreme, this can produce immiserising growth from which the price loss more than offsets the volume gain. For most countries, however, there will be an individual gain from cutting prices in order to expand volume, but a collective loss if such behaviour becomes widespread. A monopoly price requires an effective cartel.

There are always problems with a cartel in the longer run (Frankel, 1946). The most important of these is that newcomers are always tempted into the industry in order to enjoy the high prices available without having to submit to the discipline of volume restriction; during the 1960s, for example, independent US oil companies operating in Libya did much to undermine the volume control arrangements of the major companies (Penrose, 1968; Jacoby, 1974; Adelman, 1973). These problems, however, are compounded when the cartel is operated by nation states, particularly those which became powerful only through their control of the oil market. There are three main reasons for this which will be clear if we compare the OPEC 'cartel' with the company cartel which preceded it.

To begin with, co-operation between states over a long period is much more difficult to achieve than is co-operation between international oil companies. At the higher levels, oil companies are run by men of similar educational background, similar bureaucratic skills and a similar instrumental approach to the business of producing oil. Differences of outlook between the leaders of different OPEC countries, however, are so great in some cases that they have contributed to war, as for example between Iraq and Iran. Thus, while all countries may have some interest in maintaining high oil prices, they may not all attach the same priority to this. To take a current example, the Iranian government may regard it as more important to win the war against Iraq than to restrain its oil exports; it may be willing to cut prices to maximise revenue for the war effort even at some long-term economic cost to itself. Less dramatically, Saudi Arabia's oil production decisions have had a good deal to do with the state of its arms negotiations with the USA.

Secondly, OPEC countries are a good deal less homogeneous internally than oil companies, and their governments less autonomous than oil company managements. It would be almost inconceivable for shareholders to exert serious pressure on oil company production or pricing policies; even parent governments rarely exert this kind of pressure. Some OPEC governments are not so fortunate. They instead experience a desperate need, particularly when the market is bad, to find sufficient revenue to meet their budgetary plans. Failure to do this may lead to political upheaval. It may therefore be politically impossible for some OPEC governments to hold back their oil production as much as they would like and forgo short-term revenue for the long-term benefit of the cartel. Analysts have generally responded to this point by dividing OPEC members into two groups:

176

those with large populations which are in no position to hold back production, and those with small populations and large reserves who are the true controllers of the cartel. However, it is no longer clear that even if the small population countries (Saudi Arabia, Kuwait, Abu Dhabi and, to a lesser extent, Libya) were to hold back oil production to the minimum there would be a major world shortage of oil. Moreover, the effect of military budgets and development plans initiated when expectations were high, combine to increase the minimum revenues which these countries now require. In 1981 even Libya was reported to have balance of payments difficulties.

Thirdly, the international oil companies did not merely control a substantial part of world production; they were also actively engaged in exploration in other parts of the world and also in developing oil-transforming industries in consuming areas. The major companies never controlled these areas completely, but they were in a position to influence them significantly in a direction which protected their own holdings in the main exporting countries. The OPEC countries, however, are in no position to exercise such influence. On the contrary, one of the less noted consequences of the mid-1970s wave of oil company nationalisations has been to free the companies for activity elsewhere. Naturally there has been a good deal of diversification out of oil, but it remains true that the major oil companies have been willing to explore in non-OPEC areas on terms which they would never have accepted prior to 1973 (Philip, 1982). Partly for this reason, an unexpectedly large amount of oil has been discovered and developed in the non-OPEC world since 1973.

Indeed, the more one looks at the evolution of the world oil market over the last ten years, the more it is clear that OPEC has not succeeded in establishing an effective cartel. During the 1970–75 period, when the oil-exporting countries sharply increased their per barrel price, production decisions continued to be made by the international oil companies who were in a position to pass on these price increases to the consumer. Given the vertically integrated structure of the industry, the major companies had few incentives to combat the demands of producer governments; consumer countries were also ineffective in this respect (Sampson, 1975; Weisburg, 1977). Only from the mid-1970s did OPEC members begin to exercise effective control over how much to produce and to sell; the process only became complete after the Iranian Revolution. The second oil price 'shock' of 1978–79 was made possible partly by the Iranian Revolution, which brought about a sharp reduction in oil productive capacity, and partly by the fragmentation of the market as a result of the change in trading conditions; the new environment led to the rise of a plethora of small traders, all of them eager to build up their stocks at the same time. A serious weakening of the market in 1980 was prevented by the outbreak of the Iran—Iraq war (further reducing OPEC's production capacity) only to occur later, in 1981—82 when OPEC's output was already very much below peak. Some OPEC governments showed considerable skill in creating a psychology of shortage and forcing up prices when the opportunity arose, in 1973—74 and again in 1978—79, but OPEC's ability to maintain these prices in hard times has not yet been seriously tested.

One might well argue also that the very high price of oil prevailing in 1974 and again in 1979—80, and also the abruptness of the increases, were not in the long-term interests of the oil exporters themselves. The international companies, although charging oil prices well above the tax-paid cost of production during the 1950s, were always careful to avoid abrupt transformations of this kind. The double shock of the 1970s appears to have persuaded a number of net importing countries, for example Brazil and the United States, that the oil situation was indeed serious and that efforts needed to be made to promote domestic exploration and realistic domestic pricing policies. Moreover, the recent history of the Middle East has made it natural for importing countries to attach a premium to breaking undue dependence on what is seen as a highly unreliable source of supply. In order to avoid this, importing governments may deliberately protect high cost domestic energy industries and continue to prefer them even if OPEC prices should fall.

The post-1973 world recession also has serious long-term implications for the oil market. For several years, it was widely believed that this recession would be no more than temporary; this belief is now less commonly held. Thus, oil exporters who have held back production in the expectation that world conditions would eventually permit an increase in export volume, may now believe instead that a market share, once lost, is gone for ever. The conflict between the level of production desired by oil-exporting countries and the level which the market can actually accept at any given price may consequently become increasingly acute. There was a tendency to over-production of oil from around 1950 to the late 1960s even though world demand was growing at around 7—8 per cent per annum; this tendency, despite being loosely controlled by cartel, brought about a considerable fall in the international price level. In the 1930s, it is true, price reductions were largely suppressed by cartel arrangements, but the oil companies' cartel in the 1930s was genuinely well organised and cuts in output were seriously enforced. It is likely that, if oil prices are not to fall considerably during the 1980s, OPEC really will have to form itself into a disciplined cartel, with all of the political drawbacks which this entails.

Nobody can predict the future with certainty and political developments may once again destroy so much oil-producing capacity in the

Middle East that sharp price increases again become possible. Mexico and Venezuela, however, would be most unwise to rely on this. Instead, it is more likely that the main exporting countries, not necessarily only those in OPEC, will make increasingly determined attempts to reach formal agreement to restrict output in order to maintain the price level. If these are successful, Mexico and Venezuela will be unable to expand their output during the 1980s by as much as they would like. If they are not successful, export revenues are likely to fall even if there are considerable increases in export volume.

World market conditions, therefore, are likely to become increasingly difficult for Venezuela and, even more so given its need to increase production, for Mexico. Moreover, even at present prices, truly monopoly profits are available only on oil which has already been developed or which can be developed at very low cost. Development cost is the crucial barrier to entry into oil production, much more so than exploration or maintenance cost (Adelman, 1964). During the 1980s Venezuela and, to a lesser extent, Mexico, will need to increase their spending on exploration and development as known and developed oil reserves in the areas of easier extraction become depleted. At present prices, such investment would still prove highly rewarding, but not so much so as to generate windfall profits of the kind available in the 1970s.

Venezuela and Mexico may respond to problems in the oil sector by trying to develop other related exports. Other oil exporters, however, are likely to follow a similar strategy and some already have. As a result, the outlook for industries closely related to oil (natural gas exports, oil refining and petrochemicals) is for continuing surplus and a buyers' market. Diversification plans of this kind, together with the world recession, have already led to considerable world overcapacity in oil refineries and petrochemical plants.

It may be much more promising for Mexico and Venezuela to develop instead their rich mineral reserves; as we shall see below, they are to some extent already doing so. However, given the absolute size of the oil industry in both countries, any new exports would have to be of truly vast proportions if they were to alter the trade account significantly. It is not clear that world markets, in their present condition, could take such increases in mineral production unless the countries concerned were willing to cut prices aggressively with corresponding damage to export revenue. Moreover, the high valuation of the exchange rates of almost all oil-exporting countries makes them relatively uncompetitive in anything involving a significant labour cost. In practice, increasing oil exports have often been associated with the relative and sometimes absolute decline of both visible and invisible non-oil exports (cocoa and coffee in Venezuela and Nigeria, tourism in Mexico). Once oil export revenue declines, non-oil exports may become increasingly competitive, but it is difficult to arrange for this to happen beforehand. In sum, therefore, Mexico and Venezuela are likely to face a difficult outlook for their exports over the next decade in so far as international factors are involved. Internal factors will be considered in more detail below.

*Level of domestic industrialisation*

The second variable mentioned above, the degree of success with domestic industrialisation, takes on added significance in this context. Exports can never be ignored completely, but an effective process of import substitution may go far to offset the damage done by a fall-off in export revenue, as happened in several Latin American countries during the 1930s. There may once more be some reason for optimism here.

Oil exports generate income on a very large scale and thus expand the domestic market more effectively than any redistributionist measures ever could. The sheer pressure of demand is likely to generate some degree of industrial growth in even the most backward economy, particularly if this is fostered by tariffs or other protective measures. Moreover, in Venezuela as well as Mexico, there already exists an industrial sector of some sophistication. In Mexico the oil boom permitted economies of scale and also further development of technical and industrial experience in partially developed industries such as automobiles, steel and shipbuilding. These may no longer be particularly profitable at current international prices, particularly if the local exchange rate is overvalued, but they are at any rate substantial employers of labour and help to make up the industrial base of most developed or near-developed countries. It is also quite possible that some genuinely high-technology industries will be developed within the country. In Venezuela, as we shall see below, this increase in demand has strengthened the more dynamic local companies and may make a number of new industrial processes viable (and some old ones less unviable) even though much local industry will remain basically uncompetitive.

*Government spending*

There are two courses that the last factor, government spending, can take, redistributive or conservative. If conservative, government policy will seek to strengthen industrial capitalism by emphasising important 'bottleneck breaking' infrastructural investments which require heavy capital outlays for a low financial return. Most less developed countries find it difficult to finance these, except at high international interest rates, and so they are either delayed for too long, or paid for at a high price in terms of future resources.[4] Oil-exporting governments do not have this problem. A policy of strengthening capitalism is also likely to require a high level of investment in social infrastructure, particularly since rapid population increase and movement of people to the larger cities are likely to be typical of most oil-exporting countries. There will thus be vast pressures on social welfare services and on human capital forming sectors such as education, particularly since a high proportion of the population is likely to be young and financially dependent. Mining and oil economies, indeed, are likely to urbanise more quickly and more thoroughly than those based on the export of agricultural products.

The option of redistribution, more ambitious than the first, is to seek a policy of growth with social justice with the emphasis on employment creation, small-scale public works projects, support for small farms and businesses, and income redistribution. This requires even more detailed planning and effective policy making than a more straightforward pro-capitalist strategy if it is not to lead simply to rhetoric without results, to a consumer boom with no matching increase in production or to waste on a massive scale.

In fact, according to any economic criterion, the historical record of government spending in export economies has rarely been impressive. Yet, because it is a focal point in the spending of the surplus, the state apparatus within such exporting countries is of more than usual importance. On the face of it a state which controls a fairly high proportion of GDP without the need to tax or otherwise inconvenience high domestic income earners may appear to be an ideal instrument for enlightened and reformist policies. However, governments presiding over such states have rarely even approached these expectations. It is perhaps worth seeking some general reasons for this.

One of these stems from the nature of politics itself. The state bureaucracy has, throughout Latin America, always been made to depend heavily on political appointments, particularly when the form of politics has been electoral. Where jobs are scarce, it is only natural that newly elected governments find it necessary to reward supporters with places within the administration and prefer to expand the bureaucracy rather than upset the political balance by dismissing supporters of the preceding government. It is perhaps also natural for state functions to be expanded for political advantage and a genuine belief in social reform may also play a part here. When times are good and the economy appears prosperous, there are few limits to the kind of promises that can be made. When times are bad, procedures can be tightened up, public sector salaries can be held down and payment delayed; bureaucracy, in other words, can be used to cut actual spending without any need for previous policies or promises to be openly repudiated.

Apart from money actually spent on the bureaucracy, political criteria are likely to influence the nature of government projects. Those which are visible, particularly large constructions in the capital city, will count strongly. Those which offer people immediate financial benefit will be more attractive than those which take longer to show results; thus, the provision of subsidised wage goods will be more attractive than higher spending on health or education. Projects of an extra-ordinary character have the added advantage that they can be entrusted to a specially created organisation which can be made comparatively efficient; objectives which require continuing expenditure and no obvious end product are harder to extract from the day-to-day bureaucracy which, if appointed in a clientelistic way, may not be capable of overseeing programmes which require efficiency and co-ordination.

Finally, there is a point which is true of the governments of all oil-exporting countries. If oil or other raw material exports can be said to 'distort' an economy, then government spending will either have to reflect these distortions and, in doing so, reinforce them, or it will have to suffer the financial costs of trying to discount them. In practice, ill-considered attempts to diversify an economy away from a particular export dependence may end up reinforcing it if the effect is to set up inefficient and loss-making ventures which need to be subsidised by tax payments and thus by export earnings. A shadow pricing system may in theory resolve this problem but few bureaucracies possess the necessary degree of sophistication to operate this. In practice, the quality of government spending in export economies during periods of bonanza has not really been high enough to support even the conservative economic strategy satisfactorily. let alone to meet the very demanding requirements of the redistributive strategy.

**Venezuela and Mexico**

This section offers a brief sketch of the economic situation of these two countries focusing on the three variables considered above – the export economy, the state of domestic industrialisation and the quality of government spending.

*Venezuela*

Venezuela has been exporting oil since the 1920s and there are increasing signs that its resource base is less strong than it was. Exploration in Venezuela was heavy in the years up to 1960, but subsequently fell off quite sharply under the more severe tax and regulatory systems set up by post-1958 democratic governments (Tugwell 1975). Consequently although oil production continued to increase until 1970, few new oil discoveries were made and reserve increases were overwhelmingly the result of the increased development of existing fields. During the 1970s oil production fell from 3.5 to around 2.2 million barrels daily, but the effect of this was more than offset by price increases so that oil export revenue increased from US$1.4 billion in 1970 to around US$16 billion in 1980. However, in order to stabilise oil production roughly at present levels and to prevent the quality of the oil produced from deteriorating further, it was necessary to step up investment considerably. This perceived need largely explains why the oil nationalisation was brought forward to 1975 from 1983 (when the old oil concessions were in any case due to expire). Thus, investment in the oil industry increased from US$323 million in 1976 to around US$2,250 million in 1980 without any corresponding increase in production (Petroven, Annual Reports).

Thus unless real oil prices increase sharply in the 1980s or unless there is a major new oil discovery in Venezuela, which would not be totally surprising but of which there is as yet no sign, the oil revenues available to the government would be likely to fall during the 1980s, even without taking the world market into consideration. A further factor contributing to such a fall is mounting domestic oil consumption, at the moment some 320,000 barrels daily (of which one half is gasoline), which will cut increasingly into the country's exportable surplus, particularly if the present highly subsidised price levels are not changed. In the long term the vast deposits of very heavy oil which are to be found in the Orinoco oil belt may well restore Venezuela to the front ranks of the oil-exporting countries, but it is most unlikely that any significant surplus can be realised from this source until the 1990s at the very earliest. In any case, the Orinoco development will only yield a positive financial return if oil prices rise which, as we have seen, can by no means be regarded as certain.

Given the importance of the public sector in the Venezuelan economy, it may be easiest to consider government spending and the degree of domestic industrialisation together. Fundamentally, Venezuela suffers from a lack of symmetry between its abundant resource base, the development of which generally requires capital-intensive projects, and an over-supply of unskilled and only partially educated labour. Until 1974 the oil industry was the country's only natural resource which had been fully developed, although there was a small iron ore export trade. Under the presidency of Carlos Andrés Pérez, however, the public sector moved strongly into 'heavy' industrial projects with a strong natural resource component (hydro-electricity, steel, aluminium smelting, petrochemicals, railway development) as well as beginning the recapitalisation of the oil industry. These new projects have not been an unqualified success. Although some have worked better than others, the general picture has been one in which completion dates have been significantly delayed, costs have been higher than expected (in some cases much higher) and those projects which are onstream are running at a loss because of poor management or technical difficulties. It has not helped that many of them were financed internationally and have thus encountered unexpectedly high capital costs as world interest rates remained high. Even so, many of them are likely to be useful projects which will in time add to Venezuela's resource base.

If raw material export sectors have been regarded as a priority, however, there has been much tolerance of inefficiency in areas of the economy which have spent rather than earned foreign exchange. This is particularly true both of manufacturing and the public sector itself. The public sector, particularly the central bureaucracy, is overmanned and poorly organised with salaries within it tending to be low. The manufacturing sector itself is heavily protected and controlled, with the effect of controls serving to maintain the position of the oligopolists who control the most important markets as well as depressing the general level of productivity. Price controls may be a nuisance for an established producer, but the impossible series of bureaucratic obstacles facing any new entrant to an industry provide those already established with valuable protection. Established trade unions similarly benefit from such restrictive policies, particularly since employment is strongly protected by law.

The organisation of manufacturing in Venezuela, therefore, permits a convenient accommodation of established interests. The local bourgeoisie is certainly not interested in a dynamic or competitive industrial structure. Intersectoral in character, it is better identified with its financial rather than its industrial presence; almost all of the main industrial families are also associated with banks or financial

184

houses. Such a class is only too willing to rely on close associations both with foreign, overwhelmingly US, sources of capital and technology and with friendly sections of the state bureaucracy or influential political figures. If the effect of these associations is to congeal the domestic market, then any spare capital can always be exported. There can be no doubt that the Venezuelan private sector is a major exporter of capital (Wilkins, 1981), and no government has yet dared to attempt the introduction of exchange controls. Thus, if the Venezuelan state can be said to have many *rentista* characteristics, the same can certainly also be said of the local bourgeoisie.

This pattern of economic organisation has had its advantages. For one thing, it has kept employment at a much higher level than would otherwise have been the case; in 1980 the government sector employed nearly 1 million and the manufacturing sector almost another 500,000. Venezuela is now the only Latin American country where manufacturing has a proportionately lower share of GDP (11.4 per cent in 1979) than of the labour force (16.3 per cent in 1979) (Banco Central de Venezuela). In the absence of any kind of welfare state, these employment practices coupled with a policy of keeping wage goods fairly cheap have enabled some redistribution of income away from the export sector, although wages are fairly low in both the public and manufacturing sectors and income distribution remains regressive. The artificially induced tightness in the labour market has not only benefited those employed in the protected sector but also those in the labour absorbing service sector of the economy who thus have fewer competitors. During the 1973—77 boom there was an actual shortage of unskilled labour and there is still comparatively little open or disguised unemployment despite a slowing of the economy and an increase in illegal immigration. Open unemployment remained as low as 5.2 per cent in 1979.

Moreover, this set of policies has not led to complete economic stagnation. There has been significant economic growth both in agriculture and in some sections of manufacturing due largely to direct government support. The more successful Venezuelan companies have also had the opportunity to strengthen their technical and financial capacities and there are signs that they are beginning to invest and operate more ambitiously than previously. The oil industry may provide an example of this. Before the 1960s Venezuelan capital was hardly involved in oil-related activities. In the subsequent fifteen years the industry declined and so provided very little attraction to domestic entrepreneurs. With the post-nationalisation expansion, however, domestic companies became increasingly interested in undertaking the comparatively demanding and technical work required by the state oil company. Even so, the state company has become so locked into dealing with its former international suppliers that the

185

task is proving difficult. Thus, in 1980 Petroven set up a purchasing subsidiary known as Bariven with head offices located in Houston, so that local companies wishing to sell to Petroven had to travel to Houston to make the necessary arrangements. This anomaly reflected not so much any obstinacy or conservative mentality on the part of Petroven as the traditional division of the Venezuelan economy into the efficient raw-material exporting sector and the protected foreign exchange-using sector. Supply to Petroven has now become a political issue – the first major Orinoco development contract was awarded in March 1981 to a Venezuelan-American consortium – and it is likely that domestic companies will be given an increasing role during the 1980s.

A heavily protected and subsidised domestic economy was also a part of the price that had to be paid for the successful restoration of democracy after 1958. Prior to 1958, Venezuela had enjoyed only some three years of real democracy in the mid-1940s and the economic élite was highly suspicious of anything which might threaten its privileges. In order to win acceptance, the leaders of the main political parties had to agree, at any rate implicitly, not to act in too threatening a manner. At the same time, they needed to find a way of rewarding their own supporters. Consequently, post-1958 governments have sought to use co-optation and spending policies in order to reward their supporters and maintain their popularity while taking care not to threaten the economically powerful.

This type of economic organisation, however, is not without its dangers. There is a real possibility, especially now that the commanding heights of the economy are firmly under government control, that the inefficiency afflicting much of the public sector will spread to all of it. In 1981 Venezuela suffered some serious international embarrassment when the chronic confusion of its public finances led to a formal default being declared against a minor public sector agency whose accounts were in complete disarray; for a time Venezuela had to pay more for its international loans than its underlying economic position might warrant purely because of poor management. Similarly, if the efforts of domestic Venezuelan companies to enter the oil industry lead simply to the disqualification of better-equipped foreign competitors, then it is likely that the performance of Petroven will suffer, along with the Venezuelan balance of payments; although it may be that the better domestic companies will develop their expertise quickly enough to make a significant degree of protection unnecessary. Finally, Petroven itself may be vulnerable to political attack, particularly if its financial results suffer from low international oil prices: such attack may lead to the wrong kind of political control being exercised with growing bureaucratisation and a cut in the real resources made available to the company.

186

It is already true that the limitations and inefficiencies of the public sector are proving costly. Relatively full employment and the provision of cheap wage goods have been insufficient to combat the absolute poverty that affects perhaps one-third of the Venezuelan population. The Venezuelan state is also an inept tax-collector, which contributes significantly to the fact that income distribution in Venezuela is among the most unequal in Latin America. For as long as oil income is available at present levels this need not matter but effective fiscal reform will become increasingly important if oil revenue falls off. Moreover, the provision of education in Venezuela, while rather better than the Latin American average, is not outstandingly good, particularly when the country's per capita income is taken into account. The vast majority of Venezuelans have no more than a primary education and there is a major shortage both of skilled workers and medium-level professionals and managers. Although recent governments have reaffirmed education as a priority, it remains true that public spending has generally accorded higher priority to the accumulation of physical capital than to the development of human resources.

During the rest of the 1980s, then, the real income provided for Venezuela by the oil industry will amost certainly fall. Unless ways are found of raising alternative sources of revenue, public spending will also fall, perhaps after a period in which the government seeks to resolve its problems by borrowing. At the same time, the government will need to maintain the momentum of some state investments, notably those relating to oil, if it is not to face the prospect of a dramatic deterioration in its balance of payments a few years later. The attempts made by the Pérez government to overcome this situation by developing major new capacity in non-oil exports appear unlikely to resolve the difficulty since the new ventures will be far less profitable than the oil industry. It may just be that Venezuela will have to reconcile itself to a much lower rate of economic growth during the 1980s than in the previous decade, but there is also some danger that the situation will worsen dramatically.

*Mexico*

If we exclude the pre-1938 period, Mexico has only recently become a major oil exporter. Since 1976, however, the growth of its oil industry has been among the world's fastest. Proven reserves have gone up from 5 to 72 billion barrels, with a new category of 'potential reserves' put at some 250 million barrels. Meanwhile oil exports have increased from US$206 million (net) in 1976 to around US$15,000 million in 1981. There have also been major investments in downstream projects such as refining and petrochemicals and, albeit on a deliberately limited scale, an export natural gas trade has been created.

In 1981 oil and gas were expected to make up 75 per cent of Mexico's export revenues (Pemex, Annual Reports). There is undoubted potential, moreover, for major increases in export volume during the next decade and as we shall see, the Mexican government may have little option except to keep producing to the technical maximum.

As these figures suggest, Mexico has become an oil-exporting country on a scale which has worried some of the more cautious members of its own government. The country is now undergoing many of the classic symptoms of oil-led growth.[5] These include a sharp upward movement in the real exchange rate (at least until early 1982), rendering uncompetitive many non-oil exports and key invisible items such as tourism, and working against any move to open the protective structure of the country: Mexico in 1979 formally decided not to enter GATT. Imports have been increasing dramatically and in 1980 accounted for 15.7 per cent of total supply (up from 12.3 per cent in 1976). There has been an investment boom; in the three years 1978–80 investment in real terms grew by 15.8 per cent per annum. At the end of 1980, investment made up 25.6 per cent of total GDP — an unprecedented figure for Mexico. Real government spending increased sharply although not so much as to greatly increase the government's role in the economy which itself grew at over 8 per cent per annum during the four years 1978–81. There was a fall in unemployment but the very high rates of return on capital suggest some further worsening of an already grossly unequal income distribution. Meanwhile inflation has continued at an historically high rate of nearly 30 per cent annually until the end of 1981 (Banco de Mexico, Annual Reports).

The large Mexican market and Mexico's relatively sophisticated industrial structure may well allow the country to use its oil wealth to generate self-sustaining industrial development in a way that has not been possible for the smaller and poorer oil-exporting countries. Mexico already has a public sector capable of planning and managing complex projects coupled with a number of large and ambitious companies in the private sector. There remain, however, a few potentially serious problems which are worth exploring.

One may begin with the trade cycle. The Mexican political élite is generally committed to the view that economic growth rates should be raised to the maximum sustainable in order to reduce the stresses of social transformation and the politically explosive danger of unemployment. Moreover, the Mexican private sector (and many public sector managers and civil servants) have radically shifted their expectations upwards as a result of the new oil wealth. Consumption has boomed and private investment has been committed on highly optimistic assumptions; within the public sector, the momentum of government spending has been difficult for the political élite to check even to the extent that it has wished to do so. In other words, even when oil export revenues have been increasing sharply, the growth rate has been high enough to threaten balance of payments, budgetary, money supply and inflation rate objectives. In 1981, all of these indicators, and particularly the first two, were dangerously off target.

Correction of this tendency is by no means a simple matter. The Mexican private sector has borrowed very heavily in dollars in order to increase its sales in pesos. The 1982 devaluation and the major slowdown in growth expected to follow during that year will threaten the more reckless private-sector companies with bankruptcy and default. Already in 1981 Mexico's largest private group, Alfa, required a major government loan after it had borrowed too fast and expanded too furiously. It was believed at the time that a number of other companies were in varying degrees vulnerable and that a significant slowdown in the economy would lead to major casualties.

The political implications of this situation are also interesting. It is hard to see how the political élite could afford to see a major slump in Mexico or even serious damage to entrepreneurial confidence. Political stability is believed by the political élite to require rapid growth in which private investment must play a part. On the other hand, there are obvious dangers in bailing out large private companies, particularly if public spending on other projects is being cut back. The government may instead be tempted to take over sections of ailing private companies, and there are at least a few holdings in steel and other basic industries presently in private hands which the government would be happy to bring under state control. Or at least the threat could be made; private companies might be allowed to enjoy soft loans from the government subject to an implicit guarantee of good political behaviour. This might free the government's hands for reform in other directions which might normally prove controversial, particularly the long-overdue reform of the tax system. A benign outcome on these lines might prove relatively beneficial to Mexican development, but there is always the danger that a clumsily engineered emergency slowdown of the economy might lead to serious damage both to private sector confidence and to political relationships at the élite level. Private capital might then come to prefer the security of the USA to the growth potential of the Mexican economy.

In the longer term, potential problems have mainly to do with the quality of government spending. Well before 1976, economists were turning their attention to the 'fiscal gap' which threatened Mexican development. Put briefly, the argument was that the upper limit on the government's ability to tax profits was set by the rate of return on capital within Mexico, which had to be allowed to remain well above US profit rates in order to discourage capital flight; the same was also true of interest-bearing deposits. Meanwhile, there are not enough middle-class employees to make income tax or sales taxes rewarding from a fiscal standpoint. This constraint both increased Mexican inequality substantially (Van Ginnekin, 1980) and also made it increasingly difficult for the state to finance necessary development spending, to say nothing of social welfare spending, which might also be presented as a requirement for political stability. The problem would be compounded if profit rates decline over the long run. At first sight, oil wealth has narrowed the fiscal gap by increasing the resources directly available to the public sector. However, as we have seen, oil wealth has also led to rising expectations and increased demands being made on the public sector which may well face, after a few years, a similar bottleneck as before, but at a higher level of economic activity and with higher popular expectations.

It is therefore clear that the political élite will increasingly be faced with some fairly sharp choices over its spending policies (Tello and Cordero, 1981). Thus far, such choices have not really been made. Instead everything has been expanded at once while the government has emphasised such inoffensive, if not vacuous, themes as opposition to corruption and the importance of planning. Nor has any serious effort been made to improve tax collection and thus to reduce the government's direct dependence on oil revenues. At the end of 1981, however, the government did permit a large increase in the domestic price of gasoline. This went some way towards reducing the amount spent by the state in subsidising domestic oil product prices, which at a cost of US$16,000 million in 1979 alone, amounted to vastly more than all other state subsidies combined (Corredor, 1981).

The question of public spending ties in closely with the informal division of Mexican state managers[6] into 'technocrats' and 'politicians'. The nomination of de la Madrid in 1981, as presidential successor to Lopez Portillo, was widely interpreted as a victory for the 'technocrats'. These have become identified with an emphasis on public spending in a conservative form, towards the provision of physical and social infrastructure, and on the use of large or medium-sized units to develop agriculture and industry. Pressure from below is likely to be met by increasing the toleration granted to opposition parties and activities, which are unlikely to pose any serious political threat to the regime, rather than by a further extension of clientelistic politics or any major redistributionist measures. This picture may, of course, need to be modified once the new government takes office. The political question is, to some extent, still open.

*Some concluding speculations*

It is by no means unknown for a country to fail to profit from a financial bonanza. Post-1973 Iran provides a classic case study of

190

how an unexpected inflow of wealth led to political crisis and collapse and to the repudiation of the whole ethic of developmentalism. There are a number of other OPEC countries in which, while there has been no overt collapse, abundant revenue has led to conspicuous waste and mismanagement rather than to planned, or even unplanned, economic progress. Nor is the story a new one. Spain was able to make very little of the inflow of bullion from the New World in the sixteenth and seventeenth centuries. Postwar Argentina exchanged a strong foreign exchange position for an economy notoriously prone to balance of payments and inflationary crisis. Other examples are not difficult to find.

Mexico and Venezuela are rather better placed in some respects. In 1973 they already enjoyed per capita income levels which were high by Latin American standards and much higher than the third world average. They had no serious external security problems and military spending has never been allowed to spiral out of control. International power politics, therefore, has affected them only marginally. Both countries have enjoyed comparatively stable currencies and neither has suffered, for many years, from hyperinflation. Both countries, in addition, have relatively stable forms of government — Venezuela has held free elections regularly since 1958 while Mexico has gradually evolved its own party system from around 1920. Both, therefore, are free from several obvious sources of weakness.

Even so, there may well be difficult times ahead for both countries. As we have seen the world price of oil is, in real terms, likely to fall during the 1980s. This is not to suggest that there will be any catastrophic drop to, let us say, US$1 or US$2 per barrel; the natural geological characteristics of Mexico and the main OPEC countries are therefore likely to provide a permanent source of at least moderate wealth since oil can be produced far more cheaply here than in other parts of the world. Moreover, Mexico and Venezuela, because of their relative political stability and Western Hemisphere location, will always be able to enjoy at least a small premium on average Middle-Eastern oil prices. Furthermore, the United States, while doubtless happy to see some fall in the oil price, will not wish to see either country become seriously impoverished or politically unstable as a result of collapsing oil revenue. Even in 1981 the US government was quietly willing to favour Mexico with purchases for its strategic stockpile.

Yet even a limited fall in oil export revenues (or, in the case of Mexico, a lower than expected rise) to levels which many other Latin American countries would regard with envy, might still cause serious problems to economies structured around oil. Governments will not be able to offer satisfaction to all groups at once; they will be forced to make clear choices which will leave some disappointed and may even trigger forceful political resistance. In the case of Venezuela, questions will be asked about what the government has actually 'done' with the oil revenue; it has succeeded in preserving social stability but has not pursued even a conservative spending strategy with much determination or success, and certainly has made no serious effort to pursue a strategy of redistribution-with-growth. In Mexico the crucial decisions have yet to be made, but any shortfall in government revenue will reduce further the already limited possibilities of a genuinely redistributive strategy.

The real potential danger, however, is the development of *rentista* attitudes both within the government and among the population at large where such attitudes consist of an obsession with state-provided services. A two-part definition of a *rentista* state is necessary: one whose main source of income is the rent or quasi-rent stemming from an export surplus (the 'objective' part of the definition) and which has a high time preference and no effective strategy of economic development (the 'subjective' part of the definition). Such states may be oligarchic, middle-class or mass, according to who benefits from state services. Many economists on the moderate left (and *a fortiori* many dependency writers) have advocated policies whose effect was to create mass consumption *rentista* states in agricultural or raw material exporting economies. The classic example is Uruguay prior to 1973 where the result was economic stagnation, political decline and eventually the imposition of brutal dictatorship.

The aim of this chapter is not to predict that Mexico or Venezuela will suffer similar disaster but to indicate the dangers. In both of these countries, government policy may be more enlightened and the private sector more dynamic than the pessimists suggest; the easier, short-term options may be rejected in favour of some genuinely strategic thinking. Given that the export sector is unlikely to provide much joy, such strategies must be focused on raising the quality of domestic industrialisation and government spending. A relatively conservative but seriously planned and thought-out strategy of the traditional import substitution type may achieve comfortable growth rates but will leave a large part of the population very poor and outside the real benefits provided by oil income. In the long term this may prove politically dangerous given the way in which expectations have been aroused in both countries during the past few years. A more radical strategy involves more immediate political dangers, particularly if total government revenues are affected by falling oil prices, and there is always the danger that governments will relapse into naive consumptionism in order to extract short-term political rewards. Nevertheless, policies aimed at spreading the benefits of oil by means such as rural public works and electrification and primary and secondary education may prove to have greater value in the long run, particularly if relatively free market conditions provide the necessary

192

impetus to industrial growth. This is surely better than the pointless proliferation of controls and purposeless public sector expansion so often typical, though sometimes temporarily, of prosperous raw material-exporting countries.

From the discussion it is clear that there are indeed important structural weaknesses facing mono-product export economies which are only alleviated in part by producers' control of the export product and high international prices. These weaknesses can best be grouped under three headings. First, there are the difficulties arising from the need to create an effective cartel. These difficulties are well known to conventional micro-economists. At worst, the cartel may collapse if its members do not exercise sufficient discipline or if it fails to incorporate a high enough proportion of production; in particular if it fails to integrate new producers. At best, the cartel will restrict output and encourage substitution among consumers so sacrificing considerable growth potential. This second effect may be disguised by rapid international economic growth or by the competitive advantage of the product as a whole as, for example, oil enjoyed advantages over coal, or by the rapid development of complementary industries. In many cases, therefore, members of a cartel, particularly of such a comparatively homogeneous product as oil, will face at best semi-stagnation in demand and at worst a sharp reduction in real income.

The second weakness can also be explained in conventional economic terms. This concerns the effect of a mineral export on the general price level. A successful export will lead to an over-valued exchange rate rendering production of other tradeable goods less competitive. It will also tend to make investments at the service of the export 'enclave' more profitable in relation to the rest of the economy and will bias government projects and spending plans in the same direction. Under such circumstances, export diversification will be no simple matter.

The third weakness is more general and political. When the main link from the export sector to the domestic economy is the tax system, a *rentista* state may develop. Such a state will over-regulate the economy and thus create dangerous rigidities. It will also contribute towards the over-politicisation of civil society with the subsequent danger of polarisation and political decay when the export sector finally begins to decline.

# Notes

1   For a discussion of the ECLA (Economic Commission for Latin America) model and its influence as 'economic ideology', see Chapter 5.

2   From the Spanish acronym for ECLA, CEPAL. 'Cepalistas' are those who have been linked to or influenced by the ECLA school.

3   For a complimentary interpretation of authoritarianism related more to the need to check hyperinflation than to restore export led growth, see Chapter 2 and Appendix.

4   For the implications of the resulting fiscal crises, see Chapter 5.

5   This piece was written before the Mexican financial crisis of August—September 1982. The reader may judge how far the analysis has been overtaken by events.

6   See Chapter 1, note 3, for use of this term and also Chapter 5.

# 8 The relative autonomy of the state and capital accumulation in Latin America: some conceptual issues*

CARLOS FORTIN

The proposition that the state plays a central role in the process of capital accumulation in peripheral societies is not seriously disputed among development analysts. By contrast, views about the definition of that role, its determinants and, particularly, the deeper logic that underlies it vary considerably.[1] Those observers that adhere to a class theory of the state tend to look for conceptual guidance in the Marxist notion of the relative autonomy of the capitalist state. But attempts at applying it to the Latin American context also raise complex theoretical issues, stemming both from unresolved problems in the concept itself and from the peculiarities of dependent capitalist development. The concept is, however, a potentially very powerful analytical tool, and relating the debate around it to concrete discussions of Latin America can help clarify the issues raised in the latter and open avenues for further research.

This chapter reviews some of the problems that the use of the concept of the relative autonomy of the state presents in the Latin American context. It does not purport to offer solutions to those problems, or even to discuss them exhaustively. It is, hopefully, a contribution to an ongoing debate and might help put the chapters in this volume in a broader perspective. After a brief review of the notion of relative autonomy of the state in classical Marxist writing, two sets of distinctions will be introduced: one suggesting that the

* I am grateful to Diana Tussie for comments on an earlier draft.

state can be conceptualised as either a 'pact of domination' or a set of institutions and personnels; the other concerning the fundamental logic underlying its role in society, which can be categorised either as deriving from the movement of capital or from the class struggle. These distinctions will be linked generally to the notion of relative autonomy in the context of peripheral capitalism and specifically to the contributions of Evans and FitzGerald in this volume. The remarks will conclude by identifying some areas for further exploration.

### The relative autonomy of the state in classical Marxist writings

The concept of relative autonomy of the state emerges in the context of a class theory of the state. As is well known, Marx's powerful challenge to liberal-bourgeois political theory hinged precisely on his rejection of the notion that the state is an independent actor in society, an embodiment of the common interest and neutrally arbitrating among the various contending interest groups and classes (Miliband, 1977, ch.IV). For Marx, of course, the state in general and the capitalist state in particular is an essential means of class domination. In as much as capitalist society is a class society, there is in reality no 'common interest'; the 'common interest' only appears as a part of the ideology which masks the reality of bourgeois domination. The state represents the interests of the bourgeoisie and is an essential mechanism for the imposition of those interests, through a combination of coercion and ideological manipulation, on the subordinated classes.

But this fundamental class character of the capitalist state does not mean that it is simply a direct instrument of the dominant class. Two basic reasons for this can be found in the political writings of Marx and Engels. Firstly, in capitalist social formations the dominant class itself is composed of different fractions whose immediate interests while not contradictory, are often in conflict. The state must be in a position to express the interest of the dominant class as a whole, irrespective of the particular interests of fractions of that class; it must, therefore, enjoy a degree of freedom or autonomy with respect to the various fractions of the dominant class. This line of reasoning, while not always explicit, can be clearly derived from Marx's analyses of the French state in the mid-nineteenth century (Marx, 1850, pp. 139–43, 189–90; 1852, pp.264, 272–3, 312). It is also the essential element in the often quoted dictum in the *Communist Manifesto* whereby 'the executive of the modern state is but a committee for managing the common affairs of the whole bourgeoisie' (Marx and Engels, 1848, p.36).

The second reason has to do with the relations between the dominant and the dominated classes in the capitalist state. Capitalism purports to be a society of equals, governed by the freedom of contract. The natural expression of that society in the political sphere is parliamentary bourgeois democracy (Engels, 1884, p.291) which allows the dominated class, the workers, some say in the running of the political system. This means that at least some of the interests of the dominated class must be taken into consideration by the state; the latter will need some autonomy to incorporate those subordinated interests which will in all likelihood conflict with the immediate interest of the dominant class. Furthermore, the fact that the actual political practice increasingly expresses the egalitarian aspects of the ideology of bourgeois domination, leads to the practice becoming increasingly contradictory with that domination. The workers will be able to achieve growing degrees of participation and influence in the system, notably through universal suffrage, and will begin to mount a challenge to the system itself. When the challenge reaches a certain level, a reaction to defend the system as such is required, and for that the state must, again, acquire a high degree of autonomy from the various fractions of the dominant class. This is the Bonapartist state and it is in this sense, as a response to a set of contradictions inherent in bourgeois domination, that it was characterised by Engels as 'the normal form' of the bourgeois state (Engels, 1866, p.171).[2] Bonapartism represents for Marx and Engels the extreme case of state autonomy vis-à-vis the dominant class. 'Only under the second Bonaparte', writes Marx in *The Eighteenth Brumaire*, 'does the State seem to have made itself completely independent' (Marx, 1852, p.333).

This apparently straightforward line of reasoning hides, however, some tricky conceptual difficulties. What is precisely meant by the state being autonomous from the dominant class? The clearest answer in the writings of Marx and Engels has to do with the class origins of the state personnel. The Bonapartist state is autonomous from the bourgeoisie in so far as it is not members of the latter that occupy the positions of power in the state apparatus. When the bourgeoisie sees its rule imperilled by the upheaval of the proletariat, Marx writes:

> in order to preserve its social power intact, its political power must be broken; . . . the individual bourgeois can continue to exploit the other classes and to enjoy undisturbed property, family, religion and order only on condition that their class be condemned along with the other classes to like political nullity (Marx, 1852, p.288).

It is difficult, however, to extend this reasoning to other forms of state. Marx himself notes instances in which the actual running of the capitalist state apparatus is completely in the hands of a class other than the bourgeoisie. Yet nevertheless the state is not specially autonomous from the bourgeoisie. This is the case of England in 1855, when, according to Marx, the bourgeoisie 'was on the whole acknowledged also *politically* as the *ruling* class' but only on condition that 'the entire system of government in all its details . . . remained safely in the hands of the landed aristocracy' (Marx, 1855, p.54). Marx is here, of course, reiterating the central notion that belonging to a class is not equivalent to carrying out the objective interests of that class; the latter, furthermore, are independent of the subjective perceptions of the members of the class. While important, the class origin of the state personnel is therefore not the decisive factor to character-ise the autonomy of the capitalist state. What, then, is?

By definition, the capitalist state must, in the last analysis, carry out the interests of the bourgeoisie; its autonomy can only be *relative*. On the other hand, there are *objective* but particular interests of frac-tions of capital which might be in conflict with each other and also with the general interest of the bourgeoisie as a whole. The state must be relatively autonomous in so far as it must ignore those par-ticular interests to carry out the common interests of the class. This is, however, an ambiguous formulation (how relative is 'relative'?) which represents an unresolved conceptual problem in the notion of relative autonomy. The problem is compounded in the analysis of peripheral capitalist societies because one of the relevant fractions of capital, in fact arguably the most important fraction of capital, is defined not in sectoral terms but in terms of its national affiliation: international capital. Furthermore, this is an aspect on which classical Marxist writings are of little help; the issue of the relative autonomy of the state is not discussed in those writings in its international di-mensions. The central point to be retained from this brief discussion of the classics is that the idea of relative autonomy is firmly derived from the analysis of class domination and the class struggle; from the identification of the conflictive nature of the dominant class and from the challenges to the hegemony of the dominant class posed by the proletariat.

# The relative autonomy of the state in Latin America: some distinctions

A first issue to be addressed in any attempt at applying the notion of relative autonomy of the state to the Latin American context is that the concept of the state in Marxist thought contains two meanings which are closely linked, to be sure, but different. On the one hand, the state refers to a 'pact of domination', i.e. a pact among the dominant classes and their different fractions in order to impose their domination and their interests on the rest of civil society. Expressions such as 'the social bases of the state' or 'the class nature of the state' refer to the state in this sense. On the other hand, the state is a set of institutions and personnel through which the fundamental class domination is expressed. The institutions include the repressive, bureaucratic and ideological apparatuses as well as productive organisations. The personnel include the top executive and legislative office-holders, sometimes termed 'state managers' (Block, 1980); the civilian and military bureaucracies, often partially overlapping with the former; and the managers of state enterprises, whose position is peculiar in as much as they are also posited as one of the components of the 'pact of domination', a view to which we shall come back later (Cardoso, 1979, pp.38–40; Cardoso and Faletto, 1979, pp.209–10).

From the viewpoint of this first distinction, the relative autonomy of the state can be defined as the degree of independence of the state managers vis-à-vis the social bases of the state; the extent to which they are free to pursue the common interests of the classes and fractions of classes that make up the pact of domination even against the particular interests of any of them separately, and the extent to which they can further their own interests *qua* distinctive social group.[3] A full exploration of the level of relative autonomy of the state in Latin America should therefore start by characterising these two aspects of the state. And it is here that the peculiar features of dependent capitalist societies begin to emerge in force.

To begin with, the local bourgeoisie in the Latin American countries appears to have been unable to consolidate its economic domination and its political hegemony (Nun, 1967; Weffort, 1968; Ianni, 1975). This is due to the weakness of the process of development of productive forces and capital accumulation under local control; in turn, this is a function of the insertion of the economy in a dependent position in the world capitalist system. The counterpart of this insertion is the presence of international capital as one of the fractions of capital, one that combines great economic power with some limitations to its political power due to its being foreign. An important effect of the absence of a dominant and hegemonic local bourgeoisie

and its coalescence with international capital *within* the social formation is that the state, in its institutional sense, acquires a growing role
in the productive sphere proper, not only providing infrastructure
or covering low profit areas, but in effect competing with private
capital in high profit sectors. Thus, the peculiarity of the dependent
capitalist state in the more industrialised Latin American countries
is that its social basis is composed of the internationalised fraction
of capital, the local bourgeoisie and the managers of the state enterprises. The latter are at times called:

> the 'state bourgeoisie', to emphasize that these social agents
> are not simple bureaucrats nor do they simply implement the
> 'public good'. They function sociologically as the 'office-holders
> of capital', for they support the accumulation of capital in the‹
> State enterprises (Cardoso and Faletto, 1979, p.210).

In this sense, the state in Latin America generates in part its own social
bases. This can be said to increase the relative autonomy of the 'state
managers' on two counts: firstly, it can make them more independent
of the non-state fractions within the pact of domination, i.e. international capital and local private capital. After all, the state bourgeoisie
are, in the last analysis, state employees, and while they have economic
power of their own through their direct control over state accumulation, they in turn depend, in a non-trivial sense, on the state office
holders; secondly, the degree of control of the state over economic
resources, including productive capital, increases the bases of power
of the state managers.

The second distinction that is relevant to our discussion refers to
the fundamental logic underlying the emergence, the role and the
forms of state in society. Two basic, distinctive approaches have been
put forward in this connection within contemporary Marxist theory.
What has been called the 'class-theoretical' approach, associated with
the name of Poulantzas, starts from the proposition that 'the task
of the state is to maintain the unity and cohesion of a social formation divided into classes' (Poulantzas, 1975, p.78). This the state
does by providing the conditions for the political organisation of
the dominant class and the political disorganisation of the dominated
class. The organisation of the dominant class proceeds through the
constitution of a 'power bloc' composed of its various fractions under
the overall direction, 'hegemony', of one of them. The state, however,
must take into account not only the interests of the hegemonic fraction but those of the non-hegemonic fractions in the power bloc as
well. The disorganisation of the dominated classes proceeds through
the masking of the class nature of economic relations and the claim
by the state to represent the general interest of individual subjects

who are equal before the law. This claim, in turn, requires that some of the interests of the dominated classes be taken into account by the state. On both counts, therefore, the state requires a degree of autonomy vis-à-vis the interests of the dominant classes (Poulantzas, 1973, Pt. IV, pp.255–321; 1978, pp.127ff).

The logic of operation of the state, and its relative autonomy, in this approach are therefore firmly rooted in class conflict and the class struggle (Poulantzas, 1976, p.73). To be sure, class conflict in capitalism is in turn rooted in accumulation and exploitation; but the class-theoretical approach is less interested in exploring the relationship between the state and accumulation than in understanding the 'relatively autonomous' dialectics of coercion, hegemony and ideology, and the political class struggle. This has led its critics to accuse it of having a 'political' bias; Poulantzas, in turn, is at pains to insist that his notion of the class struggle does not refer solely to the political level but also to the economic and ideological, and that the political is, in the last instance, determined by the economic (Poulantzas, 1976). By contrast, the approach that has been termed 'capital-logic', associated with the names of Altvater, Müller and Neussüs and Hirsch, takes as its starting point the analysis of the contradictions of the process of capital accumulation. The task of the state is to overcome those contradictions and allow for the continuing expanded reproduction of capital. Its emergence, its form, its functions and the possibilities and constraints of its actions can in this sense be derived from the logic of movement of capital. The starting point for the analysis of the state is therefore the exploration of the laws of motion of capital and its contradictions, notably the tendency for the rate of profit to fall.[4]

The extent to which there are fundamental differences between the class-theoretical and the capital-logic approaches tends to be exaggerated, not least by their respective supporters engaged in vigorous polemics.[5] As suggested above, any Marxist analyst would accept that the class struggle in capitalism stems from the exploitation of the working class through the extraction of surplus value, and this in turn is the essential mechanism of capitalist accumulation; conversely, the process of accumulation proceeds in concrete terms through the complementary/contradictory relation between workers and capitalists and among fractions of capital, i.e. through class conflict and the class struggle. There are, nonetheless, significant differences in starting points and in emphases between the two approaches, and relating those to the discussion of the Latin American context would appear worthwhile.

How can we, then, relate these two sets of distinctions to some of the contributions in this volume? It would not be sensible to try to categorise in a simple fashion what are complex and sophisticated pieces of social science analysis. Some broad correlations, however, can be offered.

Evans' analysis of the 'triple alliance' in Brazil focuses on the social bases of the Brazilian state rather than on institutions and bureaucracies — although to be sure, the latter are introduced at crucial points; and in this respect it essentially incorporates the characterisation of the 'pact of domination' suggested above. At the same time, his fundamental line of reasoning seems to follow class-theoretical lines. Evans does not employ a Marxist frame of reference, and does not use notions such as power bloc, hegemony or even relative autonomy, in the sense defined above; in fact, he puts great emphasis on the importance of the contradictions in the process of dependent capitalist industrialisation for understanding the vicissitudes of the triple alliance in the late seventies and the early eighties. The underlying logic, however, *is* that of class relations (of power alliances and conflict among the TNCs, the local capitalists and the state bourgeoisie) and of the relations between the institutional apparatus of the state — and its personnel, the state managers — and the three fractions that constitute its social bases. In spite of clear conflicts of interests, the three partners in the alliance were bound together by a complex calculus of costs and benefits, made possible by the exclusionary policies implemented by the post-1964 Brazilian state, by the internal dynamism of the process of capital accumulation and by the favourable international economic environment. When the internal dynamism begins to show signs of exhaustion and the external environment takes a dramatic downturn in the mid-1970s the conflicts become paramount and the political tensions within the alliance intensify. The most affected partner, and the one who reacts most vocally, is local private capital. The local bourgeoisie feels threatened both by the growing penetration of the TNCs and by the expansion of the state productive sector. Some groups within it respond by taking a more nationalistic stance; others by emphasising the dangers of statism. However, the common defining element in the 'entrepreneurial rebellion' is the opposition to the political structure of the state: the local bourgeoisie, excluded from decision making alongside the workers, begins to mount a challenge to the autonomy of the military state and to campaign for redemocratisation.

As the state cannot afford the disaffection of international capital, the paradoxical possibility emerges of the state attempting to support both TNCs and local capital by sacrificing the state productive sector. Evans highlights the dialectical nature of the concept of 'state bourgeoisie' when he suggests that 'state enterprises have enjoyed, on the whole, a high degree of "relative autonomy" vis-à-vis the central state apparatus'. Here we have one of the constituents of the social bases of the state being 'relatively autonomous' from the state institutional apparatus and its personnel, an unexpected inversion of the use of the term relative autonomy as compared with our previous definition. He then goes on to say:

> the division between state capital in its entrepreneurial guise and the central bureaucratic apparatus also opens the possibility that the latter could turn against the former . . . it has become increasingly clear in recent years that trimming the wings of state enterprises could be an attractive project for a regime anxious to build support simultaneously among both local capital and the TNCs.

What Evans is then saying is that the Brazilian state in the late 1960s and early 1970s enjoyed a significant degree of relative autonomy vis-à-vis both the TNCs and the local bourgeoisie because of the peculiar nature of the 'pact of domination', which included in addition the state bourgeoisie. The power of the latter within the pact grew as did the role of the public sector in direct accumulation; but the state bureaucracies were still able to pursue autonomous policies in as much as the interests of the other two partners also had to be taken into account. When the accumulation process in the mid-1970s loses dynamism and the alliance comes under stress, the relative autonomy of the state is imperilled; international capital reasserts its hegemony and the pressures of local capital tend to lead the state managers towards an attack on state enterprises and therefore the state bourgeoisie, which would further reduce the basis of their own autonomy.

Evans discusses the impact of changes in the external environment on the stability of the triple alliance, but does not treat specifically the issue of the relative autonomy of the Brazilian state vis-à-vis the world economy. From his overall analysis, though, it is clear that he avoids the trap that both Cardoso and, in a different context, Poulantzas warn against, namely that of considering inter-state relations as if states were self-contained and homogeneous actors. Here, the class nature of the state reappears as the crucial element. The question, as Cardoso and Faletto put it, is not whether Latin American states have become less dependent; the concern is to ask:

> less for whom? for which classes and groups? Which classes have become more sovereign? Which alliances and class interests within each country and at the international level lead the historical process of economic development? (Cardoso and Faletto, 1979, p.201).[6]

In the 1960s and early 1970s the Brazilian state was increasingly able to further the common interest of the triple alliance, broadly defined in terms of local accumulation, in its relationship with other national capitalist classes and the state managers of those nations as representatives of the common interests of those classes. In the process, the Brazilian state managers increased their own relative autonomy with respect to the 'world system', an outcome which might be taking place also in Mexico and Venezuela, as Chapter 7 suggests.

Yet the preceding discussion seems to be inapplicable to some of the other Latin American countries in which military regimes exist that are relatively autonomous from the internal class structure. In Chile, Argentina and Uruguay the state bourgeoisie is precisely being dismantled by the state itself through the privatisation of public enterprises. The triple alliance à la Brazil does not exist. The peculiar nature of the alliance in power cannot explain the relative autonomy of the state in the way in which Evans' analysis (Chapter 6) explains it for Brazil and similar cases.

It is at this point that FitzGerald's approach (Chapter 5) to the concept of relative autonomy of the state becomes apposite. By contrast to Evans, FitzGerald focuses on the state managers, rather than on the power bloc, and on what he calls the 'macroeconomic management' tasks – the regulation of the economy, notably of foreign trade and finance – rather than on the direct production of commodities. By the same token, his view is that the fundamental logic of the relative autonomy of the state lies less on the dialectics of the class struggle than in the movement of capital, particularly in the sphere of circulation. The central constraint to accumulation in the periphery is the realisation problem understood in terms of the availability of foreign exchange for the purchase of both consumption and capital goods. This bottleneck can only be broken by the state becoming a 'financial intermediary in its own right'. This both requires and gives the state increased relative autonomy internally; on the other hand, it might reduce its autonomy vis-à-vis the world system, except in the case of very large borrowers. It further reproduces within the state the financial contradictions that it is attempting to solve in the economy as a whole; it thus exacerbates the fiscal crisis brought about by the growing requirement of state expenditure in support of accumulation and in keeping down the cost of wage goods, e.g. through food imports, coupled with political difficulties to expand the tax base. A result is a 'special relationship' between the state and the financial fraction of the bourgeoisie, whose central role in the alliance in power is highlighted by FitzGerald when he notes that finance capital, in Hilferding's sense, is the main form in which domestic capital is organised. He questions the notion of 'industrial bourgeoisie' and instead suggests that industrial, agrarian, trading and construction groups as well as foreign firms have developed forms of co-ordination mediated by the banking system. This does not preclude some degree of conflict among those various sectors; indeed, FitzGerald suggests that elements of those conflicts penetrate the structure of the state, where the state managers in charge of the financial sector collide with those in charge of planning offices, industry ministries and state enterprises. But it is certainly not a mere reflection of the underlying conflict among fractions of the capitalist class. The state managers are relatively autonomous of their social bases because of the requirements of macroeconomic management in peripheral capitalism; they develop their own ideologies in response to those requirements and taking into primary consideration their own interests *qua* distinctive group. Thus, the ECLA approach of the 1950s and 1960s, with its emphasis on industrialisation, reform, redistribution and state intervention is said to have been 'objectively in the interest of these managers themselves'.[7] And it is against this approach that the 'financial fraction' of the state managers reacts by pressing a monetarist approach, albeit of the Stanford or structuralist kind rather than of the Chicago variety. This approach also entails considerable state-imposed discipline on both workers and capitalists, the latter being forced to subject themselves to international competition. It thus requires 'a relatively autonomous state and powerful state managers'.

FitzGerald approvingly quotes Evers as saying that:

> the relative autonomy of the Latin American state as to its socio-economic environment − and also to the world market − is a necessary premise for the fulfilment of its function of guaranteeing the insertion of the local economy into the world economy.

The nature of this autonomy can only be explained in terms of the 'organic necessities of capitalism'. There is, however, need to supplement this explanation with elements relating to the political class struggle in order to fully understand the emergence of relatively autonomous military regimes in countries such as Chile, Argentina or Uruguay. FitzGerald, to be sure, is very sensitive to the importance of the internal class struggle in the dialectics of peripheral capitalism; in fact, he sees his contribution as providing a much needed corrective to the view that different models of accumulation are a function of the logic of the international division of labour rather than of the domestic class struggle. However, the issue here is the role of increased class polarisation, with the attendant threat to the system, leading to an increasingly repressive response. Elements of the 'Bonapartist' view of the relative autonomy of the state can be of help; the military and the techno-bureaucracy in those countries acquire a degree of autonomy with respect to both the local and the internationalised bourgeoisies in so far as they represent the only perceived way of confronting the challenge to the system posed by the subordinated classes, expressed either in mass movements such as *Unidad Popular* in Chile or Peronismo in Argentina, or in guerilla activity, as in Argentina and Uruguay in the early 1970s. O'Donnell's explanation of the emergence of bureaucratic authoritarianism (Collier, 1979) seems therefore more relevant than FitzGerald is prepared to admit. Indeed, it is also relevant to Evans' approach as a supplement to the latter's emphasis on the conflicts and tensions within the dominant class.

## Conclusion

We have suggested that the two most detailed treatments of the question of the relative autonomy of the state among the contributions to this volume, those of Evans and FitzGerald, seem to occupy opposite places in each of the dichotomies introduced above. While Evans emphasises the question of the social bases of the state and adopts broadly a class struggle approach, FitzGerald concerns himself primarily with the state institutions and personnel and favours a capital-logic explanation. Hopefully, two points should have emerged from our discussion: firstly, that this characterisation simplifies what are considerably more complex and subtle analyses combining, albeit in different proportions, all the conceptual components of the notion of relative autonomy presented above; secondly, that a truly satisfactory explanation should persevere along the path of combining the various approaches and explanatory factors. In this vein, several issues for further research seem to emerge from our attempt to link Evans' and FitzGerald's contributions to the debate about relative autonomy in the Marxist tradition. To begin with, Evans' emphasis on the relationship between the state bureaucracies and the managers of state enterprises raises important questions on which further empirical work is required. No doubt because of the constraints of a summary piece, Evans' own brief discussion of the issue seems to present a relatively unproblematic picture of the relationship: state bureaucracies and the state bourgeoisie appear as independent and self-contained actors. It would be extremely interesting to pursue this issue asking questions such as: what is the actual class composition and otherwise of the two groups? What is their degree of cohesiveness and self-perpetuation? Do they hold distinctive social projects? Do they overlap? What are their relationships? The inquiry would then probably try to answer similar questions in the relationship between state managers and the local bourgeoisie. Some work addressing these issues is already available,[8] but considerably more research seems to be necessary.

FitzGerald's line of approach opens up different kinds of concerns. One that is discussed by Griffith-Jones (Chapter 3) has to do with the extent to which the relative autonomy of the state managers vis-à-vis the world system is affected by the growing involvement of the state in external and internal financial management. More generally, the application of the concept of relative autonomy to the relation with the world system (discussed in Chapter 4) is one that could profit from additional theoretical and empirical work.

Lastly, as we have already suggested, in both Evans and FitzGerald there tends to be a concentration on the dynamics of the relationship among fractions of the dominant class and between them and the state managers. This is fully justified given the more specific foci of the contributions. On the other hand, one should not lose sight of the fundamental dynamic of capitalism, central or peripheral, the relation between the dominant and the dominated classes.[9] Work along these lines, that can take advantage of contributions of the kind contained in this volume and discussed here, is a crucial future task of Latin American development analysts.

## Notes

1  For Latin America, collections of articles containing both overall treatments and case studies include: FitzGerald, Floto and Lehman (1977); Carrière (1979); Collier (1979). Hamilton (1981) has an up-to-date bibliography. For Africa and South Asia relevant discussions can be found in various issues of *Review of African Political Economy* and *The Socialist Register*. The debate on the 'overdeveloped post-colonial state' is particularly important; see Leys (1976) for a summary and critique with bibliography.

2  The contradiction between this statement and the previous one, that the natural form of bourgeois domination is parliamentary democracy, is often noted. We are suggesting that they express two different moments of a dialectical process.

3  There is, of course, a serious question as to the extent to which the state managers can be said to constitute a coherent group with identifiable common interests and some degree of continuity, as opposed to a changing functional social category comprising various interests. A distinction between the top, political office-holders and the bureaucracy might be required; the latter are probably more cohesive and continuous than the 'political élite' in many Latin American countries. Block's treatment in this connection appears deceptively straightforward.

4  Holloway and Picciotto (1978) is an excellent collection of relevant articles.

5  For a rather extreme example see Clarke (1977).

6  Poulantzas' obverse question has to do with the extent to which the internationalisation of capital could have made the European states more subordinate to the centre of capitalism, the US; his answer is also that the question should be posed in class, not state terms (Poulantzas, 1975, p.70).

7  FitzGerald draws an interesting comparison with Keynesianism, described as corresponding to the 'outlook of the senior permanent civil service, regarding them as 'above' the direct pressures of the class struggle and responsible for the survival of capitalism in the long run'.

8  See article by L. Martins cited in the bibliography.

9  Evans does discuss some of the implications of heightened political activity and unrest among Brazilian workers, but does not link the discussion specifically to the question of the relative autonomy of the state.

# Appendix: Authoritarianism and militarism in contemporary Latin America

Some scholars have compared the totalitarian governments of the Western Hemisphere with European fascism. Whatever the analogies and differences may be, it is undeniable that these totalitarian regimes replace the full exercise of democracy by authoritarianism, despotism, the limitation and even the suppression of civil liberties. The implementation of class discrimination, harsh treatment of the opposition and the systematic rejection of the just demands of the majority of the population to improve their precarious living conditions are all accompanied by the control of the mass media and the suppression of all critical thought.

Behind this image of repression the underlying reality is the confrontation between two capitalist models which correspond to two stages in the historical continuum of capitalist development: inward-oriented and outward-oriented growth.

Until the 1960s it was the first of these models that prevailed in Latin America. This model, known as 'import substitution' or 'endogenous development', was characterised by relative technological backwardness with respect to the industrialised countries; by the predominance of national capital in industrial development mainly oriented towards the production of direct consumer goods for the domestic market; by the predominance of foreign capital in the export

* Statement prepared by B. Osorio-Tafall and A. Briones of CEESTEM (Centro de Estudios Económicos y Sociales del Tercer Mundo) and delivered at the Millennium Conference held at the London School of Economics on 30 April and 1 May 1981.

sector; and by an import list made up fundamentally of capital goods and luxury consumer goods.

The interaction of the different social elements present in the import substitution model resulted in a shift towards the configuration of a new development pattern characterised by the concentration of capital and higher technology in order to achieve higher levels of output. This new model of development requires access to foreign markets for manufactured goods and increased inputs of foreign capital. Foreign markets are needed because of the narrowness of the domestic market, a narrowness which even an eventual redistribution of income would fail to correct. Foreign capital is necessary in order to obtain the higher technology and investment levels required by the new model. Consequently the new growth model responds exclusively to the interests of transnational enterprises and domestic big business.

The previous model of 'endogenous development' involved the establishment of a diversified industrial structure protected by high tariff barriers. These allowed the subsistence of a significant number of small and medium-sized enterprises with low productivity, and elicited the political support of the 'middle sectors'. On the level of labour relations, a system of dialogue with the working class alternated with periods of repression. This economic policy, and the role played in it by the land-owning oligarchy and the less dynamic sectors of the industrial bourgeoisie, was called into question in the mid-1960s, due to the obstacles it imposed to the new growth model.

The path towards the consolidation of a new dominant bloc to exclude the land-owning classes and the industrial bourgeoisie linked to the local market followed alternative courses according to the previous degree of independence from the state attained by the working classes. In those countries where the working classes were politically dependent upon the state, the reforms required by big national and transnational capital were relatively bloodless. But where trade unions showed a high degree of independence, such 'peaceful transfer' of power between social blocs was not possible.

The first situation has emerged in the northern countries of Latin America, with the exception of the Central American nations. The second can be found in the extreme south. Here, the transition towards the new growth model, and thus a power shift, has had as a necessary condition authoritarian and highly repressive regimes. The armed forces in these countries have been instrumental both to the policy shift and to the interests of the social minority which pursues the shift.

Despite differences between countries in the Southern Cone of Latin America, there are three constant policy elements: monetary stabilisation, measures which favour capital concentration and measures

212

geared towards a new insertion in the world economy. The stabilisation efforts draw heavily upon the quantity theory of money. They aim at a reduction in aggregate demand, through a fall in real wages, and at a reduction of government deficit spending. Capital concentration is caused by the bankruptcies of small and medium-sized enterprises whose assets are absorbed by the big industrial and financial enterprises. The reduction in aggregate demand as a result of the stabilisation policies creates an overstocking crisis to which smaller enterprises are especially vulnerable. The damage to the small and medium-sized enterprise is compounded as previous protectionist policies are replaced by drastic reductions in customs tariffs and the elimination of import restrictions which render them uncompetitive. Such structural change brings about a new form of insertion in the world economy. As the measures described above increase both the technological level and the efficiency of the industrial sector, the economy changes its export profile from one heavily reliant on primary commodities to one with a greater share of manufactured goods. But the structural change has as a necessary condition an increased role for foreign capital. Hence the economic policy also includes measures oriented to attract foreign investment.

## Results

The socio-economic structure resulting from the above mentioned policies can be characterised by deep internal inequalities, increased concentration of wealth, consumerism and domination by a small social minority. This small fraction rules via the military. Logically, a situation of this nature can only be sustained by the establishment of anti-democratic regimes.

In practice, of course, things are not as blunt as we have described them here. Dictatorships do not openly reveal their nature nor their inclination to defend the interests of a small minority of the population against those of the people. Instead, they make use of a dense network of ideological postulates in an attempt to justify their actions. Thus, totalitarian regimes claim that constraints to Latin American growth are reinforced by so-called subversive ideologies; by the frequency and intensity of social conflicts, many of which are provoked by political parties; by governmental instability; by the weakness of the political parties; and by the want of charismatic leaders. This, they believe, is compounded by weak governments unable to contain social movements which threaten to change the status quo drastically.

The truth, however, is that the changes sought by authoritarian regimes have only led to increased inequalities. In countries such as Argentina, Brazil, Chile and Uruguay there now is a part of the population whose falling standard of living was unimaginable a few years ago. In Latin America today, despite capitalist development, no military government has raised the standard of living of the population as a whole or achieved solutions to the multiple problems confronting these countries. The social cost of their economic policies has been enormous.

214

# Biographical notes on contributors

**Carlos F. Díaz Alejandro** is a Professor at the Department of Economics of the University of Yale. He has been a consultant to several international committees and organisations. His publications include *Essays on the Economic History of the Argentine Republic* and *Foreign Trade Regimes and Economic Development*.

**Peter B. Evans** is the author of *Dependent Development: The Alliance of Multinational, State and Local Capital in Brazil* and numerous articles on multinational corporations and development. He has taught at the University of Brasilia and currently teaches sociology at Brown University in Providence, Rhode Island.

**Aldo Ferrer** has taught at the University of Buenos Aires and has held several government positions in Argentina. He has published books and articles on the international economy and on Argentine economic development.

**E.V.K. FitzGerald** has been Assistant Director of Development Studies at Cambridge and is currently Professor of Development Economics at The Hague, and an advisor to the Nicaraguan government. His main research interest is the role of the state in capital accumulation and income distribution, and he has recently published *The Political Economy of Peru, 1956–78*.

**Carlos Fortín** has taught at the Latin American School of Political Science and Public Administration (FLACSO) in Santiago, where he was also Director of Studies. He was Head of the European Bureau of the Chilean Copper Corporation from 1971 to 1973 and is currently Deputy Director of the Institute of Development Studies at the University of Sussex. He has published numerous articles on the international political economy of natural resources and on the role of the state in economic development.

**Stephany Griffith-Jones** is currently a Research Fellow at the Institute of Development Studies. Her research focuses on international finance and on national adjustment policies. She has recently published *The Role of Finance in the Transition to Socialism*.

**George Philip** is Lecturer in Latin American politics jointly at the Institute of Latin American Studies and the London School of Economics. He is co-editor of the *Bulletin of Latin American Research* and has recently published *Oil and Politics in Latin America*.

**Diana Tussie** has taught at the University of Buenos Aires and at the Technological University of Argentina. She was Deputy and then Associate Editor of *Millennium* and is currently doing her doctoral research at the London School of Economics where she also teaches.

# Bibliography

Abel, C. and Lewis, C., *Economic Imperialism in Latin America*, London University Press, London, 1983.

Abranches, Sérgio, *The Divided Leviathan: State and Economic Policy Formation in Authoritarian Brazil*, PhD dissertation, Cornell University, 1978.

Adelman, M., 'The World Oil Outlook' in M. Clawson (ed.), *Natural Resources and International Development*, John Hopkins, Baltimore, 1964.

Adelman, M., *The World Petroleum Market*, John Hopkins, Baltimore, 1973.

Amin, S., *Accumulation on a World Scale*, Monthly Review Press, New York, 1974.

Araújo, José Tavares and Dick, Vera, 'Governo, Empresas Multinacionais, e Empresas Nacionais: O Caso da Industria Petroquimica', *Pesquisa e Planejamento*, vol.4, no.3, 1974, pp.629–54.

Baer, Werner, *The Brazilian Economy: Its Growth and Development*, Grid Publishing, Columbus, Oh., 1979.

Baer, Werner, Newfarmer, R.S. and Trebat, T., 'On State Capitalism in Brazil: Some New Issues and Questions', in *Inter-American Economic Affairs*, vol.30, no.3, 1977, pp.69–96.

Banco Central de Venezuela, Reports.

Banco de México, Annual Reports.

Bank for International Settlements, *Annual Report*, Basle, 1981a.

Bank for International Settlements, *The Maturity Distribution of International Bank Lending*, Basle, July 1981b.

Baran, P., *The Political Economy of Growth*, Stanford University Press, 1957.

Bernstein, H., *Underdevelopment and Development: The Third World Today*, Penguin, Harmondsworth, 1973.

Billerback, K., and Yasugi, Y., *Private Direct Investment in Developing Countries*, World Bank Staff Working Paper no.348, July 1977.

Bilson, John F.O., 'Civil Liberty – An Econometric Investigation', in *Kyklos*, January 1982.

Blackhurst, R., Marin, N. and Tumlir, J., *Trade Liberalization, Protectionism and Interdependence*, GATT, Geneva, 1977.

Block, Fred, *The Origins of the International Economic Disorder*, University of California Press, California, 1977.

Block, Fred, 'Beyond Relative Autonomy: State Managers as Historical Subjects', *The Socialist Register 1980*, Merlin Press, London, pp. 227–42, 1980.

Braun, Oscar, *Comercio Internacional e Imperialismo*, Siglo XXI, Buenos Aires, 1973.

217

Brenner, R., 'The Origins of Capitalist Development: A critique of neo-Smithian Marxism', in *New Left Review*, no.104, 1977.

Brett, E.A., 'The International Monetary Fund, the International Monetary System and the Periphery', in *IFDA Dossier*[5], Geneva, March 1979.

Brunhoff, S. de, *The State, Capital and Economic Policy*, Pluto Press, London, 1978.

Buira, A., 'Recession, Inflation and the International Monetary System', in *World Development*, vol.9, no.11/12, 1981.

*Business Latin America*, (referred to as *BLA*), *Business International Corporation*, New York, 1979, 1980, 1981, various issues.

*Business Week*, 9 November 1981.

Camps, Miriam and Gwin, Catherine, *Collective Management: The Reform of Global Economic Organisations*, McGraw-Hill Book Company, New York, 1981.

Canitrot, A., 'Discipline as the Central Objective of Economic Policy: an Essay on the Economic Programme of the Argentine Government since 1976', in *World Development*, vol.8, 1980.

Cardoso, Fernando H., *Autoritarismo e Democratizaçao*, Editora Paz e Terra, Rio de Janeiro, 1975.

Cardoso, Fernando H., 'The Consumption of Dependency Theory in the United States', in *Latin America Research Review*, vol.12, no.3, 1977.

Cardoso, Fernando H., 'Capitalist Development and the State', in *Ibero-Americana*, Special Issue, 1978.

Cardoso, Fernando H., 'On the Characterization of Authoritarian Regimes in Latin America', in D. Collier (ed.), 1979, pp.33—57.

Cardoso, Fernando H. and Faletto, E., *Dependencia y Desarrollo en America Latina*, Siglo XXI, Mexico, 1969.

Cardoso, Fernando H. and Faletto, E., *Dependency and Development in Latin America*, University of California Press, Berkeley, 1979.

Carrière, J. (ed.), *Industrialization and the State in Latin America*, CEDLA, Amsterdam, 1979.

Clarke, S., 'Marxism, Sociology and Poulantzas' Theory of the State', in *Capital and Class*, no.2, 1977, pp.1—31.

Collier, D. (ed.), *The New Authoritarianism in Latin America*, Princeton University Press, Princeton N.J., 1979.

Corredor, J., 'El Petróleo en México', in *Uno Más Uno*, 18 March 1981.

Daniel, P., 'The New Recycling: Economic Theory, IMF Conditionality and Balance of Payments Adjustment in the 1980s', in *Monetarism' and the Third World*, *IDS Bulletin*, vol.13, no.1, 1981.

Dell, S. and Lawrence, R., *The Balance of Payments Adjustment Process in Developing Countries*, Pergamon, United Nations, New York, 1980.

Díaz Alejandro, Carlos F., 'Trade Policies and Economic Development', in Peter B. Kenen (ed.), *International Trade and Finance*, Cambridge University Press, Cambridge, 1975a.

Díaz Alejandro, Carlos F., 'North-South Relations: The Economic Component', in *International Organization*, vol.29, no.1, Winter, 1975b.

Díaz Alejandro, Carlos F., 'Delinking North and South: Unshackled or Unhinged?', in A. Fishlow, et al., *Rich and Poor Nations in the World Economy*, McGraw-Hill Book Company, New York, 1978.

Díaz Alejandro, Carlos F., 'Latin America in Depression, 1929–1939', in *Yale Economic Growth Center Discussion Papers*, no.344, March 1980a.

Díaz Alejandro, Carlos F., 'Latin America and the World Economy in the 1980s', in *Economic Forum*, vol.11, no.2, Winter 1980b.

Díaz Alejandro, Carlos F., 'The Less Developed Countries and Transnational Enterprises', in Sven Grossman and Erik Landberg (eds), *The World Economic Order: Past and Prospect*, Macmillan Press, London, 1981a.

Díaz Alejandro, Carlos F., 'Stories of the 1930s for the 1980s', in *Yale Economic Growth Center Discussion Papers*, no.376, April 1981b.

Díaz Alejandro, Carlos F. and Bacha, E., 'Financial markets: a view from the periphery', paper presented at International Seminar on External Financial Relations, Santiago de Chile, Mimeo, 19–21 March 1981.

Diniz Cerqueira, Eli and Renato Boschi, 'Elite Industrial e Estado: Uma Análise de Ideologia do Empresariado Nacional nos Anos 70', in Carlos Estevan Martins (ed.) *Estado e Capitalismo no Brasil*, Editora Hucitec–CEBRAP, pp.167–88, 1977.

Diniz Cerqueira, Eli and Renato Boschi, *Empresariado Nacional e Estado no Brasil*, Editora Forense Universitaria, Rio de Janeiro, Brazil, 1978.

Dixit, Avinash, 'The Export of Capital Theory', in *Journal of International Economics*, vol.11, no.2, May 1981.

Dorfman, A., 'Los nuevos grupos de poder y el sector industrial público' in J. Carrière (ed.) *Industrialization and the State in Latin America*, CEDLA, Amsterdam, 1979.

Dos Santos, T., 'The Structure of Dependence', in *American Economic Review*, vol.60, no.2, May 1970, pp.231–7.

Dreifuss, Rene, *1964: A Conquista do Estado: Ação Politica, Poder e Golpe de Classe,* Editora Vozes, São Paulo, 1981.

ECLA, *Economic Survey of Latin America 1951–52*, United Nations, New York, 1953.

ECLA, *Economic Survey of Latin America: 1974*, United Nations, New York, 1976.

ECLA, *Economic Survey of Latin America: 1978*, United Nations, New York, 1980.

ECLA, *Economic Survey of Latin America: 1979*, United Nations, New York, 1981.

*Economist Quarterly Report*, 1981, p.153.

EEC, *Un Projet pour l'Europe*, Brussels, 1978.

Engels, F., *The Origins of the Family, Private Property and the State*, (1884) in K. Marx and F. Engels (1949), pp.155–296.

Engels, F., Letter to Karl Marx, 13 April, 1866, in K. Marx and F. Engels (1965), p.171.

*Estado de São Paulo*, pp. 156 and 160.

Evans, D., 'Monopoly Power and Imperialism: Oscar Braun's Theory of Unequal Exchange' in *Development and Change* vol.12, 1981.

Evans, P.B., *Dependent Development: The Alliance of Multinational, State and Local Capital in Brazil*, Princeton University Press, Princeton N.J., 1979.

Evans, P.B., 'Collectivized Capitalism: Integrated Petrochemical Complexes and Capital Accumulation in Brazil', in T.C. Bruneau and P. Faucher (eds), *Authoritarian Capitalism: The Contemporary Economic and Political Development of Brazil*, Westview Press, Boulder, CO, 1981, pp.85–125.

Evans, P.B., 'Recent research on Multinational Corporations' in *Annual Review of Sociology*, 1981, pp.199–223.

Evers, T., *El estado en la periferia capitalista*, Siglo XXI, Mexico City, 1979.

*Express, L'*, p.97.

Feinberg, R.E., *Subsidizing Success: The Export-Import Bank in the United States Economy*, Cambridge University Press, New York, 1982.

Ferrer, A., 'The Structure of the World Economy: Southern Perspectives' in E. Lazlo and J. Kurtzman (eds), *The Structure of the World Economy and the Prospects for a New International Economic Order*, Pergamon Press, New York, 1982.

Fiechter, Georges-Andre, *Brazil Since 1964: Modernization Under a Military Regime*, John Wiley and Sons, New York, 1975.

Findlay, Ronald, 'Commentary' in R.C. Amacher, G. Haberler and T.D. Willett (eds), *Challenges to a Liberal Economic Order*, American Enterprise Institute for Public Policy Research, Washington, 1979.

FitzGerald, E.V.K., 'The Fiscal Crisis of the Latin American State' in J.F.J. Toye (ed.), *Taxation and Economic Development*, Cass, London, 1978.

FitzGerald, E.V.K., 'Aspects of Finance Capital in Latin America' in C. Abel and C. Lewis (eds) 1983.

FitzGerald, E.V.K., Floto, E. and Lehman, A.D. (eds), *The State and Economic Development in Latin America*, Cambridge University Printing House, Cambridge, 1977.

Flores de la Peña, H., *Teoría y práctica del desarrollo*, Fondo de Cultura Económica, Mexico City, 1976.

Fragoso, J.M., *El poder de la gran burguesía*, Editorial Cultura Popular, Mexico City, 1979.

Frank, A.G., *Capitalism and Underdevelopment: Historical Studies of Chile and Brazil*, Monthly Review Press, New York and London, 1967.

Frankel, P.H., *Essentials of Petroleum*, Allen and Unwin, London, 1946.

Fröbel, F., Heinrichs, J. and Kreye, O., *The New International Division of Labour*, Cambridge University Press, Cambridge, 1980.

Galbraith, J.K., 'The Economic and Social Consensus and the Conservative Onslaught', *Millennium: Journal of International Studies*, vol.11, no.1, 1982, pp.1–14.

*Gazeta Mercantil*, Brazil; discontent with state apparatus, p.152.

Gereffi, Gary and Evans, Peter, 'Transnational Corporations, Dependent Development and State Policy in the Semi-periphery: A Comparison of Brazil and Mexico' in *Latin American Research Review*, vol.16, no.3, 1981.

Griffith-Jones, S., 'The Alliance for Progress: An Attempt at Interpretation' in *Development and Change*, vol.10, no.3, July 1979.

Griffith-Jones, S., 'The Growth of Multinational Banking, the Eurocurrency Market and the Effects on Developing Countries' in *Journal of Development Studies*, vol.16, no.2, June 1980.

Griffith-Jones, S., 'The Impact of the 1981 Saudi Arabian Loan to the IMF', *IDS Discussion Paper*, no.170, Sussex University, 1982.

Hamilton, N., 'State autonomy and dependent capitalism in Latin America' in *British Journal of Sociology*, vol.32, no.3, September 1981, pp.305–29.

Haberler, Gottfried, 'The Political Economy of Regional or Continental Blocs' in Seymour E. Harris (ed.), *Postwar Economic Problems*, McGraw Hill Book Company, New York, 1943.

Haberler, Gottfried, 'Postscript' in R.C. Amacher, G. Haberler and T.D. Willett (eds), *Challenges to a Liberal International Economic Order*, American Enterprise Institute for Public Policy Research, Washington, 1979.

Helleiner, G.K., 'Intra-firm Trade and the Developing Countries: An Assessment of the Data' in *Journal of Development Economics*, vol.6, 1979, pp.391–406.

Herrera, J.E. and Morales, J., 'Opening Up to the Outside World and its effects on the national recovery: the case of Chile' in *IFDA Dossier*, 11, Geneva, Switzerland, September 1979.

Hilferding, R., *Finance Capital*, Routledge and Kegan Paul, London, 1981.

Hirschman, Albert, 'The turn to authoritarianism in Latin America and the search for its economic determinants' in David Collier (ed.), 1979.

Holloway, J. and Picciotto, S. (eds), *State and Capital: A Marxist Debate*, Edward Arnold, London, 1978.

Huntington, S., *Political Order in Changing Societies*, Yale University Press, 1968.

IDS, 'Monetarism: and the Third World', *Bulletin of the Institute of Development Studies*, vol.13, no.1, 1981.

IMF, *Direction of Trade Yearbook*, Washington DC, 1970–71/1978–79.

IMF, *International Financial Statistics*, Washington DC, 1980.

IMF, *IMF Survey*, Washington DC, 18 May 1981.

IMF, *World Economic Outlook*, Washington DC, 1981a.

IMF, *IMF Survey*, Washington DC, 8 February 1982.

Ianni, O., *La formación del estado populista en América Latina*, Era, México, 1975.

Inter-American Development Bank, *Economic and Social Progress in Latin America*, Washington DC, 1979.

Jacoby, N., *Multinational Oil: a Study in Industrial Dynamics*, Columbia University Press, New York, 1974.

Jenkins, R., 'Latin America and the New International Division of Labour: a Critique of Some Recent Views' in Abel and Lewis (eds), 1983.

Kaplan, M., *Formación del estado nacional en América Latina*, Editorial Universitaria, Santiago, 1960.

Kay, G., *Development and Underdevelopment: A Marxist Analysis*, Macmillan, London and St Martin's Press, New York, 1975.

Knight, Peter T., 'Brazilian Socioeconomic Development: Issues for the Eighties' in *World Development*, vol.9, no.11/12, 1981.

Kregel, J.A., *The Reconstruction of Political Economy*, Macmillan, London, 1973.

Krugman, Paul R., 'A model of innovative technology transfer and the world distribution of income' in *Journal of Political Economy*, vol.87, no.2, April 1979.

Lal, Deepak, *The Resurrection of the Pauper-Labour Argument*, Thames Essay no.28, Trade Policy Research Centre, London, 1981.

Lamfalussy, A., 'Changing attitudes towards capital movements', paper presented at Conference on Changing Perceptions of Economic Policy, Oxford, 27–29 March, 1981.

*Latin American Weekly Report* (formerly *Latin American Economic Report*, referred to as *LAWR, LAER*), London, 1979, 1980, 1981, various issues.

Lechner, N., *La crisis del estado en América Latina*, Editorial El Cid, Caracas, 1977.

Lessa, Carlos, *A Estratégia de Desenvolvimento 1974–1976: Sonho e Fracasso*, Reproarte, Rio de Janeiro, 1979.

Levinson, J. and Onis, J., *The Alliance That Lost Its Way: A Critical Report on the Alliance for Progress*, Archangel Books, Chicago, 1970.

Lewis, W. Arthur, *The Evolution of the International Economic Order*, Princeton University Press, Princeton, N.J., 1978.

*L'Express*, 'Special Allemagne', Paris, 17–23 March 1979.

Leys, C., 'The "Overdeveloped" Post-Colonial State: A Re-evaluation' in *Review of African Political Economy*, no.5, Jan–April 1976, pp.39–48.

Lindblom, Charles E., *Politics and Markets: The World's Political–Economic Systems*, Basic Books, New York, 1977.

Love, J.L., 'Raúl Prebisch and the Origins of the Doctrine of Unequal Exchange' in *Latin America Research Review*, vol.15, no.3, 1980.

Lustig, N., 'Some Considerations on the Theories of Underconsumption and Latin American Economic Thought' in *Review of Radical Political Economy*, 1980.

Mainwaring, L., 'A Neo-Ricardian Analysis of International Trade' in Steedman (1979).

Malan, Pedro and Bonelli, Regis, 'The Brazilian Economy in the Seventies: Old and New Developments' in *World Development*, vol.5, no.1/2, 1977, pp.19–45.

Mandel, E., *The Second Slump*, New Left Books, London, 1978.

Martins, Luciano, 'A Expansão Recente de Estado no Brasil: Seus Problems e Seus Atores', working document, 1977.

Marx, K., *The Class Struggles in France 1848–1850* (1850), in K. Marx and F. Engels, 1962, pp.118–242.

Marx, K., *The Eighteenth Brumaire of Louis Bonaparte* (1851), in K. Marx and F. Engels, 1962, pp.243–344.

Marx, K., 'The British Constitution' (1855) in K. Marx and F. Engels, 1980, pp.53–6.

Marx, K. and Engels, F., *Selected Works in Two Volumes*, vol.II, Foreign Languages Publishing House, Moscow, 1947.

Marx, K. and Engels, F., *The Communist Manifesto* (1848), in K. Marx and F. Engels, 1962, pp.21–65.

Marx, K. and Engels, F., *Selected Works in Two Volumes*, vol.I, Foreign Languages Publishing House, Moscow, 1962.

Marx, K. and Engels, F., *Selected Correspondence*, Progress Publishers, Moscow, 1965.

Marx, K. and Engels, F., *On Colonialism*, Progress Publishers, Moscow, 1976.

Marx, K. and Engels, F., *Collected Works*, vol.14, Lawrence and Wishart, London, 1980.

*Mercurio, El*, Chile, p.82.

Michaely, Michael, 'Exports and Growth: An empirical investigation' in *Journal of Development Economics*, vol.4, no.1, March 1977.

Michaely, Michael, 'Exports and Growth: A reply' in *Journal of Development Economics*, vol.6, no.1, March 1979.

Migdal, J.S., 'International Structure and External Behaviour' in *Inter-*

*national Relations*, vol.4, no.5, May 1974.

Mikesell, R.F. (ed.), *Foreign Investment in the Petroleum and Mineral Industries; Case Studies of Investor-Host Country Relations*, John Hopkins, Baltimore, 1971.

Miliband, R., *Marxism and Politics*, Oxford University Press, Oxford, 1977.

Moreira Alves, Maria Helena, 'Grassroots Organizations, Trade Unions and the Church: Challenge to Controlled Abertura in Brazil', paper presented at 1981 meeting of the American Political Science Association, New York, 1981.

Mouzelis, N., *Organisation and Bureaucracy; An Analysis of Modern Theories*, Routledge and Kegan Paul, London 1975.

Naciones Unidas, *America Latina: Relacion de Precios del Intercambio* Santiago, Chile, 1976.

Newfarmer, Richard and Mueller, W., *Multinational Corporations in Brazil and Mexico: Structural Sources of Economic and Non-economic Power*, prepared for the Senate Sub-Committee on Multinationals, USGPO, Washington DC, 1975.

*New York Times*, p.166.

Nun, J., 'The Middle-Class Military Coup', in C. Veliz (ed.), 1967, pp.66–118.

OECD, *Interfutures: La Dynamique des Societés Industrielles Avancées*, Paris, 1977.

OECD, *Interfutures: Draft Final Report*, Paris 1978.

OECD, *Interfutures: Facing the Future*, Paris, 1979.

OECD, *Observer*, Paris, January 1982, no.114.

O'Brien, Philip, 'A Critique of Latin American Theories of Dependency' in I. Oxaal, T. Barnett and D. Booth (eds), *Beyond the Sociology of Development*, Routledge and Kegan Paul, London, 1975.

O'Connor, J., *The Fiscal Crisis of the State*, St Martin's Press, New York, 1973.

O'Donnell, Guillermo, *Modernization and Bureaucratic-Authoritarianism: Studies in South American Politics*, Institute of International Studies, University of California, Berkeley, 1973.

O'Donnell, Guillermo, 'Reflections on the Patterns of Change in the Bureaucratic-Authoritarian State' in *Latin American Research Review*, vol.13, no.1, 1978, pp.3–38.

Palma, G., 'Dependency: a Formal Model of Underdevelopment or a Methodology for the Analysis of Concrete Situations of Underdevelopment?' in *World Development*, vol.6, 1978.

Parkinson, F., *Latin America, the Cold War and the World Powers, 1945–73*, Sage Publications, Beverley Hills and London, 1974.

Parrinello, S., 'Distribution, Growth and International Trade' in Steedman (ed.), 1979.

Pemex, Annual Reports.

Penrose, E., *The Large International Firm in Developing Countries: The International Petroleum Industry*, Allen and Unwin, London, 1968.

Petroven, Annual Reports.

Philip, G., *Oil and Politics in Latin America: Nationalist Movements and State Companies*, Cambridge University Press, Cambridge, 1982.

Pinto, A., *Inflacion: raices estructurales*, Fondo de Cultura Economica, Mexico City, 1973.

Poulantzas, N., *Political Power and Social Classes*, New Left Books, London, 1973.

Poulantzas, N., *Classes in Contemporary Capitalism*, New Left Books, London, 1975.

Poulantzas, N., 'The Capitalist State: A Reply to Miliband and Laclau', *New Left Review*, no.95, 1976, pp.63–83.

Poulantzas, N., *State, Power and Socialism*, New Left Books, London, 1978.

Prebisch, R., *The Economic Development of Latin America and its Principal Problems*, UN, New York, 1950.

Prout, C., 'Finance for Developing Countries: An Essay' in S. Strange, *International Monetary Relations*, vol.2 of A. Schonfield (ed.), *International Economic Relations of the Western World*, Oxford University Press, 1976.

Rodríguez, O., *La teoría del subdesarrollo de la CEPAL*, Siglo XXI, Mexico City, 1980.

Sampson, A., *The Seven Sisters*, Penguin, London, 1975.

Sanford, Rose, 'Why the Multinational Tide is Ebbing', *Fortune*, August 1977.

Schlesinger, A., 'The Alliance for Progress: a Perspective', in R.G. Hillman and H.J. Rosenbaum (eds), *Latin America: the Search for a New International Role*, John Wiley and Sons, New York, 1975.

Seers, D., 'Massive Transfers and Mutual Interests' in *World Development*, vol.9, no.6, 1981.

Seers, D., 'Patterns of Dependence' in J. Villamil (ed.), *Transnational Capital and National Development*, Harvester Press, Hassocks, Sussex, 1979.

Sercovich, Francisco, 'State-owned Enterprises and Dynamic Comparative Advantage in the World Petrochemical Industry: The Case of Commodity Olefins in Brazil', Cambridge, Massachusetts, Harvard Institute for International Development, Development Discussion Paper, no.96, 1980.

Sercovich, Francisco, 'The Exchange and Absorption of Technology in Brazilian Industry' in T.C. Bruneau and P. Faucher (eds), *Authoritarian Capitalism: Brazil's Contemporary Economic and Political Development*, Westview Press, Boulder, CO, 1980, pp.127–40.

Serra, José, 'Three Mistaken Theses Regarding the Connection between Industrialization and Authoritarian Regimes' in D. Collier (ed.), 1979, pp.99–163.

Sheahan, John, 'Market-oriented Economic Policies and Political Repression in Latin America' in *Economic Development and Cultural Change*, vol.28, no.2, January 1980.

Singer, Paul and Vinícius Caldeira Brant, *São Paulo: O Povo em Movimento*, Editora Vozes, São Paulo, 1980.

Skidelsky, R., 'The Decline of Keynesian Politics' in C. Crouch (ed.) *State and Economy in Contemporary Capitalism*, Croom Helm, London, 1979.

*South*, 'GATT: Counter to 'Free Trade' ', January 1982, p.21.

*South*, 'EEC Tries to Slam the Door on Third World Footwear', February 1982, p.105.

Steedman, I. (ed.), *Fundamental Issues in Trade Theory*, Macmillan, London, 1979.

Stepan, Alfred, *The Military in Politics: Changing Patterns in Brazil*, Princeton University Press, Princeton, NJ, 1971.

Stewart, F. and Sengupta, A., *Framework for International Financial Cooperation*, Frances Pinter, London, 1982.

Strange, S., 'IMF: Monetary Managers' in R. Cox and H. Jacobsen (eds), *The Anatomy of Influence*, Yale University Press, New Haven, Connecticut, 1973.

Sunkel, O., 'External dependency and national policy of development' in *Journal of Development Studies*, October 1969.

Sunkel, O. and Fuenzalida, E., 'Transnationalisation and its National Consequences' in J. Villamil (ed.), *Transnational Capitalism and National Development*, Harvester Press, Sussex, 1979.

Sunkel, O. and Paz, P., *El subdesarrollo latinoamericano y la teoria del desarrollo*, Siglo XXI, Mexico City, 1970.

Suzigan, W., 'As Empresas do Governo e O Papel do Estado na Economia Brasileira' in F. Rezende et al., (eds), *Aspectos da Participacão do Governo na Economia*, IPEA, Rio de Janeiro, Brazil, 1976, pp.77–134.

Tello, C. and Cordero, R., *México; La Disputa por la Nación*, Siglo XXI, México, 1981.

Tendler, J., *Electric Power in Brazil: Entrepreneurship in the Public Sector*, Harvard University Press, Cambridge, Massachusetts, 1968.

Thorp, R. and Bertram, I.G., *Peru 1890–1977: Growth and Policy in an Open Economy*, Macmillan, London, 1978.

Thorp, R. and Whitehead, L. (eds), *Inflation and Stabilization in Latin America*, Macmillan, London, 1979.

Tugwell, F., *Oil and Politics in Venezuela*, Stanford University Press, 1975.

UNCTAD, *Trade and Development Report, 1981*, Geneva, 1981.

US Department of Commerce, *Survey of Current Business*, various issues.

United Nations, *Statistical Bulletin for Latin America*, New York, March 1964.

Van Ginnekin, W., *Socio-Economic Groups and Income Distribution in Mexico*, ILO, London, 1980.

*Veja*, Rio de Janeiro, various issues.

Véliz, C. (ed.), *The Politics of Conformity in Latin America*, Oxford University Press, London, 1967.

Wallerstein, I., *The Capitalist World Economy*, Cambridge University Press, Cambridge, 1979.

Wallerstein, I. and Hopkins, T., 'Structural Transformations of the World Economy' in R. Rubinson (ed.) *Dynamics of World Development*, Political Economy of the World-System Annuals, vol.4, Sage, Beverley Hills and London, 1981.

*Wall Street Journal*, p.159.

Weffort, F.C., *Clases populares e desenvolvimento social: contribuição ao estudo do 'populismo'*, Instituto Latinoamericano de Planificación Económica y Social, Santiago, 1968.

Weisburg, R., *The Politics of Crude Oil Pricing in the Middle East*, University of California, Berkeley, 1977.

Weisskopf, T.E., 'Marxian Crisis Theory and the Rate of Profit in the Postwar U.S. Economy', *Cambridge Journal of Economics*, vol.3, 1979.

Wells, J., 'State Expenditures and the Brazilian Economic "Miracle" ', pp.315–34, in E.V.K. FitzGerald et al. (eds), *The State and Economic Development in Latin América*, Cambridge University Printing House for the Centre for Latin American Studies, 1977.

Wilkins, M., 'Venezuelan Investment in Florida, 1979' in *Latin American Research Review*, vol.16, no.1, 1981, pp.156–64.

Winkler, Max, *Investments of United States Capital in Latin America*, Kennikat Press, Port Washington, New York, 1971, (first published in 1928).

World Bank, *World Development Report 1980*, Oxford University Press, New York, 1980.

World Bank, *World Development Report 1981*, Oxford University Press, New York, 1981.

World Bank, *Brazil: Human Resource – Special Report*, The World Bank, Washington DC, 1980a.

Worsley, P., 'One World or Three: A Critique of the World System of Immanuel Wallerstein' in *Socialist Register 1980*, Merlin Press, London, 1980.

Wright, E.P., 'World Bank Lending for Structural Adjustment' in *Finance and Development*, January 1980.

# Index

229

234

problems of maintaining
cartel 176–8

Palma, Gabriel 21n
Paraguay 30, 37, 42, 71
Parkinson, F. 62
Pascal, Blaise
*Pensées* 105
Pemex 188
Penrose, E. 176
Pérez, Pres. Carlos Andrés,
of Venezuela 184, 187
Perón, Gen. 35
Peru 36, 37, 44, 76, 81,
126
armed forces and open-
ness-politics link 45–6
development in 1970s 129
export promotion 40
protectionism in 1920s
33
trade trends e9
Petroven Co. 186
Philip, G. 172, 177
on dependency and oil-
exporting countries
15–16, 169–94
Pinochet, Pres. of Chile
42, 50
Poulantzas, N.
'class-theoretical'
approach 201–2
Prebisch, Raúl 62
theory of weakness
of raw material
economies 171
Prout, Christopher
on increase of US aid
in 1960s 62

Rhodia Company
at odds with Brazilian
government 157–8,
159, 161
Rhone Poulenc Co. 157

Rockefeller, David 62
Rose, Sanford 95, 97

Sampson, A. 177
Samuelson, Paul 22, 24
Sanson, David 152
São Paulo, Brazil
riots of 1981 139
strikes of 1979 162
SAREC 55n
Saudi Fund 84
Schlesinger, Arthur 58
Seers, Dudley 10, 55n, 56
Sercovich, Francisco 162
Serra, Jose 143
on paying for 'Brazilian miracle'
143
Sheehan, John 21n
on economic distortions and
authoritarianism 48
Singer, Paul and Brant, V.C. 163
Skidelsky, R. 131
Standard Electric Co. 162
State, the
and accumulation on periphery
113–19
developing ECLA model
113–17, 131–2
finance and relative autonomy
117–19
and management of accumulation in periphery 111–38
'capital-logic' approach to 202
CEMLA ideology 132
'class-theoretical' approach to
201–2
fiscal implications of intervention in support of accumulation 123
integration into international
division of labour 120–1
Marxist views on relative autonomy of 197–9
patterns of peripheral economies
125–30